Journal of the
Chester
Archaeological
Society

Volume 76 for 2000–01

Edited by
PETER CARRINGTON
Chester 2002

ISBN 0 9542563 0 1
ISSN 0309-359 X

Abbreviations
The abbreviations used in this volume follow
the system laid down in BS 4148: 1985, as
recommended by the Council for British
Archaeology in Signposts for Archaeological
Publication ed 3, 1991, Appendix A

Notes for contributors
The Society welcomes articles about the
architecture, archaeology and history of
Cheshire in its Journal. If you are interested
in contributing, please contact the Editor at
the following address for further guidance on
the scope of the Journal and for notes on
style and layout:

Chester Archaeology
27 Grosvenor Street
Chester CH1 2DD
Tel: +44 (0)1244 402028
Fax: +44 (0)1244 347522

E-mail: p.carrington@chestercc.gov.uk

For more information about the Society, see:
http://www.chesterarchaeolsoc.org.uk

Designed and produced for the Society
by Aquarium Graphic Design
+44 (0)1244 398004

Printed in the United Kingdom by Henry Ling
Limited, at the Dorset Press, Dorchester,
DT1 1HD

Contents

Illustrations

Tables

Gertrude Jones JP
Past Chairman and Vice-President

by J T Driver BLitt, MA, PhD, FRHistS

With the death of Gertrude Jones on 10 February 2001 the Society lost one of its oldest and most respected members, and one who had given it much devoted service for many years.

Gertrude Jones was very much a Cestrian and, indeed, a proud one at that — proud of the city and of its history. A major aspect of her life was her involvement in business. Her grandfather had founded a glue-works at Tattenhall, which went under the name of W R Smith and Sons. Eventually she herself became a director of the firm, which survived until quite recently. For a time she worked for Owen Owens in Liverpool, but later she and her late husband, Basil N Jones (whose own family had established the well known stores of Richard Jones & Co Ltd in Bridge Street and Eastgate Street in 1860, sold to Owen Owens in 1960), ran Henderson's furniture and furnishing business in St Michael's Arcade.

Outside her business interests Gertrude Jones had many other concerns. During Word War II she served in the Red Cross. She was closely and actively involved with the League of Pity, of which she took a turn as chairman; and she was, too, a vice-president of the Chester branch of the NSPCC. For some thirty years she was a Justice of the Peace and Chairman of the Juvenile and Family Bench.

Her love of archaeology and history, especially that of her own city, was keen and life-long. An interesting sidelight on this aspect of her career was that she took part in the grandly titled 'Chester Historical Pageant and Searchlight Tattoo' held in the grounds of Chester College in 1937. Very much in line with her real concern for the preservation of Chester's architectural, archaeological and historical heritage was her work for the Chester Civic Trust, of which she was a founder member and subsequently chairman and vice-president; her membership of the Grosvenor Museum Society; and her long and active association with the Chester Archaeological Society. Gertrude Jones served successively as vice-chairman, chairman and past chairman of the Society from 1974 to 1979 and after-wards became a vice-president. She proved a diligent, conscientious chairman, and both she and her late husband gave great support to our excursions. Nothing could better under-line her enthusiasm for the Society than her generous contribution towards the production of its *History* on the occasion of its one hundred and fiftieth anniversary in 1999 and her delight in opening the exhibition in the Grosvenor Museum to celebrate the event. Earlier

Gertrude Jones had been a voluntary worker at the museum when Robert Newstead, Graham Webster and Hugh Thompson — distinguished archaeologists — were successively curators. She was, in fact, a close friend of Graham Webster and Hugh Thompson.

In her prime, Gertrude Jones could, and did, present quite a formidable figure. She held firm views and had high standards, yet she was always down-to-earth; her enthusiasms were life-long, not transient; and her interest in what was going on, as well as her sense of humour, remained to the end. If the Society has lost a staunch friend and supporter, it can also be grateful for her having been with us for so long.

Graham Webster

OBE, MA, DLitt, FSA, AMA, MIFA
Curator of the Grosvenor Museum 1947–1955

by D J Robinson BA, MPhil

One of the great archaeologists of the twentieth century and a man with close connections with Chester, Graham Webster, passed away after a long illness on 21 May 2001. His funeral took place nine days later in Swindon.

Graham Webster was born in Stamford, Lincolnshire in 1913. Although trained as a civil engineer, he clearly felt little enthusiasm for the profession and found much more enjoyment in his hobby as an archaeologist, working in his spare time at both Canterbury and Lincoln. In 1947 on the recommendation of Ian Richmond he was appointed the first professional curator of the Grosvenor Museum, with a brief to thoroughly modernise the building and its displays. The museum had just been taken over by the Corporation from the Chester Archaeological Society, and putting Graham in the job was seen very much as a gamble by both parties, as he was to admit himself in later years.

At Chester he continued to develop his archaeological career, for amongst his other responsibilities the new position made him the successor to Robert Newstead, whose excavations had done so much to put Roman Chester on the archaeological map before the Second World War. He worked with Richmond on the legionary headquarters building (*principia*) in Goss Street, and at various points on the circuit of the Roman defences. However, not all of the archaeology was so formal — some discoveries were made by accident. When the first fragments from what was to become known as the Castle Esplanade hoard were brought to him in November 1950, he immediately rushed to rescue everything which still remained in the service trench where they had been discovered a few days earlier, ironically only a short distance from the front door of the museum. By careful detective work he also tracked down most of the workmen and schoolchildren who had made off with handfuls of what were later to prove to be Saxon pennies. By this quick response he had saved one of the most important Viking-age coin hoards ever found in England.

Above all else Graham Webster's particular talent was in communicating his love of the past to others. In Chester this can be seen in his lasting legacy to the city — the renovation, expansion and redisplay of the Grosvenor Museum between 1947 and 1954. Inevitably he will be remembered best for his two new Roman galleries. The Newstead Gallery, named after his predecessor, told the story of the Roman army and Roman Chester in a unique style which has survived, with minor improvements, to this day. Graham's little secret — which he freely admitted — was that he had very little original Roman material to work with: the style of the new displays, heavily reliant on graphics, was not the result of a great vision or design but dictated by a dearth of real objects. About half of the great collection of Roman tombstones and sculptures amassed by the Society at the end of the nineteenth century was redisplayed in the adjacent room, where the design and building of the supports for the stones was a chance to use his old engineering skills.

However, there was much more to his work at the museum than the Roman galleries. He incorporated a seventeenth-century house, No 20 Castle Street, into the complex, filling it with period rooms which are still a feature of the museum today. New displays about the Civil Wars and the medieval port of Chester were also put into the King Charles' Tower and the Water Tower respectively. Nor were publications ignored: three popular booklets were written about Roman Chester, the city's Roman inscriptions, and the Roman army. This was a tremendous amount of work, achieved in a very few years and with the help of a very small staff Among the latter were two promising young men called Brian Hartley and Ken Barton, later to become respectively the doyens of samian and medieval pottery studies in Britain. By the early 1950s Chester's museum was one of the most modern and admired in the country, and this was largely due to Graham Webster's energy and imagination.

By 1954 his work in Chester was drawing to a close and he was to leave the city to take up a research fellowship at Birmingham University, where he spent the rest of his working life. Graham Webster will always be associated with the Roman city of Wroxeter, where he ran a training excavation from 1955 until 1985, encouraging and inspiring a whole generation of young archaeologists with his enthusiasm for Roman Britain. He became an acknowledged expert on Romano-British pottery and also a respected historian of the earliest years of the Roman conquest, with books such as *Rome against Caratacus* and *The Rebellion of Boudicca*. His other specialism was the study of the Roman soldier, and his best known book, foreshadowed by the booklet he had produced for the Grosvenor Museum in 1956, was the seminal *The Roman Army*, first published in 1969 and still in print today. It is a fitting memorial to his stature as a scholar that it remains the standard work on the subject.

In his retirement Graham was closely associated with the formation of the Roman Research Trust, latterly the Association for Roman Archaeology, a sign of his continuing absorption in the study and excavation of the remains of Roman Britain. He was Honorary President of the Association at the time of his death.

His last visit to Chester was in June 1992 when he attended the opening by HRH The Prince of Wales of the latest reinterpretation of the museum's Roman stones collection. Graham was the guest of honour on a day which saw the new displays officially given the name 'The Webster Gallery' to celebrate and commemorate the enormous debt which the city and its museum owed to him for his work in Chester.

Note

Graham Webster's own account of his years in Chester can be found in 'Reflections on archaeology and the creation of the Grosvenor Museum 1947–55', *J Chester Archaeol* Soc new ser **72**, 37–47. *Archaeologist at large* (London: Batsford, 1991) is a collection of papers spanning his whole career, including his time in Chester.

I: The Iron Age of North-West England
A Socio-Economic Model1

by K J Matthews BA

This paper reviews the evidence for Iron Age settlement and society in north-west England as far north as the Ribble. Models based on south-eastern England are explicitly rejected, as is the view that the region was populated by an egalitarian farming society. Rather there seems to have been a politico-economic elite who based their wealth on salt and engaged in trade with the continent *via* an *emporium* at Meols.

Introduction

It is easy to assume that nothing happened and nobody lived in north-west England during the first millennium BC. In fact, this is because the period has all but been ignored by local archaeologists and rarely appears in national overviews. Explanations for this neglect are simple to find: the populations had all but given up using domestic pottery by the end of the second millennium BC and no longer built or (apparently) used ritual monuments. Archaeological evidence for people during the first millennium BC is almost confined to their construction of hilltop enclosures on the Pennine fringes and the Mid-Cheshire Ridge. Consequently, our understanding of the regional Iron Age is all too frequently based on inappropriate models imported from outside (eg Varley 1964, 84 ff). Just as in many other places, though, the patterns of settlement, trade and social organisation that the population of north-west England established in the first millennium BC endured. Their social practices were effectively masked by the swamping effect of the Roman imperial power's consumption of durable material culture, diverting the attention of archaeologists towards quite anomalous sites such as Chester or Ribchester, but they can be glimpsed again in the sub-Roman period in the middle of the first millennium AD (Matthews 1997, 130).

This paper will review the evidence for Iron Age activity in north-west England, setting up a chronological framework based, it must be admitted, on only a handful of radiocarbon dates. It will then question the core–periphery model that has dominated interpretations of the Iron Age since the late 1970s and propose an alternative model, considering how the consumption of material culture worked to create distinctive identities for the people of the Iron Age North-West. Finally, I will construct a social model for settlement patterns based on the available evidence but using models drawn from anthropology, geography and history.

The 'new' Iron Age

The 1990s were an exciting time in Iron Age studies. At the start of the decade, the study of the Iron Age seemed to have been all but exhausted as an academic enterprise (Hill 1989, 19). However, developments in cognitive archaeology and the introduction of concepts of agency began to change the established model of Celtic warrior society. There was also a recognition that the 'Celtic' model was less than helpful as it masked the considerable regional differences visible throughout Britain (Matthews 1999a, 19). Post-processual approaches have stressed the importance of studying individual sites rather than forcing them into Europe-wide normative models. Interpretative approaches have also sought to bring in new levels of hypothesis testing. By the end of the decade, the Iron Age had once

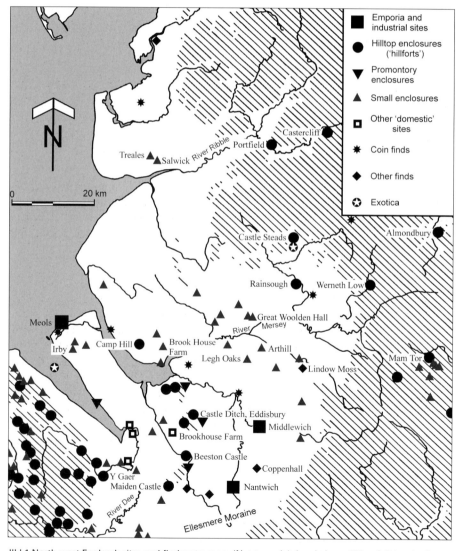

III I.1 North-west England: sites and findspots: map. (Not to scale). Land above 100m O D hatched.

again become an area of uncertainty, populated by people with strange and often incomprehensible attitudes to the world around them (Gwilt & Haselgrove 1997, 7).

Where does this leave the Iron Age of north-west England? It might be argued that the data set is too poor to allow us to indulge in what might be dismissed as 'high theory', that the best we can hope for at the moment is to synthesise the data and attempt to put it into some sort of historical perspective. This is wrong for a number of reasons. Firstly, the historical framework has to come from within the data set: it can be disastrous, as we shall see, to import frameworks from outside and try to fit our data to them. Secondly, some good data does exist. How representative it is, we do not yet know (Nevell 1999b, 63 concludes that Great Woolden Hall — the best known of the excavated enclosures in the region — cannot be used as a type site), but we can at least attempt to build on it. Thirdly, archaeology has moved away from a purely descriptive mode and now aims to explain the patterns of the past in increasingly sophisticated ways. Not to make the attempt, however provisional, would be a dereliction of our duties as archaeologists.

The first millennium BC in regional context
Definition of the region

The definition of north-west England used here differs considerably from that formulated by modern geographers. For a start, it is confessedly Cheshire-centred. The area that the Domesday survey of 1086 included within the returns for Cheshire (pre-1974 Cheshire, Flintshire, much of Wrexham Borough and Lancashire south of the Ribble) corresponds surprisingly well to cultural patterns that are visible throughout prehistory. Indeed, this remains a coherent region during the first millennium AD and into the second (as recognised, for instance, by Phillips & Smith 1994, 5). The identifiable patterns include settlement morphology, subsistence strategies and, in the later first millennium AD, when the evidence is first available, territorial organisation.

The region defined in this way has a topographic coherence that is masked to some extent by modern boundaries (Ill I.1). To the west, the Clwydian mountains form an obvious barrier and themselves contain a quite distinct settlement pattern, dominated by numerous hillforts. To the south and south-east, the Ellesmere moraine is an important watershed both hydrologically and culturally, including settlement patterns, material culture traditions and distribution, and monument types: Bronze Age burnt mounds, for instance, are common to the south, but only one (at Hampton Green, Cheshire) has been found to its north. To the east, the Pennines form a clearly separate region, with very different settlement patterns and a typically upland agricultural régime. The north of the region is more difficult to define, but beyond Lancaster there are none of the lowland plains with occasional hills, marshy estuaries and numerous mosses that are characteristic of the area to the south, while settlement patterns and subsistence economy are more typical of upland regions.

Historians have generally assumed that the region remained thinly populated and economically backward until the industrial revolution. The *aestuaria ac siluae* (estuaries and forests) mentioned by Tacitus (*Agricola* 20, 2), which are usually — and no doubt correctly — located here, have been used as evidence to demonstrate that the region was inhospitable and virtually uninhabited, with vast tracts of uncleared natural forest. This reads too much into three bland words used by a writer whose knowledge of the region was, at best, second-hand through his father-in-law. Instead, palaeoenvironmental evidence suggests that the Roman army passed through an open landscape with areas of light woodland and arable fields. Arable fields presuppose farmers and light woodland implies a population widely dispersed throughout the landscape.

The state of current knowledge
Hillforts
In terms of settlement sites, the first millennium BC is known primarily from the hillforts situated on the Pennine fringes and Mid-Cheshire Ridge. They have been subject to a number of excavations during the twentieth century, although large-scale work has been uncommon. The only recent large-scale work to take place on the Mid-Cheshire Ridge was at Beeston during the 1980s. When work began, the existence of the prehistoric site was not even suspected. It was soon found that the outer bailey wall of the medieval castle sits on a Late Bronze Age rampart, which originated as a palisade before 1000 Cal BC[2] (Ellis 1993, 21). It was later strengthened to create a formidable box rampart and ditch in Period 2 (Ill I.2). Occupation continued through to the Middle Iron Age, with a range of dates centring on 500 Cal BC. Although grains of bread wheat and other cereals from the site have been dated to the Iron Age, the nature of the stratigraphy made it impossible to assign structures to this period with any certainty, although two postholes belong to the Middle Iron Age. Consequently, it is the Late Bronze Age occupation of the site that is better understood.

Ill I.2 The Period 2 rampart at Beeston, with the ruins of the medieval castle sitting on it

The form of the rampart at Helsby on the northern end of the ridge also suggests an early date (Bu'Lock 1956, 110), although this is not confirmed by artefacts or radiocarbon dates. An excavation by Graham Webster and T G E Powell at the apparently 'unfinished' site at Woodhouses, Frodsham, took place in 1951, but was never published (Longley 1987, 114); unfinished, in this context, means merely that the rampart was never completed, but says nothing about occupation of the site. Similarly, an excavation at Kelsborrow Castle, Kelsall, in 1973 and a geophysical survey in the 1990s remain only partly published (Williams 1997, 19; Quarterman 1997, chapter iv; Ill I.3); however, the box rampart is once again of an early type. No datable material appears to have been recovered from either site. Castle Ditch, Eddisbury, also lacks radiocarbon dates, but again the form of the rampart is typologically early and is preceded by a pre-rampart palisade (Varley 1950, 51), as at Beeston. The material culture of the inhabitants belongs best in the Early Iron Age, something which puzzled earlier prehistorians (Varley & Jackson 1940, 73), who were accustomed to thinking of multivallate hillforts as belonging to the Middle Iron Age. Maiden Castle, Bickerton, further south, was subject to small-scale excavation in 1980 (Taylor 1981, 34), following more extensive campaigns in 1934/5 (Varley 1936b, 113). The inner rampart has a series of three radiocarbon dates centring on 470 bc[3] (c 860–330 Cal BC at 2σ). The outer rampart at the south entrance has two dates of 485 ± 70 bc and 280 ± 70 bc (c 770–400 and c380–10 Cal BC at 2σ). As a series, the dates are largely consistent and centre on the sixth century BC, with the single exception of one late date from the south entrance.

The hillforts of the Pennine fringe are also early. Mam Tor has produced two very early dates of 1180 ± 132 bc and 1130 ± 115 bc (c 1750–1000 Cal BC and 1650–950 Cal BC at 2σ). It is thought to have been abandoned by the eighth century BC (Coombs & Thompson 1979, 47), although this is far from certain. Castercliff has two virtually identical dates: 510 ± 70 BC (780–400 Cal BC at 2σ) and 510 ± 60 bc (770–400 Cal BC at 2σ) (Coombs 1982, 127). Both it and Almondbury were abandoned in the fifth century (Nevell 1992a, 50). Almondbury produced a series of radiocarbon dates centred on 520 bc (825–290 Cal BC at 2σ). The rampart at Almondbury has a vitrified rubble core, a suggestion that has also been made for Maiden Castle, Bickerton (Varley 1964, 95). The latest material from Portfield dates from the seventh century BC (Kenyon 1991, 36), while Castle Steads, 2km north of Bury, is a small site that has been interpreted as a hillfort (Fletcher 1986, 39), although it is more of an enclosed promontory.

The resistivity survey at Kelsborrow Castle

A resistivity survey was undertaken at Kelsborrow by Alistair Quarterman in March 1996 as part of the research for his undergraduate dissertation submitted to the University of Durham (Quarterman 1997). Approximately 2160m² were surveyed, covering the western part of the site, using a Geoscan RM-15 resistivity meter and processed using Geoplot 2.01. The results are shown here as a dot-density plot (Ill I.4) and as an interpreted plan (Ill I.5).[4] The most striking features are the western rampart and external ditch. Internally, the resolution is poor, but an area of low resistivity close to the edge of the scarp possibly represents a cluster of pits, as does a similar area to the south of the rampart. Several roughly circular areas of high resistivity may be the foundations of houses in view of their rough diameters of around 15m; the high resistance may be caused by the presence of trampled clay floors.

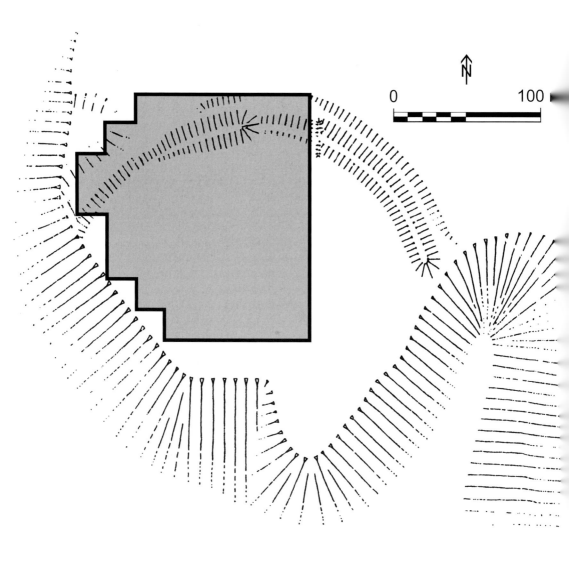

Ill I.3 The hillfort at Kelsborrow Castle: plan showing the area of the 1996 geophysical survey
(after Quarterman 1997). (Scale 1/2500)

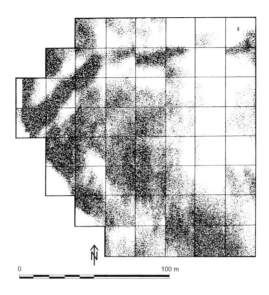

Ill I.4 Dot density plot of the resistivity survey at Kelsborrow Castle
(after Quarterman 1997). (scale 1/2500)

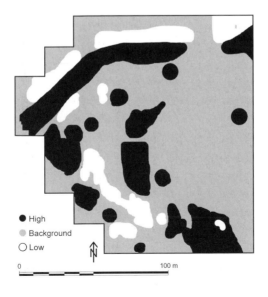

Ill I.5 Interpretation of the resistivity data from Kelsborrow Castle. (scale 1/2500)

Possible hillforts

A number of other sites have been suggested as hillforts. Eddisbury in Rainow, on the Pennine fringes of east Cheshire, is the only potential hillfort site so far identified in this part of the region. Finness Hill, a lost site in Delamere (Ormerod 1882, **2**, 11), appears on an early map in a form that suggests it was an Iron Age enclosure, but it cannot now be recognised as such on the ground. Camp Hill, Liverpool, was recorded as a circular enclosure in 1835 but was later built over. A small excavation in 1963 confirmed the presence of a site, but its character could not be determined (Forde-Johnston 1962, 13). The Cloud, near Congleton, has been considered a hillfort (Varley & Jackson 1940, schedule vi), but its form — a straight-sided trapeze — and situation away from the edge of the scarp suggest that it is not an Iron Age enclosure (Forde-Johnston 1962, 10). A similar site, Toothill in Macclesfield Forest, is probably of medieval origin (Thomas 1960, 86).

Dates

The pattern of dates for hillforts is consistent throughout the region, belonging to the Late Bronze Age to the end of the Middle Iron Age. This stands in contrast to the better known model of hillfort development in the south, where some sites continued in use through to the Roman conquest. Maiden Castle appears anomalous because of the late date of one of the radiocarbon samples (although even here, there is no suggestion of occupation after the Middle Iron Age and the single inconsistent date may be an error). The widespread view that the North-West was a hillfort-dominated region at the time of the Roman conquest (eg Shotter 1997, 6) is therefore false. The hillforts were built early and were abandoned in the Middle Iron Age, if not earlier.

Little is known about the interiors of the hillforts, as the defences have been the main focus of investigation. The circular buildings that were constructed over the demolished defences of Eddisbury, probably during the Middle Iron Age, are typical of those observed in other parts of Britain. On the other hand, we do not know if the four-posters that are characteristic of other areas were common in the Iron Age of the North-West.

Smaller enclosures

A number of smaller enclosures have been known for some years, often close to hillfort sites. Bradley can be considered a promontory site as its northern edge is formed by the steep valley of a small stream. Burton Point was formerly a coastal promontory site overlooking the Dee estuary, but following the establishment of the New Cut in the eighteenth century and reclamation of land on the north side of the estuary, it is now inland. The site appears to have suffered considerably from erosion (Longley 1987, 109), so its original extent is unclear. Despite rumours of an excavation in the early 1960s, there is no evidence for archaeological work on the site. The bank at Oakmere, a promontory site on the edge of the mere, was sectioned in 1960 and found to consist of a simple dump of soil (Forde-Johnston 1962, 22), contrasting with the structured defences of the hillforts proper. Peckforton Mere consists of a small, subrectangular ditched enclosure sitting on a low hill. Although undated, it is likely to be of Iron Age origin (Longley 1987, 109).

Oldcastle Hill, south-west of Malpas, was investigated in August 1957 following the destruction of woodland on the site during a severe storm. The site consists of a defended spur overlooking the steep-sided valley of the Wych Brook, currently the border between England and Wales. The southernmost of the two ditches across the neck of the spur was sectioned and found to be filled with a clean, undifferentiated clay that produced no finds (Thompson 1967, 5). Eight trenches were dug on the top of the platform that occupies the main part of the spur. Some six inches (0.15m) below the surface, a cobble spread was identified across the southern end of the platform. A smaller patch of cobbles including a possible hearth was found north-east of the centre (archive notes in the Grosvenor Museum, Chester). There were no finds whatsoever. Although Thompson discounted an Iron Age date for the site on the grounds that the triple ditch system at the southern end of the spur is not a characteristically prehistoric feature, the lack of finds rules out his explanation of the site as an eleventh- or twelfth-century motte. There is no indication that the central platform is artificial at all. The other possibility is that it belongs to the early medieval period, inviting comparisons with Buckton Castle, which has occasionally been seen as a hillfort (Forde-Johnston 1962, 11). A recent radiocarbon determination places the rampart at Buckton in the early medieval period (*pers comm* M Nevell, 22 May 1999).

Five trenches were excavated in 1961 at the small enclosure of Y Gaer at Llay, near Rossett (Wrexham Borough) and failed to reveal any finds that would enable the site to be dated with accuracy. The recent history of the site had included its use as a plantation, resulting in the heavy disturbance of the interior, but the only traces of pre-modern activity consisted of an undated, irregular pit and several stakeholes (Bevan-Evans & Hayes 1963–4, 27–8). The ditch was found to be 3.96m wide and only 0.99m deep on the west side of the enclosure (Bevan-Evans & Hayes 1963–4, 28), while on the south side no ditch could be located. The form of the enclosure suggests a late prehistoric origin and an Iron Age date appears likely, especially in view of the lack of datable finds.

Aerial survey work by Mike Nevell, Rob Philpott and others has begun to identify enclosed lowland sites that appear to belong to the first millennium BC. Most of the sites are curvilinear and, although there are few whose complete plans are known, those not sited on promontories appear to be oval. Some subrectangular enclosures may also belong to the first millennium BC rather than AD, although typically the evidence is not clear cut. Excavated enclosures at Arthill (Nevell 1989a, 33), Great Woolden Hall (Nevell 1999b) and Rainsough (Nevell 1994, 14) have all produced evidence for Iron Age activity. Radiocarbon dates from Great Woolden Hall place its origins in the Late Iron Age, with determinations of 40 ± 25 bc (40 Cal BC–Cal AD 80) for Phase II and 60 ± 100 bc (200 Cal BC–Cal AD 350) for Phase III. In form, it closely resembles Bradley, Frodsham.

The distribution of oval enclosures extends outside the region into north-east Wales (Manley 1991, 97), Shropshire, south Yorkshire and north Derbyshire (Hart 1981, 77); there are two possible enclosures on the Fylde, at Salwick and Treales (Welsh 1992, 16), which are currently the northernmost known examples of the type. This form is quite different from the curvilinear enclosures of upland areas, such as the Lune Valley, which tend to be circular and whose economy appears to have been largely pastoral (Haselgrove 1996a, 64).

These lowland enclosed sites appear to have had diverse economies, with evidence for mixed farming and small-scale metalworking. Some sites, such as Werneth Low (Nevell

1992b, 21) or Legh Oaks enclosure A (Nevell *forthcoming*), can be dated to the later prehistoric period by analogy, while others that have produced only Roman material, such as Halton Brow (Newstead & Droop 1937; Brown *et al* 1975), may also have earlier origins. At Irby, an oval enclosure lies only a few hundred metres from the excavated open settlement at Mill Hill Road.

Open sites

The open site at Mill Hill Road, Irby, is perhaps the best known such site in the region. Apart from some very early activity, belonging to the fifth and third millennia respectively, the earliest occupation (Phase 3) is associated with VCP (Very Coarse Pottery) and other coarse, handmade pottery (Philpott & Adams 1999, 66). Radiocarbon determinations have not yet been carried out on material from this site, but there can be little doubt that two probable structures (S1 and S2) belong to this phase. In the succeeding phase, three round-houses (S3, S4 and S5) were built successively on the same spot. As these types of building seem to last a generation at least, Phase 4 ought to have lasted around 75 years. It is at this time that there is some evidence for an enclosure (although not of the types described above: the domestic space at Mill Hill Road appears to occupy an area between enclosures, probably fields and paddocks). In view of the dating of Phase 5 to the second century, it is possible that Phase 4 begins before the Roman conquest in the middle of the first century AD, so that Phase 3 should be earlier still.

Meols, on the northern tip of the Wirral peninsula, is best known as a source of unstratified material. All that remains of the site today is a series of sandbanks and mudflats close to Dove Point, as the settlement discovered there early in the nineteenth century has now been largely washed away by the sea (Cowell & Innes 1994, 26). The Iron Age material from Meols is small in quantity, but its significance is potentially huge. It is one of only a handful of sites in the North-West to have produced pre-Roman coins and other Iron Age metalwork. This material needs to be set alongside the other exotic objects from the region to provide a context for its deposition. Timber structures were reported during the nineteenth century as having been preserved in the peat and uncovered by marine erosion; they included both rectangular and circular forms, of which some may well have dated from the Iron Age. It is now impossible, however, to recognise any spatial pattern to the finds that might shed light on the morphology of the settlement. At best, we can suggest that it was an open form.

The Lousher's Lane site at Wilderspool (Hinchliffe & Williams 1992, 100) is best known for the Romano-British enclosures that produced evidence for circular, oval and rectangular buildings. These were interpreted as ribbon development along a track parallel to a major road leading east towards Manchester from the focus of the 'small town' on the brewery site to the west. However, the earliest enclosure cut the top of a small pit, 2267, which contained one coarse gritty potsherd, interpreted as being of Iron Age date. As with some of the other enclosures discussed here, it is possible that the Phase 1 enclosure originated in the Iron Age and that Lousher's Lane, not the brewery site (which is of overwhelmingly industrial character), was the original focus of the settlement. As the alleged Iron Age pottery has not been published, it is not clear if it is of VCP or one of the other types found on Early Iron Age sites in the region (*see below*).

The recently excavated site at Manchester Airport, initially thought to be of Bronze Age date, has yielded a number of surprises, not least the radiocarbon dates, which run in a series from the Neolithic through to the sub-Roman period, with all intervening periods represented (pers comm Dan Garner 22 May 1999). Phasing the site has not yet been completed, but it is clear that some of the structures, including possible four-posters, belong to the Iron Age. This is the first site at which such structures — usually interpreted as granaries — have been identified in the region. There is also a large assemblage of pottery, some of which belongs to the Iron Age phases, although no metalwork was found, despite the use of metal detectors.

Two of the radiocarbon dates from the site at Tatton Park suggest occupation during the first millennium BC (Higham & Cane 1996–7, 39). Pit 7 is dated 390 ± 120 bc (HAR-5147; 800–100 Cal BC at 2σ), while the range of dates for Building J includes one dated 80 + 120 bc (HAR-4496; 400 Cal BC–Cal AD 250 at 2σ) and another of AD 40 ± 110 bc (HAR-5111, 200 Cal BC–Cal AD 400 at 2σ), suggesting a possible pre-Roman origin, rather than the sub-Roman date suggested. The published plan (Higham & Cane 1996–7, 46) also shows a circular feature of evident Iron Age form that is not discussed in the text (*see below*).

Other sites
A number other sites can be dated to the Iron Age. The earthworks of 'Celtic' fields (now usually referred to as 'regular aggregate field systems') on Longley Hill, Kelsall (Bu'Lock 1955, 26), are undatable, but their form may belong anywhere between the Late Bronze Age and the early medieval period. Kirkby Vicarage has produced material of Iron Age date, but its character is uncertain, while a supposed prehistoric site near Raw Head, Bickerton, was observed only as parch marks and remains unconfirmed. Nevertheless, the observation of circular structures some nine metres in diameter suggests that an Iron Age or Romano-British site awaits discovery here (Robinson 1978–9, 58).

The salt towns of the first and second millennia AD are likely to occupy sites that were the centres of production during the Iron Age. Indeed, the source of clays used in the manu-facture of Cheshire VCP is the Middlewich/Nantwich area of the Cheshire plain. Nothing certain is known of these sites, however. It is very unlikely that salt production was centralised in the way it was during the Roman period, when there was intense state interest in mineral extraction and exploitation. Nevertheless, the distribution of Cheshire salt (as shown by the distribution of VCP) and the exchange networks it helped maintain must have involved some form of élite control, direct or otherwise.

Structures
The diagnostic late prehistoric architectural form is the round house (often, and quite unfairly, referred to as a 'hut'). A number of such buildings have been excavated in the region, mostly showing a great uniformity of design, in common with those known from other regions of Britain (Ill I.6). Examples range from 11m and above in diameter (as at Great Woolden Hall Farm and Brookhouse Farm, Bruen Stapleford) to 4m at Tatton Park. One peculiarity of the region is the occurrence of oval (or bow-sided) structures. Found elsewhere in Britain, they have been interpreted as a Romano-British innovation in north-

west England (Cowell & Philpott 2000, 198), but the occurrence of examples in an Iron Age phase at Mill Hill Road, Irby, and in a purely Iron Age context at Brookhouse Farm, places their origin in the first millennium BC. Most of the examples of architecture known so far from the region are timber, but it is notable that the roundhouses overlying the infilled ditches at Eddisbury had stone floors and stone foundations. Varley (1950, 57) believed them to be of sub-Roman date, but their association with VCP places them firmly in the Iron Age.

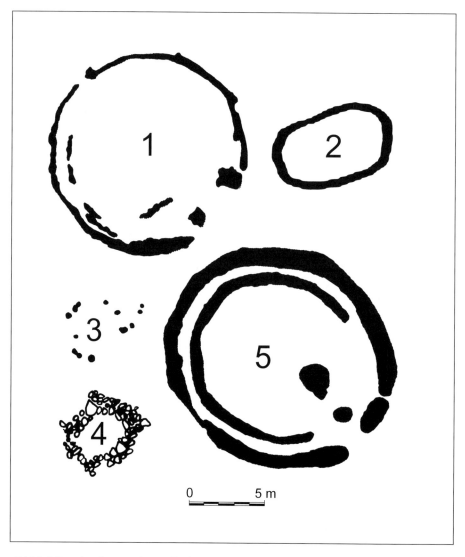

Ill I.6 Building plans from north-west England. 1: Great Woolden Hall Phase II (after Nevell 1999b, 52); 2: Mill Hill Road, Irby, Phase 3 (after Philpott & Adams 1999, 65); 3: Tatton Park building B (after Higham & Cane 1996–7, 46); 4: Castle Ditch, Eddisbury (after Varley 1950, 12); 5: Brookhouse Farm, Bruen Stapleford (after Fairburn 2002). (Scale 1/250)

Finds

Ceramics

Late prehistoric pottery is extremely uncommon in the region, the only widely represented locally made form being so-called VCP. It is thought to have been a form of briquetage used in salt production; it has a sandy fabric with inclusions that form a temper designed to resist thermal shock. The form is handmade with a flat base and a truncated, flared cone profile with a widely flared rim (Ill I.7) and its date range runs from about 1000 BC at Beeston Castle to the early Roman period (sherds were found in a Roman roadside ditch at Tarvin). One sherd among the residual prehistoric pottery from Abbey Green, Chester, was of VCP. Several large pieces, including part of the flared rim, have been found at Handbridge, south of the River Dee at Chester. At Beeston, excavation revealed substantial quantities of VCP, while at Eddisbury, where W J Varley (1950, 58) incorrectly surmised that it was of 'Dark Age' (ie sub-Roman) date, it was associated with structures built over the slighted ramparts.

VCP has been associated with salt production in Cheshire, although no single site has yet been established for the activity in the county (Morris 1985, 352). Recent observations at Coppenhall (now a suburb of Crewe) found VCP close to Romano-British salt production (Price 1994, 4). It is probable that the industry was as widespread in the Iron Age as in later periods. At this early date, it was probably based on the natural brine springs found predominantly in the south of the county. The Droitwich salt industry provided a focus for ceramic exchange (Hurst 1992, 132) and it is likely that the exchange included other types of goods. This was probably also the case in Cheshire and the pre-Roman coins occasionally found in the region are evidence for external contacts (Matthews 1996, 21).

A growing number of sites have produced a variety of pot forms of uncertain affinity. Pottery with finger-tip impressions was found at Eddisbury (Varley 1964, 90 describes it as of 'Wessex first A' type, now more generally called All Cannings Cross type); the form, although not the fabric, has parallels in the West Harling–Staple Howe group of eastern England. A high-shouldered, flat-rimmed jar from Maiden Castle, Bickerton (Varley 1964,

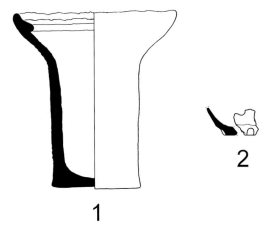

Ill I.7 Cheshire VCP forms. 1: 'Classic' Cheshire stony VCP (after Morris 1985); 2: variant ('sandy') VCP (after Ellis 1993, 75). (Scale 1/4)

101), is of the same general type (Varley 1936a, 105 adds that it was found in 'association with a small piece of iron', although he does not expand on the point). These vessels have clear affinities with the Late Bronze Age/Early Iron Age pottery from Mam Tor. The one sherd from Wilderspool (Hinchliffe & Williams 1992, 100) has not been published and is of uncertain type.

The largest assemblages from the region are from Beeston Castle, Irby and Brookhouse Farm, Bruen Stapleford. The former is dominated by Late Bronze Age types (accounting for 92.7% of the assemblage by weight), suggesting a considerable reduction in the use of pottery during the Early Iron Age. Of the remainder, 86.3% consists of stony VCP, although a small group of material classed as Fabric 19 (Ellis 1993, 71) with small bases and an outward flare appears to belong to another VCP tradition, perhaps more akin to Droitwich VCP types in shape, although they are of local manufacture. This second VCP type is also found at Irby and Brookhouse Farm, although only body sherds were represented. A large quantity of prehistoric material in seven or eight different fabrics has been recovered from Mill Hill Road, Irby, with 590 sherds weighing over 3.5 kg (Philpott & Adams 1999, 69). As well as two types of VCP, there are barrel-shaped jars and vessels with widely flared rims, again similar to the early material from Mam Tor. The assemblage from Brookhouse Farm consisted of 289 sherds with a total weight of 1363 g. Here, though, classic Cheshire stony VCP accounted for only 40% of the assemblage by weight, whilst all three fabrics of VCP made up less than half the total. The most common fabric was a domestic type, evidently belonging to a single barrel-shaped jar.

Some of the residual prehistoric pottery from Abbey Green, Chester, although of un-diagnostic form, consists of fabrics of similar type, as does material from Poulton, south-west of Chester. Pottery from excavations at Middlewich in 2001 includes an almost complete plain jar; although found in a Roman period context, the material is clearly of Iron Age date. The excavators have compared it with Malvernian Ware of the mid-first century AD, but the fabrics do not match and one of the vessels from Brookhouse Farm is more closely comparable. The large assemblage of material from Manchester Airport has not yet been published, but appears to contain some material of Late Bronze Age and Early Iron Age affinities. There is also unpublished material from Hessle Drive, Heswall (Wirral), of Iron Age type. All the closely dated pot forms — apart from VCP — belong to the Early Iron Age and have close similarities with the more plentiful material from Mam Tor.

As well as the locally made pottery, there are two very unusual ceramic items from the region. One is a fifth-century BC Massaliote amphora in the Grosvenor Museum, Chester, said to have been dredged from the River Dee around 1900 (Ill I.8). It was presented to the museum some seventy years after its discovery, raising suspicions about its alleged provenance, and it has been thought to be an illegal import of recent date. However, the encrustations on the vessel, consisting of small oysters and marine worms, are more consistent with its having lain in the Dee estuary than the Mediterranean Sea. The principal distribution of these amphorae is along the southern coast of Gaul and the Rhône–Saône valley, although examples have been found in the upper Seine and upper Danube valleys. The example from the Dee estuary may have reached north-west England by way of the Seine or, in view of some of the other imports discussed below, along the

Atlantic seaboard. A contemporary Greco-Roman earthenware pot from Bury, found in 1903 (Nevell 1993, 48), is usually seen as problematical for the same reasons. At first sight, these exotic finds appear entirely anomalous, but there are other objects from the region that are no less unusual and whose presence adds weight to a model of Iron Age exchange that will be developed below; they need not therefore be discounted as evidence for the Iron Age archaeology of the region, as some have done.

Ill I.8 Massaliote amphora dredged from the River Dee c1900, now in the Grosvenor Museum, Chester. (Reproduced by permission of Chester City Council, Grosvenor Museum)

It is now evident that the Early Iron Age was not completely aceramic and that the material has affinities with Yorkshire and the east Midlands, although there are sufficient differences from these areas to recognise a separate tradition. We are perhaps now in a position to propose a 'Bickerton–Mam Tor jar continuum' (Ill I.9) for the north-western Early Iron Age (using the convention of naming it after early excavations on sites where this material was found). It is in the Middle Iron Age that domestic pottery types become more uncommon. In view of the chronological evidence, we need to re-examine some of the Mersey valley types defined by Mike Nevell (1993, 44). In particular, his association of Type 4 from Great Woolden Hall (Nevell 1999b, 58; Ill I.10) with the very early material from Mam Tor is highly problematical in view of the radiocarbon dates that place the occupation at Great Woolden Hall in the Late Iron Age.

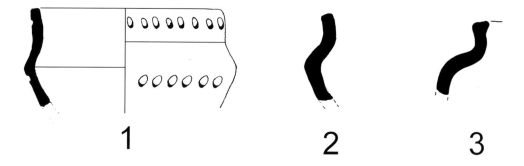

Ill I.9 Bickerton–Mam Tor jars. 1: Eddisbury (after Varley 1964, 101; NB the diameter shown is highly conjectural); 2: Maiden Castle, Bickerton (after Varley 1964, 101); 3: Beeston Castle (after Ellis 1993, 72). (Scale 1/4)

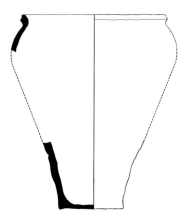

III.I.10 Late Iron Age jar from Great Woolden Hall (after Nevell 1994, 35). (Scale 1/4)

Coins

Although the population of north-west England in the Iron Age is not known to have minted coins, some minted elsewhere have nevertheless been found. They are uncommon and it is therefore difficult to comment on their distribution, but they include some very surprising exotics. Even the more banal British types raise interesting questions about how and why people brought them to the region. Steven Willis (1994, 144) has rightly pointed to the way in which exchange studies have treated deposition as a simple phenomenon, whereas recent examinations of Iron Age structured deposition demonstrate that many complex factors affect the deposition of objects, be they exchanged items or otherwise.

The most extensive identifiable collection comes from Meols. The pre-Roman assemblage (Hume 1863, 292; 290) consists of three Carthaginian half-shekels, two silver coins of the Coriosolites (a tribe of northern Brittany), one very worn gold coin of uncertain origin, although of British Late Iron Age type, and a Syrian coin of the first century BC. Of the nineteenth-century finds, only the Coriosolite coins can now be located in Liverpool Museum, as it suffered bomb damage during the Second World War and its collections were badly affected, perhaps by looting. A silver tetradrachm of Tigranes II of Armenia (20 BC–*c* 6 BC) was found about 1987 at Leasowe Common, to the south-east of Dove Point.

The Coriosolite coins are of billon, a type of base silver, and date from the early first century BC, well before any direct Roman interest in Britain or even northern Gaul. Margaret Warhurst thought it unlikely that they 'could have reached the North-West at or soon after their date of issue' (Chitty & Warhurst 1979, 35) and suggested that they were lost by an antiquarian collector during the eighteenth or early nineteenth century. This is typical of the prevailing discourse of Iron Age studies according to which all the interesting developments were confined to England south of the Thames. In fact, coins of the Coriosolites have also been found at Hexham (Northumberland) and Lesmahago (Lanarkshire) (Allen 1960, 273). These coins do not appear to be recent losses, so we can probably accept the examples from Meols as prehistoric imports, as Margaret Warhurst now does.

Detailed descriptions of the lost coins allow their types to be identified, and these types contribute to the acceptability of the Coriosolite material. The Carthaginian half-shekels were minted in the third and second centuries BC (Watkin 1886, 284 gives a good description of them). Another Carthaginian coin was found in the nineteenth century together with a coin of Pyrrhus (King of Epiros 295–275 BC) on the bed of the River Irk at Cheetham Hill, Manchester (Nevell 1993, 49). Other finds of Carthaginian coins cluster predominantly along the south and west coasts, with a few in the Home Counties (Laing & Laing 1983, 6). The gold coin from Meols was similar to British L or M type, Mack (1975, 73) 138A or Mack (1975, 75) 148, dating from the last half of the first century BC. This makes it the latest of the Iron Age coins from the site. The low weight recorded ($7\frac{1}{4}$ grains or about 0.47 g) suggests a quarter stater type.

Coins of the Corieltauvi (the people of the north-east Midlands attested in the Roman period, formerly known incorrectly as Coritani) have been found at Halton Castle in Runcorn (Allen 1963, 18) and at Brindley, near Nantwich (Tindall 1993, 3). This is much further west than usual, as the main distribution is to the south and east of the Pennines, although there are further finds from the Great Orme (Llandudno, north Wales) and Cardiganshire (Allen 1963, 14). The distribution of these coins in the region is interesting in view of the recently discovered VCP from east of the Pennines (pers comm J Evans 15 May 1999). There is also a poorly recorded hoard of Iron Age coins from Liverpool, containing at least one Gallo-Belgic bronze piece (Allen 1960, 277).

Coins began to be exchanged in Britain during the second century BC, initially as imported pieces, usually of high value, but by the end of the first century BC also as potin coins of low value. The distribution of most pre-Roman coins in Britain is strongly weighted to the south and east coasts, whether they are imports from continental Europe or of British origin. These were the areas that minted coins themselves in the later centuries BC. However, they are not the only areas where such coins are found, and isolated examples have been retrieved from as far north as the Scottish lowlands.

The purpose of Iron Age coinage is disputed. Ethnographic parallels make it clear that coinage circulates as payment for a wide variety of goods and services (Orme 1981, 179), and in a recent overview Colin Haselgrove (1996b, 67) suggests that early, high-value issues served as payment for social and political obligations. By contrast, the later bronze issues were designed for exchange transactions. However, symbolic currency (in the form of coins) is almost uniquely associated with commercial exchange and there is little anthropological justification for regarding coinage as part of a gift-exchange system, as many have done. It remains possible, if unlikely, though, that the historically specific context of the late first millennium BC could have created a system not found in any contemporary societies.

Other metalwork
There are a few pieces of metalwork that can be dated to the first millennium BC in addition to coins. The best assemblage of material comes from Beeston Castle, where there are both copper alloy and iron objects (effectively disproving Nick Higham's (1993, 28) unsupported suggestion that iron did not reach the region until the Roman conquest). There is a clearly high-status leather drinking vessel with copper alloy fittings (J Foster *in* Ellis 1993, 50) together with other material that appears to date largely from the first half of the millennium. The ironwork includes a La Tène I (conventionally dated *c* 450–325 BC) dagger and a La Tène II (*c* 325–150 BC) spearhead together with a swan's neck pin, an Early Iron Age type (Dunning 1934, 269).

The excavations at Eddisbury produced evidence for iron gate-post shoes (Varley & Jackson 1940, 74), but the nature of the excavation makes it very unclear if these belong to the prehistoric or tenth-century phase of occupation on the site. The roundhouses dated by Varley (1950, 75) to the sub-Roman period, but which clearly belong to the Iron Age in view of their association with VCP, were also related to spreads of iron slag, demonstrating the ubiquity of smithing on this part of the site.

A number of bronze pins from Meols appear to be of Early Iron Age date rather than Early Medieval, the period to which they have usually been assigned (Griffiths 1991, 303–4), although David Longley (1987, 104) mentions two swan's neck pins without further reference. Three of the pins in the Potter Collection at the Grosvenor Museum in Chester do not conform to the Early Medieval type of ring-headed pin, which has a separate ring and shaft; although broken, they are single pieces of early Iron Age form. In addition, Hume (1863, pl xxii.7) illustrates a clearly Early Iron Age ring-headed pin which is now in Warrington Museum (pers comm Rob Philpott, 24 September 2001).

Elsewhere, the discoveries are generally without context, having been discovered either residually or as metal detector finds. Varley & Jackson (1940, 73) refer to an iron billhook without giving a provenance; Ormerod (1882, **2**, 3) mentions a fragment of iron sword from Kelsborrow Castle, Kelsall. Most spectacular is a La Tène bull's head escutcheon from Crewe, belonging to the Late Iron Age. A terret ring from Stamford Bridge, although published as Roman (Robinson & Lloyd-Morgan 1984–5, 95), is a La Tène type of the first half of the first century AD and is therefore a very Late Iron Age product. The two iron wedges from Maiden Castle, Bickerton (Varley 1935, 107), are probably of post-medieval date.

Other objects
There are several loomweights from Mill Hill Road, Irby, that are similar to Late Bronze and Early Iron Age types in Britain (Philpott & Adams 1999, 70). There is also a steatite bead with La Tène decoration that enables it to be dated to the second century BC. As the nearest source of steatite is Anglesey, the object must be regarded as a further import to the region. It was found embedded in a Roman wall; it is not clear if it was simply residual and incorporated as general, undifferentiated rubble, or if it were part of a structured and symbolic deposit placed there purposefully. Spindle whorls and whetstones are relatively common finds but very difficult to date. A number of supposedly later prehistoric spindle whorls from Cheshire have been shown to be post-medieval in date, so it is difficult to accept stray finds of this character as evidence for Iron Age activity in an area.

Objects from stratified contexts show the difficulty of recognising specifically later prehistoric artefacts, as with a pounder from Brookhouse Farm, Bruen Stapleford. Some are completely unexpected, such

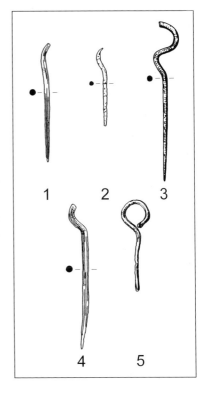

Ill I.11 Iron Age pins from Cheshire. 1: copper alloy swan's neck pin from Meols (Grosvenor Museum CHEGM: 1999.86); 2: iron swan's neck pin from Meols (Grosvenor Museum CHEGM: 1999.87); 3 iron swan's neck pin from Beeston (after Ellis 1993, 54); 4: copper alloy ring headed pin from Meols (Grosvenor Museum CHEGM: 1999.85); 5: iron ring headed pin from Meols (after Hume 1863, pl xxiii.7; now in Warrington Museum). (Scale 1/2)

as the wooden base from Brook House Farm, Halewood, with its radiocarbon date of 2720 ± 50 bp (980–790 cal BC at 2σ), which appears to have been at least five centuries old when discarded (Cowell & Philpott 2000, 46).

Bog bodies

The bodies that have been found in lowland peat bogs, particularly in the Mersey Basin, are the best known Iron Age finds from the region. They have been reported from at least ten sites, most famously Lindow Moss, but also including Meols (Turner 1995, 110). Recent analyses have suggested that we are wrong to treat them as a single phenomenon and that different explanations can be adduced for individual bodies (Turner 1995, 122; Briggs 1995, 181). They certainly belong to very different periods. Although they remain a fascinating source of information about individual people, whose remains have not otherwise been identified, they should not be allowed to dominate our accounts. In particular, attributions of 'Celtic' religious practice need critical examination in view of current debates about Celticity (James 1999, 94).

Environment and subsistence economy

Palynological evidence shows that major woodland clearance began throughout the region late in the second millennium BC, probably for cereal cultivation (Schoenwetter 1982, 11; Leah et al 1997, 152). The North-West Wetlands Survey identified increasing intensification of landscape use during the first millennium, becoming particularly marked after 500 BC, so that by the time of the Roman invasion in the first century AD there was little wild-wood left. Even so, Mike Nevell (1999a, 17) suggests that there was a period of woodland regeneration during the early first millennium, which brings the subsistence role of hillforts into question.

Evidence for agricultural practices in the form of plant or animal remains has been very difficult to identify. Cereal grains from Beeston (G Jones & R Moss in Ellis 1993, 80) can now be matched by others from Mill Hill Road, Irby (Philpott & Adams 1999, 70); while they demonstrate that arable farming was practised, it remains impossible without further evidence to determine if this was anomalous or characteristic. Several species are represented, including bread wheat (*Triticum aestivum*), emmer (*T dicoccum*), spelt (*T spelta*), barley (*Hordeum sp*), oats (*Avena sp*) and possibly rye (*Secale cereale*). In upland areas, stock rearing may have been more common, although it has been suggested (Hall et al 1995, 119) that conditions at this time were too wet for settlement above the 200m contour. No Iron Age plant remains or animal bone assemblages have been recovered from sites north of the Mersey (Huntley 1995, 41; Stallibrass 1995, 128), with the exception of the small assemblage from Brook House Farm, Halewood (M Robinson in Cowell & Philpott 2000, 49). This group is dominated by cattle mandible fragments, with some frog and the fragment of a tooth from a sub-adult pig. The cattle bone shows good evidence for butchery practice, including the likely removal of the tongue and the extraction of marrow, while charring is indicative of cooking. The animals all appear to have been fully adult at the time of their death (presumably by slaughtering). How representative this small assemblage is of the pattern throughout the region is unknown and the recovery of more environmental remains is an important research priority (Stallibrass & Huntley 1995, 201).

Exchange

Salt

Cheshire salt was exchanged over a wide region during the first millennium BC. It is impossible for obvious reasons to detect the salt itself, but the VCP containers mentioned above are distributed throughout north-west England, the north Midlands and Wales. Elaine Morris (1985, 355) was the first to characterise the material as a type of Iron Age briquetage, and she was able to distinguish early and late patterns by comparing distributions of stratified sherds from sites with secure radiocarbon dates. Larger quantities of material have become available since she published her work, largely confirming her analysis and extending the distribution east of the Pennines. In the early phase, covering the Early Iron Age, Cheshire VCP is the only type found in the area north of the River Severn (Ill I.12). Sites in the middle reaches of the Severn valley contain a roughly equal mixture of Cheshire VCP and Droitwich salt containers. Further south, Droitwich salt containers are the only forms to be found. This is exactly what would be expected from an overland or riverine distribution. The pattern shows this to have been a very simple form of exchange, belonging to the period in which the hillforts were in use.

The later distribution pattern — covering the Middle and Late Iron Age — shows that Cheshire salt was exchanged throughout north Wales, the north Midlands and the Marches (Ill I.13). Sites in Herefordshire, Worcestershire and Gloucestershire that had only Droitwich salt containers in the Early Iron Age now have some Cheshire VCP, although it is never the dominant form. The south-western distribution of Cheshire material is separated from the northern by an area in northern Worcestershire where only Droitwich material is found. This clearly indicates a more complex distribution mechanism than in the earlier period, presumably with a redistribution centre somewhere on the lower Severn and the existence of maritime exchange routes. This has important social implications.

Trade and Emporia

The term 'trade' has value-laden implications of profit as a motive for exchange and other reasons can be more important. It can be suggested that the main reason for using this term is that it fits the evolutionary scheme of Polanyi (1944), who associated redistributive trade with centralised polities. Other models of exchange may be suggested, including models of reciprocity, social embeddedness and so on. Nevertheless, Barry Cunliffe's (1978, 67) model of redistributive trade through *emporia* continues to dominate our understanding of long-distance exchange during the Iron Age.

Cunliffe defines *emporia* as trading settlements with good harbours, forming points of contact between traders and the populations in their hinterlands. There were essentially redistribution centres in what Thomas Beale (1973, 142) defines as 'regional organised trade'. The Coriosolites were evidently an important link in exchange in western Britain. Cunliffe presents the major *emporium* at Hengistbury Head, Dorset, as the sole aim of the Coriosolite traders. In Cunliffe's model, the distribution patterns outside Hengistbury are explained as a result of trade by locals into a 'hinterland' (Cunliffe 1988, 103). He completely disregards the admittedly limited Irish Sea evidence, but further trading posts can be identified along the western coast of Britain, that may have been served either by local traders or by Coriosolite merchants. The Rumps, a cliff-top defended site in north

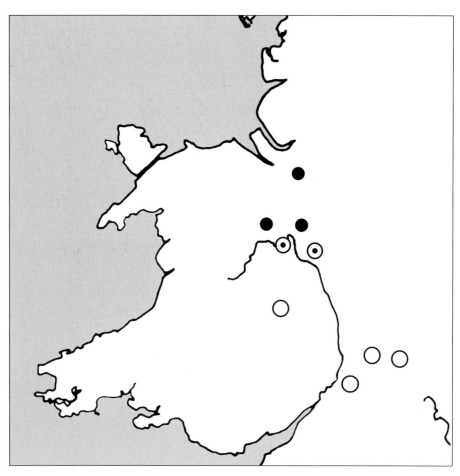

Ill I.12 Distribution of Cheshire and Droitwich VCP before 300 BC (c 300 Cal BC) (after Morris 1985, with additions): map. (Not to scale) • = Cheshire (stony) VCP; ● = Droitwich VCP; ⊙ = both types.

Cornwall, has produced imported pottery. Coastal sites at St David's Head and Merthyr Mawr in south Wales are similar in character but have not so far produced exotic material. Meols is the next identifiable site to the north. Beyond it lies a major site at Whithorn (Cowley 2000) and, beyond this, Stevenston Sands near Ayr is the most northerly of these coastal *emporia* so far to have been identified; there may be others in the Western Isles and north-west Scotland.

Cunliffe's model is entirely Mediterranean-based: the classical Greco-Roman cities comprise his core area and reduce the north to a periphery useful only for the procurement of raw materials. This is particularly evident in the subtitle of his recent book, casting Pytheas as 'the man who discovered Britain' (Cunliffe 2001), when it had been continuously settled for almost eleven thousand years in Pytheas's day! However, viewed from the so-called 'periphery', imports of any kind from distant centres of production would have been exotic and rare, items traded in stages on the back of the more important exchanges of everyday

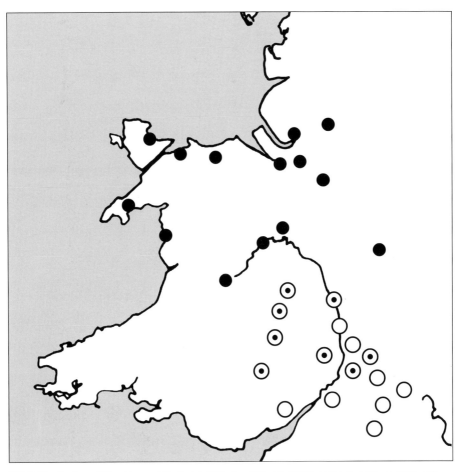

Ill I.13 Distribution of Cheshire and Droitwich VCP after 300 BC (c 300 Cal BC) (after Morris 1985, with additions): map. (Not to scale) • = Cheshire (stony) VCP; ● = Droitwich VCP; ⊙ = both types.

local produce. Moreover, such trade need not be restricted to purely local populations trading within a small hinterland, as the distribution of Coriosolite and other exotic coins hints that an international merchant class was operating by this date.

For a number of reasons, the exotic items from the region are difficult to explain in terms of down-the-line exchange, in which goods are passed from community to community or individual to individual, involving many separate exchanges (Renfrew 1973, 207; Beale 1973, 141). The fall-off in numbers of exotica in Britain to the west and north of Mount Batten at first sight suggests that this was the westernmost point at which they were an important component of exchange, and it could be that beyond Mount Batten they ceased to have commercial or symbolic value (the two are linked anyway) and were exchanged only as curios. (Incidentally, Barry Cunliffe has recently shown (2001, 79) that there is good evidence for activity at Mount Batten throughout the first millennium BC, a situation remarkably similar to Meols). However, in north-west England these exotica — metalwork, ceramics (the pots from Longdendale, Great Woolden Hall and, less certainly, Bury) and, possibly wine (as evidenced by the drinking vessel from Beeston and the amphora from the Dee estuary) — can be seen to have been elements in a trade which involved the exportation of salt to south Wales and the southern Marches but which probably included other products as well. Much of the trade remains invisible: it presumably concentrated on perishables but with a small amount of durable material culture.

The pattern of exchange that is visible, with the export of a locally produced rural resource and the importation of high-status exotica, has been characterised as 'upwardly mobile' and requires the presence of social stratification, with class unequals within the system of production and exchange at the local level (Gregory 1994, 932, 935). Greg Woolf (1998, 180) has pointed out that in Gaul 'before the conquest, Iron Age populations did purchase Mediterranean goods, but for their own ends, not in order to reproduce classical cultural processes'. These practices, as is well known, included feasting and drinking, with the consumption of imported wine by the elites, a feature remarked on by Roman writers (Woolf 1998, 184).

The six exotic coins from Meols, which is the only one of the *emporia* beyond Mount Batten with any coins whatsoever, are further indication that the exchange was more complex than has hitherto been appreciated. These coins will only have had symbolic value in coin-using societies, which north-west England's population was not. This is a strong indication that the coins were being used by people who were not local, presumably Coriosolite and perhaps even Carthaginian merchants living in distinct communities where they retained their own social practices. Ethnographic parallels for *emporia* (Macknight 1973, 201) indicate that multicultural communities of this type are common features of such places. The loss of a Massaliote amphora in the Dee estuary hints strongly at long-distance maritime exchange. These facts indicate that some form of organised exchange was taking place at Meols. Moreover, it is likely that it was carried out between local élites and foreign traders, the only two groups of people to value the imports. This kind of exchange requires a society with a much more complex economic organisation than we are accustomed to attributing to the Iron Age peoples of the region and a degree of social differentiation that has hitherto been difficult to perceive.

Consumption

Economic archaeology generally concentrates on cataloguing and classifying materials and establishing the processes of their production and distribution, as in classical economics generally (Fine 1995, 27). It is only in recent years that the effects of consumption have been studied (Miller 1994; Ferris 1995), but it is clearly an important factor in determining the cultural identities of groups at any period. In the light of the small quantities of such material in the region, it seems that the Iron Age populations of north-west England did not take part in the conspicuous consumption of durable material culture. However, the occasional finds of exotica show that there was access to international exchange. The common assumption that north-western populations were too 'poor' to acquire such goods through exchange begs a number of questions and is not an adequate explanation (Haselgrove 1996a, 69). Rather, by and large, the north-western élites chose not to procure the materials that, in the south-east, would have marked them out as members of the international set, probably because it had no meaning to their social inferiors. It may be hypothesised that they concentrated their acquisition of status from invisible social networks and practices, perhaps *via* systems of patronage, livestock accumulation, mineral control and so on. A lack of material 'wealth' is therefore not necessarily proof of a lack of economic dominance by an élite. In other words, the northern élites may have been seen as wealthy not through the consumption of continental material culture, for which they had little use, but through their archaeologically invisible social practices. The small quantities of exotic goods may be interpreted as items used by resident aliens (such as the Coriosolite coins) or as items used in peer interactions (such as the drinking-vessel from Beeston, which would have been used in situations such as feasting, where it could display signals that need not be interpreted by social inferiors).

Nevertheless, something was being exchanged for the exported salt and, like the salt, it seems to be archaeologically invisible. It may be that the north-western élites acquired exotic forms of livestock from further south, even the continent; on the other hand, the Massaliote amphora from the Dee estuary and the drinking-vessel from Beeston are suggestive of the importation of completely invisible materials such as wine.

A model of settlement

The study of rural settlement — whether by archaeologists, anthropologists, geographers or historians — is very much seen as the poor cousin of the study of urbanisation. Towns and cities are privileged in our accounts by virtue of their identification with 'civilisation', especially the civilisation which has produced the academic tradition within which archaeological researchers operate; the rural settings of the towns are in turn denigrated by being presented as 'hinterlands'. This attitude informs and reinforces the Roman specialist's view of the Iron Age as mere preface and the popular conception of pre-Roman 'Celtic' warriors. The Iron Age cannot, by definition, be 'civilised', except perhaps in south-east Britain during the century or so before the Roman invasion. There are nevertheless suggestions of hierarchies of settlement type in pre-urban settings, and the identification of possible patterns will enable predictions to be made about the types of society that produced them.

The model that will be proposed for the patterning of Iron Age settlement in north-west England will draw heavily on work in three non-archaeological disciplines: anthropology, geography and history. While the geographical and historical models — central place theory and multiple estates — ought to be familiar to archaeologists, the anthropological model is sufficiently new for its impact not yet to have been felt. However, it is a model with good claims to operate cross-culturally and ahistorically. It is this model that will be described first.

The population density model

Anthropologists working on the size and organisation of human groups began to recognise in the 1970s and 80s that there are cross-cultural thresholds of group size on either side of which different forms of social organisation and settlement are found (Kosse 1990, 287). This approach allows us to view social identity as a series of nested identities, beginning with the individual's sense of person, up through what we might care to think of as 'kinship' groups, 'friendship' groups, 'settlement' groups, 'regional' groups and finally 'ethnic' groups. These different scales of identity can be correlated with the thresholds suggested by Kosse as defining different forms of social organisation. She identifies specific organisational thresholds at populations of 150±25, 500±100 and 2500±500. The 500 threshold marks the upper limit of a gathering that does not need to be organised, while the 2500 threshold marks the difference between politically simple and politically complex settlements. The lower threshold is subtler in its effects, but can be linked with disaggregated and aggregated settlement patterns. The thresholds and their links with social formations and settlement patterns are summarised in Table I.1.

The model derives from both the anthropological data about social formation (notably drawn from Sahlins (1963)) and settlement size, and neurological tests of memory capacity. Six levels have been established for amounts of data which can be utilised and stored together by the human brain (which, owing to the binary nature of information storage and processing in the brain, are in powers of two: 2^0, $2^3\pm2^1$, $2^7\pm2^5$, $2^9\pm2^7$, $2^{10}\pm2^8$ and $2^{11}\pm2^9$). The third, fourth and sixth of these levels correspond closely to the anthropologically derived thresholds for settlement size, which strongly implies a pan-cultural nature to the phenomenon and suggests that it is rooted in the structure of the human brain. It also suggests the existence of other thresholds of group size (at around $2^3\pm2^1$ and $2^{10}\pm2^8$) whose effects have not yet been identified, although they may be relevant to small-scale societies such as those believed to be prevalent in Iron Age Britain. Importantly, the model is not deterministic: with increasing threshold size, more choices exist for social development, allowing each individual social group to have its own unique historical trajectory.

There is considerable debate within anthropology about the appropriateness of typologies of social formation and cultural evolution (Earle 1994, 941), although it is possible to

Table 1 Classificatory scheme for levels of social integration and settlement size (after Kosse 1990, 295)

Social formation	Population of largest settlement	Settlement hierarchy	Size of regional network
State	> 2500	five-tier hierarchy	-
Complex chiefdom	> 2500	four-tier hierarchy	c 1500km²
Simple chiefdom	> 2500	three-tier hierarchy	-
Peer polity type II	c 2500	minimal hierarchy	c 1500km²
'Big Man' society	< 2500	two-tier hierarchy	c 2500 people
Peer polity type I	> 500	minimal hierarchy	-
Acephalous group	500	Aggregated	c 2500 people
Family level (public)	150	Disaggregated	c 500 people
Family level (hamlet)	< 25	-	c 500 people
Family level (family)	6–8	-	c 500 people

reconcile the most popular. This is possibly because they share many features in common, particularly a broadly tripartite division (from egalitarian through ranked to stratified societies) and an origin in broadly Marxist theory. Within these broad divisions, there are nevertheless numerous variations on precise definitions. Table I. 2 summarises four such schemes together with popular (if approximate) archaeological correlates from European prehistory.

Table I. 2 Definitions of social organisation (adapted from Earle 1994, 941)

Childe (1964)	Service (1962) Johnson & Earle (1987)	Sahlins (1963) Earle (1978)	Fried (1967)	Archaeological correlates Renfrew (1973)
Savagery	Band (family level)	Head man	Egalitarian society	
				Megaliths
Barbarism	Tribe (local group)	Big man	Ranked society	Maltese temples
		Simple chiefdom		
Civilisation	Chiefdom	Complex chiefdom	Stratified society	Metallurgy
	State	State	State	Civilisation

These models of organisation are underpinned by an assumption that social differentiation has its origins in inequalities in access to power. The term 'power' is deliberately vague, because it derives from a wide variety of sources: social, military, ideological and economic. Social change and evolution are believed to occur because of the competitive nature of those who wield power, rendering societies with any form of ranking inherently unstable unless the élite is able to centralise and institutionalise its control of the sources of power (Earle 1994, 957). Of particular interest to the archaeologist are those symbols in which power is encoded: prestige artefacts, settlements and storage.

This model can be applied to the archaeologically attested settlement pattern of the north-western Iron Age. None of the sites so far identified is likely to have exceeded the 500 ± 100 threshold, except perhaps Meols and the salt-producing area in the Nantwich region, which may have reached the $2^{10}\pm2^8$ level. This can be taken to indicate that the social structure conformed to the 'Peer Polity' or 'Big Man' type. In either case, the existence of a well stratified society is unlikely. However, in the model proposed above for exchange, the presence of an élite is virtually a prerequisite; perhaps we can infer that there is a 'missing' threshold of information processing, of 1000 ± 250 and that this is a threshold at which an economic élite becomes viable, but without producing a strongly hierarchical settlement pattern.

The multiple estate model
Since its publication in 1976, G R J Jones's exposition of the historical evidence for multiple estates in medieval Wales has been enormously influential in discussions of early medieval estate organisation throughout Britain generally. Although it was without political unity, there was a basic cultural tradition of settlement organisation within early medieval Wales which suggests a common origin in the sub-Roman, Romano-British or

earlier periods. Individual principalities (*gwladau*) have frequently been seen as the successors of the Roman *civitates*, at least in south and east Wales, which in turn developed from pre-Roman polities. The most important subdivision of the *gwlad* was the *cantref* (etymologically, 'hundred *trefi* ('vills')'). These were in turn subdivided into two *cymydau* ('commotes'), which notionally each contained twelve *maenolau* (multiple estates). A *maenol* comprised four *trefi* ('vills'), so that an individual *cymyd* would have had forty-eight *trefi*; the two additional *trefi* to bring the total up to fifty were royal demesne, the *maerdref* (effectively the *caput*, or chief place, of the *cymyd*) and a *tref* consisting of waste and summer pasture.

Table I.3 Hierarchical structure of the multiple estate (after Jones 1976, 15)

Maenol (estate)

Tref (vill)	*Tref*	*Tref*	*Tref*
4 holdings	4 holdings	4 holdings	4 holdings
16 sharelands	16 sharelands	16 sharelands	16 sharelands
64 homesteads	64 homesteads	64 homesteads	64 homesteads

This numerical precision is a reflection of the nature of the evidence: in its fullest form it is preserved in Welsh legal texts of the thirteenth century. However, the concept was already ancient, and the system was clearly more flexible than the legal texts imply. As with the anthropological model, there is a five-tier hierarchy. However, this is based on territorial organisation in a society without significant concentrations of population. In the legal texts, four homesteads are defined as the constituent parts of a shareland; four sharelands form a holding, four holdings a *tref* or *villa* (vill) and four *trefi* a *maenol* (estate). Although medieval Wales has often been characterised as a land without towns or villages (even by contemporaries, such as Giraldus Cambrensis), there is evidence to show that there were a few nucleated settlements (Davies 1982, 20). Nevertheless, the terms used in the hierarchical structure refer not to settlement size but to settlement status: in early medieval Britain the administrative centres were not necessarily the largest settlements.

Central Place theory

Although much in vogue among archaeologists in the 1970s, Central Place theory became unfashionable during the 1980s, arguably because of the inappropriate uses to which it had been put (Collis 1986, 38). However, the theory, developed by Walter Christaller in the 1930s, is based on a number of commonsense hypotheses with cross-cultural applicability. Firstly, that a non-agricultural settlement needs a rural hinterland (best thought of in terms of a provisioning area) to support it; secondly, that the bigger the settlement, the bigger its hinterland; thirdly, that tributary areas focused on small settlements will be found in the hinterlands of large settlements. Early applications of the theory in archaeology simply followed Christaller's models and were not found to be useful except in rare specific cases because they ignored the historically specific nature of the original data set and often failed to apply relevant historically specific models to the archaeological data.

The basic premise of the theory is that the locations of settlements of different rank can be predicted according to the nature of the ranking system. Christaller proposed three basic rank types: one based on market activity, one based on transport and one based on administration. In the first type, second-order places are situated in the best location to be accessible to three first-order places, maximising access to markets. In the second, second-order places are located on the communications routes between two first-order places, minimising travel costs. In both these instances, the second-order places are to be found on the borders between the territories of first-order places. In the last, second-order places lie entirely within the territory of the first-order place on which they are dependent. Third, fourth-, fifth-, sixth- and seventh-order places also exist in this scheme, nesting within the larger patterns but conforming to one of the three organisational patterns discussed. The nature of the rank types is historically specific: other situations, for instance settlement location according to 'irrational' or symbolic principles (such as Feng Shui), are historically attested.

It has been possible to characterise the functions of different sizes of settlement and to correlate these with their market functions, their average spacing and their relative administrative importance. This is summarised in Table I.4. It is possible to spot the seven-kilometre spacing which is the ideal distance between places of specialised activity — in this instance the lowest rank of market. Clearly, we cannot take this model wholesale and apply it to the Iron Age, based as it is on nineteenth-century south Germany. The types of market product, administrative level and population size are undoubtedly historically con-stituted and have no claim to universality of application. However, the distances proposed between settlements are based on the ease of movement of human beings through a land-scape. The modelling of hierarchies in Christaller's hypothesis does not depend on changes brought about by the transport revolution of the nineteenth century, as they apply to an earlier period.

Table I.4 Correlation between consumer products, settlement hierarchy, spacing and size (after Jones 1966, 86 and 88)

Product	Settlement rank	Distance	Population
Expensive jewellery	Regional capital city	186km	300,000
Display clothing	Provincial centre	108km	90,000
	Small state capital	62km	27,000
Quality clothing	District city	36km	9,000
Children's clothing	County town	21km	3,500
Work clothing	Small town	12km	1,500
Food necessities	Village	7km	800

Christaller's model must be regarded as incomplete, largely because of his assumption of a capitalist market economy (Wagstaff 1986, 121). This led him to presuppose the primacy of the market principle in the distribution of places and the subordination of the transport and administrative organising principles. Clearly, in a society where the free market system is unknown, the marketing principle may be subordinate to one or both of the other principles. If, for instance, the Iron Age settlement pattern were dictated by the needs of a dominant élite, then we might expect the administrative principle to be fundamental. Had it grown up as a result of exchange networks in a socially embedded economy, we might expect it to conform most closely to the transport principle. Had it been designed to serve the needs of maintaining a symbolic landscape, we might find the hierarchy more difficult to model. In practice, we might find that it corresponds not to one system alone, but to a combination, varying over time and distance.

The spacing of settlements is relevant to the interpretation of their hierarchy. Seven kilometres is the distance accepted by anthropologists as an average day's return journey by foot to a location at which a specialised activity will take place. In the geographical model used here, it is the average spacing of village-type settlements whose principal economic function is the provision of food necessities. It can be recognised, for instance, in the sub-Roman settlement patterns of south-western England as the spacing of estate centres located in re-used hillforts (Dark 1994, 162). I have suggested elsewhere (Matthews 1994, 53) that the eight-kilometre spacing of hillforts in Cheshire reflects this type of administrative arrangement in the early first millennium BC. In a subsistence economy of Early Iron Age type, it is unlikely that hillforts were centres for the acquisition of food necessities and it may be suggested that they were centres for the distribution of other necessities, such as livestock, everyday metalwork and salt. This suggests the gradual development of specialisation during the Late Bronze and Early Iron Ages, which may form the background to the growth of an economic élite.

Synthesis of the models

It will be obvious that these three models are mutually compatible as they deal with essentially exclusive aspects of settlement. The first is concerned with the organisational abilities of the human mind and the numbers of people that can be encompassed within social transactions. The second examines a historically specific form of territorial organisation that is probably much earlier than its first documentation The third attempts to explain settlement location within networks of supply, communications and political control. In each of the three models there is a hierarchical view of settlement and comparisons can be made between the models, allowing the partial data of the archaeological record to be examined as if it were more complete.

Discussion

The nature of the data

The data are more incomplete than is usual in archaeological data sets as a result of a number of factors. These include the nature of the region's soils and agricultural practices, neither of which is conducive to the formation of the crop marks that would enable the easy detection of sites, and a chronic lack of interest in the regional Iron Age until the 1980s. Even so, there is a considerable if disparate body of data: it has been the lack of a theoretical framework for interpreting it which has rendered it so intractable. Models for understanding the period are now starting to be proposed (Nevell 1999a, 23; Matthews 1999b, 33; Cowell & Philpott 2000, 169). The data have a real existence and properties that can be quantified; frameworks can be proposed for giving these data structure and meaning without making claims for their 'truth'. The results of these readings can then be tested against different models and *vice versa*, establishing a dialectic. Whilst remaining in the realms of theory, it is possible to set up hypotheses capable of testing by fieldwork. Two apparently rival theories have emerged in recent years, based on the same data set. One, that the regional Iron Age was essentially egalitarian, with subsistence farmers nevertheless engaging in salt production and exchange, perhaps organised by outsiders. The second, that an economic élite emerged during the Early and Middle Iron Age, basing its wealth on developing and organising the long-distance exchange of salt and other products, and with direct continental contacts.

The distribution of the material

It is necessary to construct models of the relative values of different classes of data before hypotheses about settlement patterns can be tested. If the data were complete or rich, this would present few problems. However, it has been suggested that we are not yet in a position to accept our data as anything like a representative sample because there is not enough (Nevell 1999b, 63). Nevertheless, the attempt is worthwhile and has the potential to open up new areas for research. The models presented here will be at best provisional. A sustained research programme of investigation into sites of first millennium BC date must be a priority for the immediate future.

Early Iron Age settlement sites cluster on higher ground and include both hillforts and promontory enclosures. The two forms appear to be closely linked within the social land-scape, being under an hour's walk apart. Given the climatic deterioration of the Late Bronze Age, it appears curious that the visible elements of the settlement pattern are con-centrated on higher ground, especially on the Pennine fringes, where it has been suggested that conditions were too wet for arable farming (Nevell 1999a, 17).

The sole *emporium* identified in the region — Meols — is likely to have been the only one. The distribution of these sites across western Britain strongly suggests that they served hinterlands of many hundreds of square kilometres. If, as suggested here, these regions had a socio-political as well as economic coherence, these types of site would necessarily have been closely supervised by local élites (although this need not imply actual control).

The lowland sites so far investigated appear to belong to the Late Iron Age, although there are hints (as at Legh Oaks and Brookhouse Farm, Bruen Stapleford) that some have earlier origins. It is evident that they became more numerous at this time. This may point to a movement away from concentrations of population on the higher ground to a more dis-persed settlement pattern during the later centuries BC; on the other hand, it also coincides with a period of huge population growth across Britain generally. This occurred at a time when the climate was becoming noticeably drier. It may not reflect a newly acquired ability to work the dominant clay soils (whether through improved technology or as a result of their drying out), as these sites tend to cluster on well drained soils. On the other hand, that may be a reflection of our ability to discover sites in these places through aerial photography and their virtual invisibility in other locations. Nevertheless, the shift away from occupation of the higher ground towards the lowland plains during the latter part of the Middle Iron Age is very marked.

Explanations of the patterning

What might the changing nature of population distribution tell us about social develop-ments at this time? During the initial seminar from which this paper derives, joking reference was made to the emergence two rival hypotheses for Iron Age and Romano-British society in north-west England: the 'Nevell–Evans' hypothesis of egalitarian farmers with no complex political structure and the 'Matthews–Philpott' hypothesis of a politico-economic élite. Although the individuals concerned expressed surprise that their models could be interpreted as radically different, there are differences between them that deserve exploration. Each has it merits and problems, so they will be examined here in some detail.

Technology and the economy

The Iron Age of north-west England has traditionally been seen as economically backward and peripheral to the main social developments of southern Britain. The main reason given for this is the alleged paucity of archaeological evidence (Higham 1993, 29). This privileges durable material culture as the only type of wealth available to a population, a peculiarly modern Western perspective. We can but hope that the days are long gone when the lack of pottery could be explained as 'the movement of military pioneering groups travelling without their womenfolk, with whom the finer aspects of material culture were associated' (Varley 1936b, 120). There are plentiful ethnographic examples of very different types of wealth accumulation. Wealth may be expressed by numbers of wives, sons, goats, slaves, quantities of grain, access to mineral resources or almost any item over which the 'wealthy' individual has control; in south Yorkshire, for instance, it has been suggested that cattle were the indicators of wealth (Chadwick 1997). Unfortunately, we cannot yet see the hypothesised élites of north-west England in the archaeological record through their stored wealth.

The local population did not produce large quantities of durable material culture products such as pottery, and their acquisition and display — in other words, their consumption — does not seem to have been of any social or economic value. That such material did exist can be amply demonstrated, but it remains uncommon. The Iron Age of north-west England must be evaluated on its own terms and the terms of its contemporary neighbours, not ours. These terms allow us to see a development of international exchange at a surprisingly early date, some time around the middle of the first millennium BC. This exchange seems to have been based, insofar as it is visible, on the export of salt. Mediterranean contacts, which, by the third century, were probably direct, were part of the exchange network, although they were probably always of minor importance; they are visible because of the exotic durable material culture they occasionally brought to the region. In contrast to the south-east, long-distance trade in the west began in the Early Iron Age, was maintained until its end and implies that the social developments in the region were developed around exchange networks operating through Liverpool Bay.

Society

The egalitarian hypothesis

There is little doubt that, by the end of the Middle Iron Age, the hillforts that dominate the record of the regional Early Iron Age had fallen out of use. While some have seen hillforts as central places in a society with hierarchical ranking — whether as the residences of an élite or as symbolic centres — it remains the case that the hypothesised lower ranked settlement sites have not yet been located. If these enclosures are the sole settlement type of the Early Iron Age, as the model that sees the small enclosures as a development of the Late Iron Age would suggest, then the population density model discussed above suggests that society corresponded to either a peer polity or acephalous group type. These would allow concentrations of population of up to 500 individuals (which is presumably above the maximum size of population for the hillforts). If this were the case, each hillfort will have formed the core of a single small socio-political unit (Matthews 1994, 53).

According to this model, the changes that occurred during the Middle Iron Age took the population away from the uplands onto river terraces, which became the favoured location for a new style of settlement, the small curvilinear enclosure (Nevell 1997, 20). Again, there was little sign of differentiation, if the size of enclosure is taken as a criterion for ranking (Nevell 1999a, 23). The relative lack of social competition would have created an environment in which conspicuous consumption of display goods was irrelevant, so the acquisition of these objects would not be a priority. In this model, the small numbers of exotic items that are found must be explained as little more than curios, presumably reaching north-west England by down-the-line (or trickle-) trade, with goods changing hands many times before arriving at Meols.

The élite dominance hypothesis
Although it is possible to interpret the settlement data as indicative of a society with little or no social stratification, it is also possible to suggest the development of élites from the Early Iron Age though to the Middle Iron Age. Evidence for these élites comes principally from the evidence for long-distance trade provided by the distribution of VCP and the exotic imports that began to reach the region by the fifth century, but there may also be hints in the settlement pattern. The chronological distribution of the imports — from the fifth through to the first century BC and possibly into the first century AD — suggests sustained contact with the outside world. Indeed, the increasingly widespread export market for Cheshire salt may be taken to indicate the continuing development of these economic links. As argued above, these links suggest a degree of organisational complexity that cannot be encompassed within the acephalous groups or minimally hierarchical peer polity groups implied by an Early Iron Age settlement pattern consisting largely of hillforts.

For the Early Iron Age it is possible to suggest that the smaller lowland promontory enclosures, such as Peckforton Mere or Oakmere, were closely connected with nearby hillforts (Matthews 1994, 53). Although there is little information about the interior of any of these sites, it is likely that the hillforts were home to rather larger populations than the lowland promontory enclosures. Indeed, given the close association between the two types, the latter may have been the residences of the élites who were beginning to control the resources on which the developing exchange networks depended. Only excavation of the interior of one of these lesser sites will clarify such questions as date, density of occupation and economic status. There are also hints that some of the single-ditched curvilinear enclosures (such as Legh Oaks I) belong to this early period, while some open sites such as Manchester Airport or Brookhouse Farm, Bruen Stapleford, are certainly Early Iron Age.

We thus have suggestions of an Early Iron Age three-tier settlement hierarchy, suggestive of a simple chiefdom, according to Kristina Kosse's model. This model predicts that the largest settlement ought to have a population of between 500 and 2500; perhaps the hillforts were of the 500–1000 size. It was suggested above that the effect of one of the thresholds missing from the anthropological data about social formation (around 1000±250) would be to allow the formation of an economically dominant élite. Is there therefore evidence that the populations of hillforts grew during the Early Iron Age? At Eddisbury, round houses were built on the slighted ramparts (Varley 1950, 57) at an unknown date, although they were associated with VCP. Rather than viewing the demolition of the ramparts as a work with military or at least defensive meaning (Varley (1950, 57) saw it as the work of the Roman army, but it is clearly much earlier), might it be suggested that the population of Eddisbury simply grew too large to live inside the enclosed area?

We might therefore argue that the Middle Iron Age was a period when localised chiefdoms developed into a more complex system in this region. Increasingly large settlements re-quired a stronger political authority than earlier in the Iron Age and, in the model proposed here, the emergent rulers based their power primarily on economic control. There is a difficulty in viewing these élites as chiefdoms, whether simple or complex. Timothy Earle (1994, 957) has pointed to the cyclical nature of chiefdoms and their inherent instability. Yet we have seen how north-west England remained socially stable for an immensely long time, resisting the incursion of Roman cultural practices and retaining its coherence for more than a millennium. How do we resolve this contradiction? The easiest way is to sug-gest that the social formation of the region moved from a chiefdom into a more complex, state system during the Middle Iron Age. As with the economic model, this is considerably earlier than is usually suggested in the South.

The complexity of the way in which this exchange was organised indicates that the evolutionist models that makes the earliest state development in Britain a phenomenon of the Late Iron Age in south-east England are wrong. By the Middle Iron Age, communities in western Britain were able to organise long-distance trade, with what were evidently multicultural coastal *emporia*, which reverse the accepted geography of development. The North-West was sufficiently complex in economic and political terms to engage in this sort of trade perhaps three centuries before the South. Nevertheless, the pattern that was established did not lead to the type of acculturation seen in the South-East. After an early development, society in north-west England remained stable and probably conservative for centuries (if not a millennium or more). It has a close parallel in Iron Age developments in Galloway, where the pre-Roman cultural patterns remained intact until the thirteenth century, when it was finally incorporated into the Scottish state (Cowley 2000).

The Late Iron Age, on the other hand, appears more as a period of consolidation, even retrenchment. Socially, the construction of small enclosures represents private investment in monumental construction for the first time: the earlier hilltop enclosures were public works. This is a significant change that can be compared with the construction of home-stead moats in medieval England: in both instances, non-élites were engaged in building small 'defensive' earthwork enclosures containing farmsteads in areas that had previously not been cultivated. In the case of medieval moats, they are associated with an emergent class of small landowners seeking independence from aristocratic landlords. A similar phenomenon may account for the Iron Age 'private fortifications' of north-west England, but we would be wrong to discount other explanations. While the proliferation of such enclosures during the Late Iron Age may represent the opening up of the landscape by a new class of entrepreneurial, independent landowners, they also demonstrate an inward focusing of competition. What form this competition took cannot be determined on the evidence currently available. The effort put into the enclosures was clearly one expression of that competition, while the lack of interest in prestige durable material culture suggests some other form of wealth accumulation and display.

The Cornovii and Brigantes

Little more than a decade ago, it would have been considered appropriate to begin or end any account of Iron Age Cheshire with an exposition of the Cornovii, their territory and their material culture. Lancashire, by contrast, would be dealt with under the rubric 'Brigantes'. Recent developments in archaeological theory, especially with regard to ethnicity and group identity, have meant that such issues are now seen as more contentious than they would once have been.

The late Graham Webster's (1991) book *The Cornovii*, an account of the Romano-British *civitas*, begins with the inevitable Iron Age 'background' that all culture historical approaches to Roman Britain seem to find so necessary. Having defined his geographical area (Shropshire, much of Cheshire and part of north-east Wales), Webster surveyed the Iron Age remains and concluded that the characterisation of the people was a near impossibility. This is unsurprising. The evidence we possess for the extent of Cornovian territory is late (second century AD) and refers to Romano-British, not Iron Age, administrative arrangements. All we know is that Οὐιροκόνιον (*Viroconium*, Wroxeter) and Δηοῦα (Deva, Chester) were within the *Civitas Cornoviorum* according to the (probably late first-century) source used by the Alexandrian mathematician Claudius Ptolemaeus in compiling his *Geography*.

We cannot know whether this territorial arrangement was ancient or an innovation of Roman provincial government. Evidence that the Ellesmere moraine marked a major prehistoric cultural boundary would suggest that, if Cheshire had been part of Cornovian territory in the Iron Age, then we cannot define the people according to their material culture. On the other hand, it might suggest that the Romano-British *civitas* absorbed part of an entirely different people.

There is, of course, no evidence that a people known as the Cornovii even existed during the Iron Age. The experience of British colonial administrators in southern Africa during the nineteenth century provides an interesting analogue for the development of Romano-British political structures during the first century AD. The earliest Europeans in south Africa reported a wide diversity of 'peoples': political groupings that did not correspond to the ethnic groups they were defining on the basis of language, customs, dress and so on. By the end of the nineteenth century, though, the groups defined by the colonisers had begun to develop identities that correspond much more closely to their ethnic definitions. Patrick Harries (1989, 82) has proposed that these identities formed as a direct response to contact with the outsiders, and that self-awareness did not occur until a local bourgeoisie had developed under the influence of missionaries. He argues that the formation of ethnic identity is dependent on the differentiation of class interests and the consumption of cultural symbols. A similar situation could have obtained in first-century Britain and it is easy to see how a Cornovian identity might have been forged under these circumstances. The origins of the Cornovii might then be seen to be based more on economic opportunities and colonial administrative practices than on a shared history.

The situation is even clearer with the Brigantes. Claudius Ptolemaeus treats them as a single people occupying the land between the Mersey and Humber to the south and Hadrian's Wall to the north, with the exception of the Parisi of east Yorkshire. Modern writers have seen them as a confederacy, perhaps with its origins in the century or so before the Roman conquest (eg Kenyon 1991, 41). There is certainly strong evidence to suggest that Roman writers used the term as a catch-all for those peoples in the militarised zone of northern *Britannia*. Moreover, Claudius Ptolemaeus mentions a Σεταντιων Λιμην ('harbour of the Setantii') on the Lancashire coast, whilst there is epigraphic evidence for a *Civitas Carvetiorum* in Cumbria by the third century (Rivet & Smith 1979, 301) and a people known as the Tectoverdi (more usually given as Textoverdi, with a Greek -χ-) in the central part of Hadrian's Wall (Rivet & Smith 1979, 470). The Brigantes' core territory seems to have lain to the east of the Pennines, in the Vale of York.

What of the name Setantii, then? The location of their harbour is unknown, although some interpretations have favoured Fleetwood (Kenyon 1991, 40) and others Morecambe Bay (Strang 1997, 25). Accepting the latter identification suggests that the Setantii were the people of the Lune valley in the later first century AD, which conflicts with epigraphic evidence that this area was known as *Contrebis*. On the other hand, an identification with Fleetwood leaves open a connection between the ethnic name Setantii and Seteia, the name of the River Mersey (Rivet & Smith 1979, 457). The ethnic name would then mean something like 'people of the Mersey basin'. This intriguing suggestion raises the possibility that the name of the people considered in this paper, at least at the time of the Roman conquest, was *Setantii*. However, it would be dangerous to press the argument too far or to suggest that it could have been used to refer to the people of five centuries earlier.

The cognitive arena: beliefs and identities

Temporality

Although archaeology is directly connected with time — through the age of the material it studies — until recently, it has rarely considered the experience of time by the peoples it deals with. The anthropologist Tim Ingold's concept of 'taskscape' (Ingold 1993, 158), the space within which people do things, offers us a way of examining the rhythms of life in ancient societies. The time it takes people to perform a task will vary according to the space in which it has to be performed. For instance, the experience of walking across medieval Lancaster in less than ten minutes and of living and working in the same city-centre property will be have been very different from the experience of walking through the city in 1900, taking half an hour or more, and of travelling a mile or more to work. In the same way, if we can understand the temporal relationships between Iron Age farm-steads, their fields, the central places where people exchanged goods, paid tribute and worshipped their gods, and the places where they disposed of their dead, we will gain insights into the taskscapes of these people.

So far, the evidence we possess is limited. The spacing of hillforts on the Mid-Cheshire Ridge has previously been commented upon as apparently indicating that they were a single day's walk apart and could thus form the basis of a redistributive system for agricultural goods (Matthews 1994, 53).

Conclusions

It is abundantly clear that the first millennium BC and the first millennium AD in north-west England can only be understood through structures of the *longue durée*:[5] an enduring pattern of consumption and cultural affinity which was established in the Early Iron Age continued into the sub-Roman period. The hypothesis of an early development of long-distance exchange controlled by an emerging economic élite during the Early Iron Age may at first sight appear eccentric, but the evidence virtually forces it upon us unless we are to dismiss the data completely. It makes the distribution of a wide variety of anomalous finds from the Iron Age of north-west England much easier to explain and it places the region into an international context without making any claims for a dominance or importance it clearly did not possess. It also harks back to the economic vitality of the region as a supplier of copper during the earlier Bronze Age: Roman interest in the region may have been prompted by Clwydian silver, which was perhaps being exploited at this early date. We can now see that the region is peripheral only in terms of the lack of durable material culture; in other words, it is peripheral only in archaeologists' perceptions. By refocusing our attention on the local data rather than comparing it unfavourably with southern Britain, we can assess it without preconceived notions of 'failure' or 'backwardness'.

The hillforts that have dominated our accounts of the Iron Age belong to an early period of unsophisticated exchange in north-west England. Unlike the role Barry Cunliffe has proposed for Danebury, they were clearly not sub-regional storage or redistributive centres; their role as economic or administrative central places must be questioned and was probably negligible. Nevertheless, they were perhaps associated with political organisation at the level of the simple chiefdom from the Late Bronze Age onwards. By the time that exchange had developed a degree of complexity that appears to have involved foreign merchants residing at least semi-permanently at Meols and interacting with an economic élite around 300 BC, the hillforts were an anachronism as central places. The new élites were living in enlarged hillforts with slighted ramparts or double-ditched enclosures, their subordinates in single-ditched enclosures and open settlements; wealth was being expressed in ways that are not currently visible to our archaeological techniques; economically specialised settlements were developing at Meols and, perhaps, Nantwich and Middlewich. Central places and the conspicuous consumption of durable material culture were not important to the Iron Age élites of north-west England: how can we begin to assess the economy of the region in the first millennium BC if we do not appreciate this?

Acknowledgements

I am grateful to Peter Carrington and Mike Morris for comments on an earlier draft of this paper and to Jerry Evans for supplying information about discoveries of VCP to the east of the Pennines. I would also like to thank the staff of the various Sites and Monuments Records for their prompt responses to my very vague query ('Can you give me a list of Iron Age sites and findspots?'). I should also like to thank Neil Fairburn for sight of Alistair Quarterman's undergraduate dissertation and for his permission to use his resistivity data.

Appendix 1
Radiocarbon dates for first-millennium sites in north-west England

Site name	Sample number	Date bp	Date Cal BC[c]	Reference
Mam Tor	Birm-202	3130 ± 132	1700–1000	Coombs & Thompson 1979, 44
Mam Tor	Birm-192	3080 ± 115	1650–950	Coombs & Thompson 1979, 44
Beeston Castle: period 2B rampart	HAR-4405	2860 ± 80	1260–830	Ellis 1993, 85
Kate's Pad, Pilling Moss	Q-68	2760 ± 120	1350–750, 700–550	Middleton et al 1995, 61
Brook House Farm, wooden artefact	Beta-117717	2720 ± 50	980–790	Cowell & Philpott 2000, 58
Beeston Castle: period 3 posthole	HAR-4401	2620 ± 90	950–400	Ellis 1993, 85
Maiden Castle, Bickerton: inner rampart north	UB-2619	2620 ± 95	1000–400	Cheshire SMR341/1
Brook House Farm, silting of gully associated with VCP	Beta-118138	2560 ± 60	830–510, 470–410	Cowell & Philpott 2000, 58
Almondbury	I-5931	2540 ± 95	830–400	Coombs & Thompson 1979, 50
Almondbury: uppermost rampart	I-4542	2505 ± 100	820–390	Coombs & Thompson 1979, 50
Almondbury	HAR-183	2480 ± 110	850–350	Coombs & Thompson 1979, 50
Beeston Castle: period 3A ditch	HAR-8102	2480 ± 70	780–400	Ellis 1993, 85
Almondbury	HAR-84	2470 ± 130	850–200	Coombs & Thompson 1979, 50
Castercliff: rampart 2	S-287	2460 ± 60	770–400	Coombs 1982, 127
Castercliff: rampart 1	S-286	2460 ± 70	780–400	Coombs 1982, 127
Maiden Castle, Bickerton: south entrance outer rampart strapping	UB-2615	2435 ± 70	770–400	Cheshire SMR 341/1
Beeston Castle: period 3B rampart	HAR-6465	2430 ± 70	770–390	Ellis 1993, 85
Lindow II (Lindow Man)	HAR-6224	2420 ± 100	800–350, 300–200	Housley et al 1995, 45
Almondbury	HAR-83	2410 ± 110	800–200	Coombs & Thompson 1979, 50
Almondbury	HAR-135	2400 ± 110	800–200	Coombs & Thompson 1979, 5

Site name	Sample number	Date bp	Date Cal BC[7]	Reference
Beeston Castle: period 3B rampart	HAR-5609	2400 ± 70	780–360	Ellis 1993, 85
Beeston Castle: period 3B posthole	HAR-4402	2380 ± 100	800–200	Ellis 1993, 85
Beeston Castle: period 3B rampart	HAR-6469	2370 ± 80	800–200	Ellis 1993, 85
Maiden Castle, Bickerton: inner rampart north	UB-2618	2360 ± 100	800–200	Cheshire SMR 341/1
Beeston Castle: period 3B rampart	HAR-6503	2350 ± 70	800–200	Ellis 1993, 85
Maiden Castle, Bickerton: inner rampart north	UB-2617	2350 ± 60	800–350 300–200	Cheshire SMR 341/1
Tatton Park: Pit 7	HAR-5147	2340 ± 120	800–100	Higham & Cane 1996–7, 57
Beeston Castle: period 4	HAR-6504	2310 ± 70	800–650 550–150	Ellis 1993, 85
Beeston Castle: period 3B rampart	HAR-6464	2300 ± 80	800–650 550–150	Ellis 1993, 85
Beeston Castle: period 3B rampart	HAR-6468	2290 ± 70	550–100	Ellis 1993, 85
Beeston Castle: period 3 posthole	HAR-4406	2280 ± 80	800–700 550–50	Ellis 1993, 85
Brook House Farm, secondary ditch silting	Beta-117711	2260 ± 50	400–200	Cowell & Philpott 2000, 58
Lindow II (Lindow Man)	OxA-1041	2210 ± 60	400–100	Housley et al 1995, 45
Lindow II (Lindow Man)	OxA-789	2190 ± 100	410–AD 30	Housley et al 1995, 45
Ditton Brook, pit fill	OxA-3678	2170 ± 70	400–10	Cowell & Philpott 2000, 19
Brook House Farm, secondary ditch silting	Beta- 117716	2150 ± 60	380–40	Cowell & Philpott 2000, 58
Castlesteads	Beta-58077	2140 ± 70	370–AD 1	Nevell 1999b, 60
Brook House Farm, final silting of gully, associated with VCP	Beta-117712	2140 ± 40	360–280 260–40	Cowell & Philpott 2000, 58
Brook House Farm, stone-packed posthole	Beta-118139	2140 ± 40	360–280 260–40	Cowell & Philpott 2000, 58
Maiden Castle, Bickerton: south entrance outer rampart strapping	UB-2614	2130 ± 70	380–10	Cheshire SMR 341/1
Lindow II (Lindow Man)	OxA-605	2125 ± 80	380–AD 30	Housley et al 1995, 45
Lindow III	OxA-1524	2040 ± 90	400–AD 200	Housley et al 1995, 41
Tatton Park: structure	JHAR-4496	2030 ± 120	400–AD 250	Higham & Cane 1996–7, 57
Lindow III	HAR-9094	2010 ± 80	200–AD 150 AD 160–220	Housley et al 1995, 41
Lindow III	OxA-1523	2000 ± 100	400–300 250–AD 250	Housley et al 1995, 41
Great Woolden Hall: phase II	GrN-16849	1990 ± 25	40–AD 80	Nevell 1999b, 49

Site name	Sample number	Date bp	Date Cal BC[s]	Reference
Great Woolden Hall: phase III	GrN-16850	1970 ± 100	200–AD 350	Nevell 1999b, 49
Lindow II (Lindow Man)	OxA-790	1970 ± 80	170–AD 240	Housley *et al* 1995, 45
Brook House Farm, early disuse of ditch	Beta-117715	1970 ± 70	170–130 120–AD 220	Cowell & Philpott 2000, 58
Lindow II (Lindow Man)	OxA-782	1950 ± 80	160–AD 250	Housley *et al* 1995, 45
Lindow II (Lindow Man)	OxA-781	1940 ± 80	120–AD 260 AD 290–320	Housley et al 1995, 45
Lindow II (Lindow Man)	OxA-783	1920 ± 80	100–AD 260 AD 280–330	Housley *et al* 1995, 45
Lindow II (Lindow Man)	OxA-531	1920 ± 75	70–AD 260, AD 280–330	Housley *et al* 1995, 45
Tatton Park: structure J	HAR-5111	1910 ± 110	200–AD 400	Higham & Cane 1996-7, 57
Lindow II (Lindow Man)	OxA-1040	1910 ± 60	40–AD 250	Housley *et al* 1995, 45
Lindow II (Lindow Man)	OxA-784	1900 ± 80	60–AD 340	Housley *et al* 1995, 45
Lindow II (Lindow Man)	OxA-785	1900 ± 80	60–AD 340	Housley *et al* 1995, 45
Beeston Castle: period 3B rampart	HAR-5610	1890 ± 120	200–AD 450	Ellis 1993, 85
Lindow III	OxA-1521	1890 ± 100	100–AD 400	Housley *et al* 1995, 41

Appendix 2
Sites and finds of the Iron Age of north-west England

Name	Description	NGR			References
Abbey Green, Chester	Plough marks and pottery	SJ	4048	6667	Cheshire SMR 3015
Arthill Heath farm	Subrectangular enclosure complex	SJ	7279	8586	Cheshire SMR 2061/1/0
Baddiley Mere	Logboat	SJ	5971	5039	Cheshire SMR 363
Beeston Castle	Hillfort	SJ	5380	5920	Cheshire SMR 1732/1
Bickerton	Possible farmstead	SJ	5125	5463	Cheshire SMR 330/1
Billington	Burial mound containing iron spearheads	SD	6990	3750	Lancashire SMR
Blatchinrod	Lenticular quern	SD	9550	1730	G Manchester SMR 2715/1
Bradley	Univallate promontory fort	SJ	5394	7679	Cheshire SMR 971/1
Brereton	Bull's-head escutcheon	SJ	7650	6259	Cheshire SMR 2502
Bruen Stapleford, Brookhouse Farm	Farmstead	SJ	4975	6398	Fairburn 2002
Burton Point	Univallate promontory fort	SJ	3033	7356	Cheshire SMR 9/1
Bury, Calrow Lane	Greco-Roman earthenware pot	SD	7976	1145	G Manchester SMR 162
Camp Hill, Liverpool	Hillfort?	SJ	4241	8583	Merseyside SMR 4285-001
Castercliff	Univallate hillfort	SD	8848	3839	Lancashire SMR 224
Castle Ditch, Eddisbury	Bivallate hillfort	SJ	5530	6930	Cheshire SMR 866/1
Castleshaw	Stone spindlewhorl	SD	9980	0960	G Manchester SMR 1191/2
Castle Hill, Heywood	Possible hillfort	SD	8273	1248	G Manchester SMR 2498/1
Castle Hill, Oldcastle	Possible bivallate promontory fort	SJ	4681	4414	Cheshire SMR 1667/1
Castleshaw	Spindlewhorl	SD	0000	0970	G Manchester SMR 5931/1
Castlesteads, Walmersley	Promontory fort	SD	7969	1298	G Manchester SMR 78/1/2
Chapelhouse Poulton	Farmstead	SJ	4024	5845	Unpublished
Cheetham Hill	Coins (Epirote, Carthaginian & Roman)	SJ	8430	9920	G Manchester SMR 1393/1
Chester	Glass bead	SJ	3940	6540	Cheshire SMR 2007
Cholmondeley Castle	Dugout canoe	SJ	5300	5100	Cheshire SMR 325
Congleton Edge	Three millstone grit querns	SJ	8700	6000	Cheshire SMR 157

Name	Description	NGR			References
Deneshay Slipway	Coin	SJ	2289	0150	Merseyside SMR 2289-015
Ditton Brook, Ditton	Pit	SJ	4750	8540	Cowell & Philpott 2000
Finness Hill	Possible enclosure (now destroyed)	SJ	5350	7410	Cheshire SMR 995/1
Gawsworth	Disc-quern and fragment	SJ	9113	7094	Cheshire SMR 1538
Great Low	Possible hillfort (now destroyed)	SJ	9568	7703	Cheshire SMR 1602/1
Giant's Seat, Bolton	Univallate promontory fort	SD	7747	0484	G Manchester SMR 1461/1
Great Meols	Emporium	SJ	2310	9060	Merseyside SMR 2390-009
Great Woolden Hall	Oval enclosure	SJ	6980	9290	G Manchester SMR 1783/1
Great Woolden Hall Farm	Bivallate promontory fort	SJ	6910	9355	G Manchester SMR 1907/1
Grimsditch	Placename possibly indicating earthwork	SJ	7050	8210	Cheshire SMR 1263
Halewood, Brook House Farm	Bivallate enclosure	SJ	4730	8500	Cowell & Philpott 2000
Hangingbank, Werneth Low	Double-ditched enclosure	SJ	9650	9350	G Manchester SMR
Helsby Hill	Bivallate promontory fort	SJ	4927	7539	Cheshire SMR 1007/1
Heswall, Hessle Drive	Pottery	SJ	2690	8105	Merseyside SMR 2681-027
Irby	Oval enclosure	SJ	2544	8375	Merseyside SMR 2583-001
Irby, Mill Hill Road	Farmstead and enclosures	SJ	2520	8520	Merseyside SMR 2585-044
Kate's Pad	Wooden trackway, Pilling Moss	SD	4099	4460	Lancashire SMR 84
Kelsborrow	Univallate promontory fort	SJ	5316	6752	Cheshire SMR 833/1
Kirkby Vicarage	Excavated site	SJ	4090	9890	Merseyside SMR 4098-017
Leasowe Common	Tetradrachm of Tigranes II of Armenia	SJ	2578	9162	Merseyside SMR 2591-006
Legh Oaks Farm enclosure A	Oval ditched enclosure	SJ	6902	8318	Cheshire SMR 2062/1
Legh Oaks Farm enclosure B	Subrectangular ditched enclosure	SJ	6898	8325	Cheshire SMR 2062/2
Lindow III	Bog body	SJ	8219	8073	Cheshire SMR 1473/0/3
Lindow Man	Bog body	SJ	8202	8057	Cheshire SMR 1473/0/2
Lindow Moss	Animal jawbone (*Bos taurus*)	SJ	8183	8059	Cheshire SMR 1472/0/1

Name	Description	NGR		References
Longdendale	La Tène pot	SK	0550 9880	
Longley Hill field system	Regular aggregate field system	SJ	5294 7008	Cheshire SMR 1984
Longton Marshes	Pin	SD	4500 2600	Lancashire SMR 1692
Macclesfield	Disc- or quoit-shaped loomweight	SJ	9115 7460	Cheshire SMR 1559
Maiden Castle hillfort	Bivallate hillfort	SJ	4977 5289	Cheshire SMR 341/1
Manchester	Bronze ox-head ornament	SJ	8300 9700	G Manchester SMR 2008/1
Middlewich	Terret ring	SJ	7070 6670	Cheshire SMR 1080/0/32
Newbold Astbury	Dugout canoe	SJ	8489 6054	Cheshire SMR 1160
Oakmere	Univallate promontory fort	SJ	5760 6780	Cheshire SMR 848/1
Peckforton Mere	Subrectangular ditched enclosure	SJ	5430 5767	Cheshire SMR 314
Pilling Moss	Dagger scabbard			Lancashire SMR
Portfield (Planeswood Camp)	Bivallate promontory fort	SD	7459 3551	Lancashire SMR 181
Radcliffe	Possible univallate promontory fort	SD	7670 0700	G Manchester 3829/1
Rainow	Part of saddle quern	SJ	9527 7627	Cheshire SMR 1598
Rainsough	Farmstead	SD	8105 0213	G Manchester SMR 346/1
Rawhead Farm	Cropmarks of possible farm	SJ	5150 5490	Cheshire SMR 329
Red House Farm, Dunham Massey	Subrectangular enclosure	SJ	7736 8977	G Manchester SMR 1488/1
Red Moss, Rossendale	Gold torc	SD	8400 2700	Lancashire SMR 206
Ribchester	Pot	SD	6509 3513	Lancashire SMR 4215
River Ribble	Triple-headed bucket mount			Lancashire SMR
Calderbrook	Beaded torc	SD	9447 1839	G Manchester SMR 2702/1
Rochdale, Blackstone Edge	Iron spearhead	SD	9730 1680	Lancashire SMR
Roe Cross	Subrectangular ditched enclosure	SJ	9863 9670	G Manchester SMR
Rossett, Town Ditch	Upper half of beehive quernstone	SJ	3289 5887	CPAT SMR 100350
Shaw Brows	Enclosure	SJ	8280 9885	G Manchester SMR 1584/1
Snow Hill, Nantwich	Brine pit	SJ	6496 5243	Cheshire SMR 178/1
Tarvin	Lower half of rotary quern	SJ	4857 6705	Cheshire SMR 1894

Name	Description	NGR			References
Tatton Park	Roundhouse and yard	SJ	7570	8140	Cheshire SMR 1297
Twemlow	Lower half of rotary quern	SJ	7836	6829	Cheshire SMR 1055
Walmersley, Bury	Univallate promontory fort	SD	7970	1300	Fletcher 1986
Warrington	'Celtic' vase	SJ			Cheshire SMR 499
Warrington	Fragments of quern	SJ	6200	8752	Cheshire SMR 442
Warrington crannog 1	Timber structure supported on oak piles	SJ	6110	8821	Cheshire SMR 498/1
Warrington crannog 2	Timber piling	SJ	6070	8640	Cheshire SMR 477/1
Wepre promontory fort	Bivallate promontory fort	SJ	2888	6769	CPAT SMR 100053
Werneth Low	Ditched enclosure	SJ	9700	9320	G Manchester SMR
Wildboarclough	Subcircular enclosure	SJ	9900	6930	Cheshire SMR 2154
Winwick enclosure	Subrectangular ditched enclosure	SJ	6120	9260	Cheshire SMR 2411
Winwick enclosure	Subrectangular ditched enclosure	SJ	5940	9310	Cheshire SMR 2121
Winwick enclosure	Subrectangular ditched enclosure	SJ	6225	9418	Cheshire SMR 2410
Woodhouses hillfort	Univallate hillfort	SJ	5107	7573	Cheshire SMR 970/1
Worsley Man	Male human head from Astley Moss	SJ	7100	9700	G Manchester SMR 1961/1
Y Gaer, Llay	Oval enclosure	SJ	3555	5608	CPAT SMR 100351

Notes

[1] This paper has its origins in a conference called 'Let There Be Light!' organised jointly by the Lancaster University Archaeological Unit, Gifford and Partners and National Museums and Galleries on Merseyside and held in Liverpool and Lancaster on successive Saturdays 15 and 22 May 1999. Despite the original intention to publish the proceedings of the conferences rapidly, this has not happened and a revised and expanded version of the paper presented is published here.

[2] Details of all radiocarbon dates, including laboratory number and published source, are presented in Appendix 1.

[3] The lower-case bc convention used here indicates an uncalibrated radiocarbon date; for clarity, calibrated dates are recorded as Cal BC.

[4] It should be noted that the interpretations given here are mine, not Alistair Quarterman's, so any errors of interpretation are mine alone.

[5] The underlying structures of civilisation, according to Fernand Braudel (1993, 27), which change so slowly as to be almost imperceptible.

[6] The range is given at two standard deviations (95.4% confidence) and was calculated using the Oxford Calibration Program OxCal, version 3.5 2000, available from http://www.rlaha.ox.ac.uk/orau/06_01.htm. All dates are years BC, unless otherwise stated

Bibliography

Allen, D F 1960 — The origins of coinage in Britain: a reappraisal. *In*: Frere, S S ed. Problems of the Iron Age in southern Britain: papers given at a CBA conference held at the Institute of Archaeology, December 12 to 14 1958. London University. (Institute of Archaeology Occas Pap **11**), 97–308

Allen, D F 1963 — The coins of the Coritani. London: British Academy. (Sylloge of coins of the British Isles **3**)

Beale, T W 1973 — Early trade in highland Iran: a view from a source area. *World Archaeol* **5** (2), 133–48

Bevan-Evans, M & Hayes, P A, 1963–4 — Y Gaer,Llay. Report on rescue excavations, 1961. Flintshire Hist Soc Pub **21**, 21–31

Braudel, F 1993 — A history of civilizations. Translated by Mayne, R. Harmondsworth: Penguin

Briggs, S C 1995 — Did they fall or were they pushed? Some unresolved questions about bog bodies. *In*: Turner & Scaife eds, 168–82

Brown, A *et al* 1975 — Excavations at Halton Brow, Runcorn, 1967. *J Chester Archaeol Soc* new ser **58**, 85–9

Bu'Lock, J D 1955 — Possible remains of Celtic fields at Kelsall in Cheshire. *Trans Lancashire Cheshire Antiq Soc* **64**, 24–6

Bu'Lock, J D 1956 — The hill-fort at Helsby, Cheshire. *Trans Lancashire Cheshire Antiq Soc* **66**, 107–10

Carrington, P ed 1994 — The English Heritage book of Chester. London: Batsford

Chadwick, A 1997 — Towards a social archaeology of later prehistoric and Romano-British field systems in South Yorkshire, West Yorkshire and Nottinghamshire. *Assemblage* **2**. http://www.shef.ac.uk/~assem/2/2chad.html

Childe, V G 1964 — What happened in history. Harmondsworth: Penguin

Chitty, G & Warhurst, M 1979 — Ancient Meols: finds from the Cheshire shore. *J Merseyside Archaeol Soc* **1**, 19–42

Collis, J 1986 — Central place theory is dead: long live the central place. *In*: Grant ed, 37–9

Coombs, D G 1982 — Excavations at the hillfort of Castercliff, Nelson, Lancashire 1970/1. *Trans Lancashire Cheshire Antiq Soc* **81**, 111–30

Coombs, D G & Thompson, F H 1979 — Excavation of the hillfort of Mam Tor, Derbyshire. *Derbys Archaeol J* **99**, 7–51

Cowell, R W & Innes, J B 1994 — The wetlands of Merseyside. Lancaster University Archaeological Unit. (North West Wetlands Survey **1**; Lancaster Imprints **2**)

Cowell, R W & Philpott, R A 2000 — Prehistoric, Romano-British and medieval settlement in lowland north-west England: archaeological excavations along the A5300 road corridor in Merseyside. Liverpool: National Museums and Galleries on Merseyside

Cowley, D C 2000	Site morphology and regional variation in the later prehistoric settlement of south-western Scotland. *In*: Harding, J & Johnston, R eds. Northern pasts: the later prehistory of northern England and southern Scotland. Oxford: British Archaeological Reports. (BAR British Ser **302**)
Cunliffe, B 1978	Hengistbury Head. London: Elek
Cunliffe, B 1988	Greeks, Romans and barbarians: spheres of interaction. London: Batsford
Cunliffe, B 2001	The extraordinary voyage of Pytheas the Greek: the man who discovered Britain. London: Allen Lane
Dark, K R 1994	*Civitas* to kingdom: British political continuity 300–800. Leicester U P
Davies, W 1982	Wales in the early Middle Ages. Leicester U P
Dunning, G C 1934	The swan's-neck and ring-headed pins of the Early Iron Age in Britain. *Archaeol J* **91** (2), 269–95
Earle, T 1978	Economic and social organization of a complex chiefdom: the Halalea District, Kaua'I, Hawaii. Ann Arbor: University of Michigan. (Univ Michigan Anthropol Pap **63**)
Earle, T 1994	Political domination and social evolution. *In*: Ingold ed, 940–61
Ellis, P 1993	Beeston Castle, Cheshire: excavations by Laurence Keen and Peter Hough, 1968–85. London: English Heritage. (Archaeol Rep **23**)
Fairburn, N 2002	Unique early Iron Age and Romano-British settlements near Chester. *The Past Uncovered* February 2002, 3
Ferris, I 1995	Shoppers' paradise: consumers in Roman Britain. *In*: Rush P ed. Theoretical Roman Archaeology: second conference proceedings. Aldershot: Avebury, 132–40
Fine, B 1995	From political economy to consumption. *In*: Miller, D ed. Acknowledging consumption: a review of new studies. London: Routledge, 127–63
Fletcher, M 1986	A fortified site at Castle Steads, Walmersley, Bury. *Greater Manchester Archaeol J* **2**, 31–40
Forde-Johnston, J 1962	The hill forts of Lancashire and Cheshire. *Trans Lancashire Cheshire Antiq Soc* **72**, 9–46
Forde-Johnston, J 1976	Hillforts of the Iron Age in England and Wales: a survey of the surface evidence. Liverpool U P
Fried, M H 1967	The evolution of political society: an essay in political economy. New York: Random House
Grant, E ed 1986	Central places, archaeology and history. Sheffield University
Gregory, C A 1994	Exchange and reciprocity. *In*: Ingold ed, 911–39
Griffiths, D W 1991	Anglo-Saxon England and the Irish Sea region AD 800–1100: an archaeological study of the lower Dee and Mersey as a border area. Unpubl PhD thesis Univ Durham
Gwilt, A & Haselgrove, C 1997	Approaching the Iron Age. *In*: Gwilt, A & Haselgrove C eds. Reconstruction Iron Age societies. Oxford: Oxbow (Oxbow Monograph **71**), 1–8

Hall, D *et al* 1995   The wetlands of Greater Manchester. Lancaster University Archaeological Unit. (North-West Wetlands Survey **2**; Lancaster Imprints **3**)

Harries, P 1989   Exclusion, classification and internal colonialism: the emergence of ethnicity among the Tsonga-speakers of South Africa. *In*: Vail, L ed. The creation of tribalism in southern Africa. London: Currey, 82–117

Hart, C R 1981   The north Derbyshire archaeological survey to AD 1500. Chesterfield: North Derbyshire Archaeological Trust

Haselgrove, C 1996a   The Iron Age. *In*: Newman, R ed. The archaeology of Lancashire: present state and future priorities. Lancaster University Archaeological Unit

Haselgrove, C 1996b   Iron Age coinage: recent work. *In*: Champion, T R & Collis, J R eds. The Iron Age in Britain and Ireland: recent trends. Sheffield: J R Collis Publications, 67–85

Higham, N J 1993   The origins of Cheshire. Manchester U P

Higham, N J & Cane, T 1996–7   I: The Tatton Park project: prehistoric to sub-Roman settlement and land use. *J Chester Archaeol Soc* new ser **74**, 1–61

Hill, J D 1989   Re-thinking the Iron Age. *Scott Archaeol Rev* **6**, 16–23

Hinchliffe, J & Williams, J H 1992   Roman Warrington: excavations at Wilderspool 1966–9 and 1976. Manchester Univ. (Brigantia Monogr **2**)

Housley, R A *et al* 1995   Radiocarbon dating of the Lindow III bog body. *In*: Turner & Scaife eds, 39–46

Hume, A 1863   Ancient Meols: or, some account of the antiquities found near Dove Point, on the sea-coast of Cheshire; including a comparison of them with relics of the same kinds respectively, procured elsewhere. London: John Russell Smith

Huntley, J P 1995   Review of the botanical remains. *In*: Huntley & Stallibrass eds, 19–83

Huntley, J P & Stallibrass, S eds 1995   Plant and vertebrate remains from archaeological sites in northern England: data reviews and future direction. Durham: Architectural and Archaeological Society of Durham and Northumberland. (Res Rep **4**)

Hurst, D 1992   Pottery. *In*: Woodiwiss S ed. Iron Age and Roman salt production and the medieval town of Droitwich. London: Council for British Archaeology. (CBA Res Rep **81**)

Ingold, T 1993   Tool-use, sociality and intelligence. *In*: Gibson, K R & Ingold, T eds. Tools, language and cognition in human evolution. Cambridge U P, 429–45

Ingold, T ed 1994   Companion encyclopedia of anthropology. London: Routledge

James, S 1999   The Atlantic Celts: ancient people or modern invention? London: British Museum

Johnson, A & Earle, T, 1987   The evolution of human societies: from foraging group to agrarian state. Stanford U P

Jones, E 1966   Towns and cities. Oxford U P

Jones, G R J 1976   Multiple estates and early settlement. *In*: Sawyer P H ed. Medieval settlement: continuity and change. London: Edward Arnold, 15–40

Kenyon, D 1991   The origins of Lancashire. Manchester U P

Kosse, K 1990   Group size and societal complexity: thresholds in the long-term memory. *J Anthropol Archaeol* **9**, 275–303

Laing, J & Laing, L 1983   A Mediterranean trade with Wirral in the Iron Age. *Ches Archaeol Bull* **9**, 6–8

Leah, M *et al* 1997   The wetlands of Cheshire. Lancaster University Archaeological Unit. (North West Wetlands Survey **4**; Lancaster Imprints **5**)

Longley, D 1987   Prehistory. *In*: Harris, B E & Thacker, A T eds. A history of the county of Chester **1**. London: Oxford UP for University of London Institute of Historical Research. (Victoria History of the Counties of England), 36–114

Mack, R P 1975   The coinage of ancient Britain. Ed 3. London: Spink and Seaby

Macknight, C C 1973   The nature of early maritime trade: some points of analogy from the eastern part of the Indonesian archipelago. *World Archaeol* **5** (2), 198–208

Manley, J 1991   Small settlements. *In*: Manley, J *et al* eds. The archaeology of Clwyd. Mold: Clwyd County Council, 97–115

Matthews, K J 1994   Archaeology without artefacts: the Iron Age and sub-Roman periods in Cheshire. *In*: Carrington, P ed. From flints to flower pots: current research in the Dee-Mersey region. Papers from a seminar held at Chester, February 1994. Chester: Chester City Council. (Archaeol Serv Occas Pap **2**), 51–62

Matthews, K J 1996   Iron Age sea-borne trade in Liverpool Bay. *In*: Carrington, P ed. 'Where Deva spreads her wizard stream': trade and the port of Chester. Papers from a seminar held at Chester, November 1995. Chester: Chester City Council. (Chester Archaeology Occas Pap **3**), 12–23

Matthews, K J 1997   Immaterial culture: invisible peasants and consumer subcultures in north-west Britannia. *In*: Meadows, K *et al* eds. TRAC 96: proceedings of the Sixth Annual Theoretical Roman Archaeology Conference, Sheffield 1996. Oxford: Oxbow, 120–32

Matthews, K J 1999a   *Britannus/Britto*: Roman ethnographies and native identities. *In*: Leslie, A ed. Theoretical Roman archaeology and architecture: the third conference proceedings. Glasgow: Cruithne, 14–32

Matthews, K J 1999b   Rural settlement in Roman Cheshire: a theoretical view. *In*: Nevell ed, 27–34

Middleton, R *et al* 1995   The wetlands of north Lancashire. Lancaster University Archaeological Unit. (North-West Wetlands Survey **3**; Lancaster Imprints **4**)

Miller, D 1994   Material culture and mass consumption. New impression. Oxford: Blackwell

Morris, E 1985   Prehistoric salt distributions: two case studies from western Britain. *Bull Board Celtic Stud* **32**, 336–79

Nevell, M 1989a   An aerial survey of southern Trafford and northern Cheshire. *Greater Manchester Archaeol J* **3** (1988–9), 27–34

Nevell, M 1989b   Great Woolden Hall Farm: excavations on a late prehistoric/Romano-British native site. *Greater Manchester Archaeol J* **3** (1988–9), 35–44

Nevell, M 1992a   Tameside before 1066. Ashton-under-Lyne: Tameside Borough Council

Nevell, M 1992b   A Romano-British enclosure on Werneth Low, Tameside. *Archaeol North-West* **4**, 19–22

Nevell, M 1993   Late prehistoric pottery types from the Mersey basin. *Manchester Archaeol Bull* **8**, 40–51

Nevell, M 1994   Rainsough: a Romano-British site in the Irwell valley. *Archaeol North-West* **2** (1), 11–15

Nevell, M 1997   The archaeology of Trafford: a study of the origins of community in North West England before 1900. Altrincham: Trafford Metropolitan Borough Council

Nevell, M 1999a   Iron Age and Romano-British rural settlement in North West England: theory, marginality and settlement. *In*: Nevell ed,14–26

Nevell, M 1999b   Great Woolden Hall Farm: a model for the material culture of Iron Age and Romano-British rural settlement in North West England? *In*: Nevell ed, 48–63

Nevell, M *forthcoming* Legh Oaks Farm, High Legh: the value of sample excavation on two sites of the late prehistoric and Roman periods. *J Chester Archaeol Soc* new ser **77** for 2002

Nevell, M ed 1999   Living on the edge of empire: models, methodology and marginality. Late prehistoric and Romano-British rural settlement in north-west England. (*Archaeol North-West* 3)

Newstead, R & Droop, A Roman camp at Halton, Cheshire. *Ann Archaeol Anthropol Univ*
J P 1937   *Liverpool* **24**, 165–8

Orme, B 1981   Anthropology for archaeologists: an introduction. London: Duckworth

Ormerod, G 1882   The history of the County Palatine and City of Chester. Ed 2, rev Helsby, T. London: Routledge

Phillips, C B & Smith, Lancashire and Cheshire from AD 1540. London: Longman
J H 1994

Philpott, R A &   Excavations at an Iron Age and Romano-British settlement at Irby,
Adams, M H 1999   Wirral, 1987–96. *In*: Nevell ed, 64–73

Polanyi, K 1944   The great transformation. New York: Rinehart

Price, J 1994   The discovery of an early saltworking site near Crewe. *Cheshire Past* **3**, 4

Quarterman, A 1997   The Iron Age settlement and society of Cheshire: a survey. Unpubl BA dissertation Univ Durham

Renfrew, A C 1973   Before civilization: the radiocarbon revolution and prehistoric Europe. Harmondsworth: Penguin

Rivet, A L F & Smith, C 1979   The place names of Roman Britain. London: Batsford

Robinson, D J 1978–9   Rawhead Farm. *Cheshire Archaeol Bull* **6**, 58

Robinson, D J & Lloyd-Morgan, G 1984–5   Stamford Bridge SJ 4661 6734. *Cheshire Archaeol Bull* **10**, 95

Sahlins, M D 1963   Poor man, rich man, big man, chief: political types in Melanesia and Polynesia. *Comp Stud Soc & Hist* **5**, 285–303

Schoenwetter, J 1982   Environmental archaeology of the Peckforton Hills. *Cheshire Archaeol Bull* **8**, 10–11

Service, E 1962   Primitive social organization: an evolutionary perspective. New York: Random House

Shotter, D C A 1997   Romans and Britons in north-west England. Ed 2. Lancaster Univ: Centre for North-West Regional Studies

Stallibrass, S 1995   Review of the vertebrate remains. *In*: Huntley & Stallibrass eds, 84–198

Stallibrass, S & Huntley, J P 1995   General overview. *In*: Huntley & Stallibrass eds, 199–208

Strang, A 1997   Explaining Ptolemy's Roman Britain. *Britannia* **28**, 1–30

Taylor, J J 1981   Bickerton, SJ 498529: Maiden Castle, Bickerton Hill, interim report. *Cheshire Archaeol Bull* **7** (1980/1), 34–6

Thomas, F 1960   A fresh survey of the earthwork on Toothill. *Trans Lancashire Cheshire Antiq Soc* **70**, 84–7

Thompson, F H 1967   Castle Hill, Oldcastle, near Malpas, Cheshire. *J Chester Archaeol Soc* new ser **54**, 5–7

Tindall, A 1993   An Iron Age coin from near Nantwich. *Cheshire Past* **2**, 5

Turner, R C 1995   Recent research into British bog bodies. *In*: Turner & Scaife eds, 108–22

Turner, R C & Scaife, R G eds 1995   Bog bodies: new discoveries and new perspectives. London: British Museum

Varley, W J 1935   Maiden Castle, Bickerton: preliminary excavations, 1934. *Ann Archaeol Anthropol Univ Liverpool* **22**, 97–110

Varley, W J 1936a   Further excavations at Maiden Castle, Bickerton, 1935. *Ann Archaeol Anthropol Univ Liverpool* **23**, 101–12

Varley, W J 1936b   Maiden Castle, Bickerton: a summary of the results of the excavations of 1934 and 1935. *J Chester Archaeol Soc new ser* **31** (2), 113–21

Varley, W J 1950   Excavations of the Castle Ditch, Eddisbury, 1935-38. *Trans Hist Soc Lancashire Cheshire* **102**, 1–68

Varley, W J 1964   Cheshire before the Romans. Chester: Cheshire Community Council (History of Cheshire **1**)

Varley, W J & Jackson, J W 1940   Prehistoric Cheshire. Chester: Cheshire Rural Community Council

Wagstaff, M 1986   What Christaller really said about central places. *In*: Grant ed, 119–22

Watkin, W T 1886   Roman Cheshire: a description of Roman remains in the county of Chester. Liverpool: privately published

Webster, G 1991   The Cornovii. Ed 2. Stroud: Alan Sutton

Welsh, T C 1992   Possible prehistoric enclosures at Salwick and Treales, Fylde. *Archaeol North-West* **4**, 16–18

Williams, S R 1997   West Cheshire from the air: an archaeological anthology. Chester: Chester City Council. (Chester Archaeology Occas Pap **4**)

Willis, S 1994   Roman imports into Late Iron Age British societies: towards a critique of existing models. *In*: Cottam, S *et al* eds. TRAC 94: proceedings of the Fourth Annual Theoretical Roman Archaeology Conference, held at the Department of Archaeology, University of Durham, 19 and 20 March 1994. Oxford: Oxbow, 141–50

Woolf, G 1998   Becoming Roman: the origins of provincial civilisation in Gaul. Cambridge U P

II: Further Inscribed Roman Salt Pans from Shavington, Cheshire

by +S Penney BA & D C A Shotter PhD, FSA

In the light of the untimely death of Stephen Penney, this jointly authored paper is dedicated to his memory; his passing is a sad loss to his friends and to the worlds of history and archaeology in north-west England. (DCAS)

The discovery of two more ?fourth-century lead salt pans at Shavington confirms Roman salt production at the site; indeed they may represent its culmination rather than its beginning. The inscription FL VIVENTIUS on one pan probably refers to the same individual as the VIVENTIUS EPISCOPUS on the pan found in 1993. It implies that the saltworks was under the control of the church and adds to the small collection of evidence for early Christianity in the north Midlands. The saltworks may have continued in production into the sixth or seventh century.

Introduction

In July 1998 a metal detectorist discovered a Roman lead salt pan on farmland at Shavington near Crewe.[1] The pan (pan 1), which was lying at approximately 70cm depth, was found about 50m north of where an inscribed Roman lead salt pan had been discovered in 1993 (Penney & Shotter 1996). Having recovered the pan, the finder notified one of the authors (SP) of his discovery and reported that immediately adjacent to this find a strong metal detector signal suggested the possibility that a further pan lay undisturbed close by.

Excavation

Following the identification by metal detector of the probable position of the second pan, a trench measuring 2m x 2m was excavated.[2] At about 50cm depth a folded lead salt pan (pan 2) was found aligned north–south in a shallow pit dug into underlying fluvio-glacial sand. The backfill of the pit consisted of a yellowish grey silt sand; no finds were recovered from this context. The north-east corner of the trench cut the edge of a pit from which the finder had removed the first pan (Dodd *et al* 1998, 3–4).

The salt pans

The two salt pans are shallow, rectangular lead pans of a type in use during the late Roman period to heat naturally occurring brine in the manufacture of salt. The known occurrence of Roman lead salt pans is confined to south and central Cheshire, where at least eleven pans have been documented, seven of these inscribed with apparent indications of owner-ship (Penney & Shotter 1996; Penney 1999).

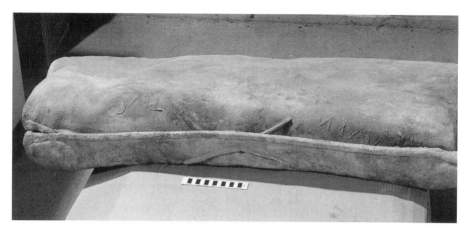

III II.1 Shavington 1998: salt pan 2

Pan 1

Pan folded to 118 x 59 x 20cm. The original dimensions were approximately 103 x 101 x 14cm; constructed from 9mm-thick lead sheet. An 11mm-wide square-sectioned moulding runs around the pan rim. Two opposite sides of the pan are centrally pierced by lifting holes beneath arched strengtheners applied to the exterior face. The pan carries low-relief inscriptions 50–60mm high on the outer face of each pierced side

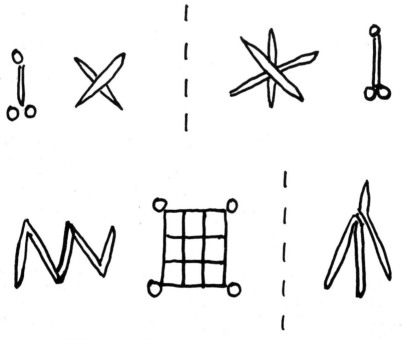

III II.2 Shavington 1998: inscriptions on salt pan 1. (Not to scale)

Pan 2

Pan folded to 127 x 51 x 15cm. The original dimensions were approximately 108 x 98 x 12cm; constructed from 8mm-thick lead sheet. A 14mm-wide square-sectioned moulding with crimped decoration runs around the pan rim. Two opposite sides of the pan are centrally pierced by 12mm-diameter lifting holes beneath arched strengtheners applied to the exterior face. The pan carries low relief inscriptions 35–50mm high on the outer face of each pierced side

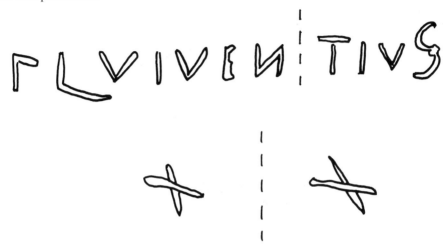

III II.3 Shavington 1998: Inscriptions on salt pan 2. (Not to scale)

Topography and Geology

All the Shavington salt pans were located in low-lying land to the east of Shavington village within a broad valley drained by Swill Brook, a minor tributary of the River Weaver.

With rock salt beds of the Northwich Halite Formation underlying this area at a depth of about 500m,[3] the conditions would have been suitable for the formation of brine springs. These emerged in river valley locations in areas of 'wet rock head', where rock salt deposits were subject to active solution beneath exposures of porous rock — in this case marlstone. Today brine springs have been almost obliterated from the Cheshire landscape by industrial brine pumping and agricultural drainage.

The geology and topography around Shavington and Swill Brook coincide to provide a convincing setting for early salt production. The discovery of a single scrapped salt pan (Penney & Shotter 1996) allowed some doubt to remain as to whether Roman salt production could necessarily be identified at this site. However, the presence of three Roman salt pans in an area which must have been conducive to brine formation now leaves little doubt that salt production on a significant scale was occurring in this valley during the late Roman period.

Shavington in its Roman context

The speed with which Roman arms moved northwards and westwards in the early years of conquest meant that the territory covered by the modern county of Cheshire rapidly became 'frontier country'. Although there are many gaps in our understanding of the political geography of the area in the pre-Roman Iron Age, there is some reason to see it as militarily sensitive from an early stage because of the known factionalism between the Brigantian leaders, Venutius and Cartimandua, and because of its proximity to north Wales. Roman armies had already penetrated the area in the 50s and 60s AD from bases such as Little Chester, Wroxeter and Whitchurch. There was probably also a base in the Chester area by the 60s to facilitate the transportation of troops by sea to locations further north. It would seem certain from coin evidence (Shotter 1998) that, by this time, Middlewich itself lay on a route which represented the earliest line of penetration from the north-west Midlands into north-west England.

There is now little doubt that permanent military dispositions were being laid out in Cheshire as early as the governorship of Quintus Petillius Cerialis (AD 71–3) and that by the late 70s–early 80s the area was well on the way to being consolidated in Roman hands, with the completion of the legionary fortress at Chester. Meanwhile, Roman forces were pushing ever-further northwards, until in the late 80s a decision was evidently taken to limit the extent of the province by the fortified road, now known as the Stanegate, which may have eventually run from South Shields (on the Tyne estuary) to Kirkbride in the west. Although the Roman historian, Tacitus, plainly regarded this limiting of territory as a 'sell-out' of Roman interests, the evidence is that consolidation behind the Stanegate was pursued with considerable vigour.

The period between *c* 90 and 120 saw the building of new forts, the establishment of civilian communities outside the forts and the development of a supporting infrastructure. Cheshire will have benefited from this, with the permanent emplacement of Legion XX at Chester: its 5,500 men, not to mention other soldiers housed in auxiliary forts, represented a large market. Industrial sites sprang up at other locations such as Holt, Heronbridge, Wilderspool, Wigan and Walton-le-Dale and, as peace settled on the area, some of the forts also evidently gave way to industrial activities — as appears to have happened at Middlewich and Northwich.

High in importance would have been the production of salt — not least because the feeding of so large a military establishment as the North-West possessed required that much of the foodstuffs supplied to them, particularly meat and fish, needed to be cured in brine as a regular part of its processing (cf Jackson & Potter 1996). Salt production is known to have remained strong in central Cheshire, and the need for this vital commodity did not decrease over the years. We can readily postulate, therefore, that sites such as that at Shavington would have developed in significance with the passage of time.

Until the discovery of the first salt pan in 1993, no Roman sites or finds had been recorded from Shavington, and little Roman material was known from the surrounding area. Whilst a scatter of Roman finds has been reported from the neighbouring parishes of Wybunbury to the south and Weston to the east, lack of fieldwork in this part of Cheshire, and generally unfavourable conditions for cropmark formation (Collens 1999, 36), are likely to have led to an under-representation of the Roman presence in this area. However, some indications of wealth in the vicinity are provided by a small hoard of *denarii* (Shotter

2000) and a stray Samian sherd (CSMR 2676), both from Weston. In addition, in Shavington itself a small number of Roman finds (coins, brooches and pottery) have recently been recorded a short distance to the south-east of the lead pans site in an adjoining field.[4] These finds can be dated to the second to the fourth centuries, a pattern which is repeated in those from Weston and Wybunbury.

As the Shavington salt pans are of apparently late Roman date, it is quite possible that they represent the culmination of Roman salt-making at the site. The evidence for an earlier presence in the vicinity, provided by the stray finds, suggests that the brine springs may have acted as a focus of activity from at least the second century. Salt-making at Middlewich (eight miles north of Shavington) at this earlier date is attested by large quantities of briquetage (Bestwick 1975), and only excavation near the salt pans' location is likely to resolve whether there was an earlier phase of salt production here as well. However, it is worth noting that the only other two Cheshire sites where Roman briquetage has been found are both in Moston parish, mid-way between Middlewich and Shavington (Price 1997). The brine supply at Shavington is, therefore, likely to have been identified at an early date.

The saltworks complex

The discovery of three buried salt pans, supported by the evidence of local geology and topography, points to the existence of a Roman saltworks at Shavington. Other excavated saltworks sites provide some indication of what other components may remain to be investigated there.

The focus of Roman saltworking units was the brine pit, dug around a brine spring to facilitate access. Circular pits were dug into the natural sand at Middlewich, where they appear to have been unlined (Bestwick 1975, 67). Prior to evaporation brine was stored in settling tanks — plank-lined pits or sunken halved barrels at Droitwich, Worcestershire (Woodiwiss ed 1992), or in some instances at Middlewich, in spherical amphorae set into the ground (Bestwick 1975, 67).

At Middlewich brine was evaporated over horizontal-draught brine kilns (evaporation hearths) constructed from clay, whilst circular kiln structures may have been used to dry the salt. Large quantities of briquetage, coarse-fired clay kiln furniture, were associated with these structures. There is no evidence that lead pans were used in association with these types of kiln. To provide sufficient support for a working set of two to three lead pans, stone-lined flues, of the type excavated in Droitwich in fifth- to seventh-century contexts (Hurst ed 1997, 17), would have been required. It is envisaged that such structures must have been present in close proximity to the presumed brine pit(s) at Shavington. Open-sided timber buildings, like those identified at Middlewich (Bestwick 1975, 66), may have provided shelter for these working units.

Lead-working would probably also have been carried out in the vicinity of the saltworks. The discovery at both Shavington (Penney & Shotter 1996) and Middlewich (Penney 1999) of stockpiled scrap lead in the form of cut pan fragments is persuasive evidence that lead was re-cycled for the manufacture of new pans. It has been argued in connection with late Roman 'baptismal' tanks that these are likely to have been made where they were wanted, since the transport of lead would have been easier if it was in pig form (Guy 1981, 273). It is similarly suggested that itinerant leadsmiths are likely to have made use of scrapped lead retained on site rather than transport complete pans, weighing in excess of 100kg, over considerable distances. It is therefore envisaged that lead-working hearths would have been located near the site. The pans would have been cast flat on a sand bed before being beaten into shape.

Inscribed Roman lead pigs provide much information concerning the extraction and trade in British lead (Still 1999); the date range for these pigs spans the mid-first to late second century. By the late Roman period significant quantities of scrap were doubtless supplementing the fresh output of lead-mining and processing areas such as Flintshire, Derbyshire and the Mendips. It is clear that the leadsmiths responsible for the late Roman salt pans in Cheshire were working at a time when some of the most spectacular examples of Roman leadworking were being produced. The circular baptismal tanks are generally accepted as fourth-century in date (Guy 1981; Watts 1988), whilst it has been estimated that some 70% of Roman lead coffins in Britain date to the fourth century (Toller 1977, 10).

A Christian enterprise?

The pan inscriptions shed some light on the ownership of this saltworks. The inscription on pan 2, FL VIVENTIVS (Flavius? Viventius), presumably refers to the same individual as that recorded on the pan found nearby in 1993. The inscription on that pan, VIVENTI [EPIS]COPI, has been taken to indicate that it may have been owned by a bishop Viventius, who was presumably based in Chester (Penney & Shotter 1996, 362–3). The extent and distribution of bishoprics in late Roman Britain is a matter of some conjecture, but it has been suggested that by the second half of the fourth century the number of British bishops may have been in double figures (Thomas 1981).

The two saltires in shallow relief on the other side of pan 2 are likely to be no more than purely decorative. However, the presence of the Christian name Viventius could just mean that these devices should be interpreted as *crux decussata* (St Andrew's cross), a Christian symbol recognised in late Roman Britain and apparently represented on late Roman baptismal tanks (Watts 1988).

The devices on pan 1 are difficult to interpret — if, indeed, there is any symbolism to interpret. Side 1 could again possibly show a *crux decussata* and the iota-chi Christian symbol. However, without any overtly Christian inscription on pan 1, any such interpretation would be hard to justify. On the other side of pan 1 the zig-zag motif could represent an MV ligatured; the other two motifs defy interpretation and again could be purely decorative.

The implication of the inscription on the 1993 salt pan find is that salt manufacture at Shavington may have been a source of income for the local Christian community. The fourth-century church in all probability benefited from gifts and endowments by wealthy benefactors. The Shavington salt pans, or at least the VIVENTI [EPIS]COPI pan, should probably be seen in this light. It is interesting to note that the wealth of another late Roman bishop is demonstrated by a silver lanx from Risley Park (Derbyshire) which carries an inscription recording it as a gift to a church from a bishop Exuperius — EXVPERIVS EPISCO[P]VS (Mawer 1995, 27–8).

The two Viventius salt pans can therefore be numbered amongst the very few Roman finds from the North-West which can be positively identified as having Christian connotations. It is now generally believed that an amphora fragment from Manchester carrying a graffito cryptogram is unlikely to have any Christian significance (Mawer 1998, 39–40). However, an inscribed silver spoon carrying the chi-rho monogram between an alpha and omega found in the late nineteenth century thirteen miles north-east of Shavington, at Whitemore Farm mid-way between Congleton and Biddulph, is unambiguously in the Christian tradition (Painter 1975; Mawer 1995, 44).

Post-Roman activity

The discovery of a sixth- or seventh-century bronze penannular brooch with punched decoration within a few metres of the first Roman salt pan find[5] suggests that the Shavington brine spring(s) may have been a focus for continuing activity beyond the Roman period. Whilst there is clear evidence of salt production at Droitwich between the fifth and seventh centuries (Hurst 1997, 17), no archaeological evidence of salt manufacture in this period has so far been identified in Cheshire. This important find perhaps provides the first tentative evidence that there may have been a sub-Roman salt industry at Shavington.

No salthouse is recorded in Domesday Shavington, where two manors were held by Godwin and Dot. The thirteenth-century reference to a *salina de Schavinton* may be significant, but does not provide conclusive evidence of medieval saltworking at Shavington, as it is possible that this could relate to a salthouse at Nantwich belonging to the manor of Shavington (Dodgson 1971, 38). The field name 'Witch-house Field' (ie wyche house = salthouse) in the neighbouring parish of Rope[6] is, however, clear evidence of a saltworks operating little more than 1km west of Shavington. This is probably to be related to the rash of small saltworks which sprang up in some salt-bearing areas away from the traditional salt towns as these lost their monopoly during the sixteenth and seventeenth centuries. There is also possibly significant field-name evidence from Shavington itself (Penney & Shotter 1996, 364).

Conclusion

The discovery of three Roman lead salt pans at Shavington clearly indicates the presence of an important late Roman salt production site nearby. The discovery of other earlier Roman material in the vicinity suggests that the Shavington brine springs may have served as a focus for activity from at least the second century, whilst the nearby discovery of a later penannular brooch also raises the possibility of a sub-Roman salt industry at this site. The Christian associations of the fourth-century saltworks gather strength from the recurrence of the name Viventius, whilst the implications of the existence of a bishop Viventius are far-reaching.

Shavington is clearly a potentially key site in our understanding of the organisation and operation of the late Roman salt industry in Cheshire. Further archaeological investigation is clearly needed to understand more fully the operation and chronology of this site.

Notes

[1] The authors are grateful to Mr Gordon Sandland for promptly reporting this find.

[2] The excavation was undertaken by Earthworks Archaeological Services under the direction of Mr Will Walker and grant-aided by Cheshire County Council.

[3] British Geological Survey 1:50,000 series, Sheet no 123 (Stoke-on-Trent).

[4] *Sestertii* of Hadrian and Antoninus Pius, two bow brooches and a stray rim sherd in Wilderspool fabric. The authors are grateful to Messrs Andy Harper, John Bailey and Phil Baddiley for so willingly making their finds available for recording.

[5] To be published by Susan Youngs of the British Museum in a study of this distinctive brooch type. Thanks to Gordon Sandland for making this find available for recording.

[6] Located at NGR SJ 696 520. Dodgson 1971, 69. Thanks to George Twigg for drawing this reference to the attention of the authors.

Bibliography

Bestwick, J D 1975 — Romano-British inland salting at Middlewich (Salinae), Cheshire. *In*: de Brisay, K & Evans, K eds. Salt: the study of an ancient industry. Colchester Archaeological Group, 66–70

Collens, J 1999 — Flying on the edge: aerial photography and early settlement patterns in Cheshire and Merseyside. *In*: Nevell, M ed. Living on the edge of empire: late prehistoric and Romano-British rural settlement in north-west England. *Archaeol North-West* **3** (13), 36–41

Dodd, L J *et al* 1998 — A Roman lead salt pan at Shavington, near Crewe, Cheshire: an archaeological investigation. Earthworks Archaeological Services unpublished report

Dodgson J McN 1971 — The place-names of Cheshire **3**. Cambridge U P for English Place-Name Society. (English Place-Name Soc **46**)

Guy, C J 1981 — Roman circular lead tanks in Britain. *Britannia* **12**, 271–6

Hurst, J D ed 1997 — A multi-period salt production site at Droitwich. York: Council for British Archaeology. (CBA Res Rep **107**)

Jackson, R P J & Potter, T W 1996 — Excavations at Stonea, Cambridgeshire, 1980–5. London: British Museum

Mawer, C F 1995 — Evidence for Christianity in Roman Britain: the small finds. Oxford: British Archaeological Reports. (BAR British Ser **243**)

Painter, K 1975 — A Roman Christian silver treasure from Biddulph, Staffordshire. *Antiq J* **55**, 62–9

Penney, S 1999 — An inscribed Roman salt pan from Middlewich. *Archaeol North West* **4** (14), 8–9

Penney, S & Shotter, D C A 1996 — An inscribed Roman salt pan from Shavington, Cheshire. *Britannia* **27**, 360–5

Price, J 1997 — The discovery of an early saltworking site near Crewe. *Cheshire Past* **3**, 4

Shotter, D C A 1998 — Roman north-west England: the process of annexation. *Trans Hist Soc Lancashire Cheshire* **168**, 1–26

Shotter, D C A 2000	Roman coins from north-west England: second supplement. Lancaster University
Still, M 1999	Metal production in Roman Britain. *Coins and Antiquities* July 1999, 47–52
Thomas, C 1981	Christianity in Roman Britain to AD 500. London: Batsford
Toller, H 1977	Roman lead coffins and ossuaria in Britain. Oxford: British Archaeological Reports. (BAR British Ser **38**)
Watts, D 1988	Circular lead tanks and their significance for Romano-British Christianity. *Antiq J* **68**, 210–22
Woodiwiss, S ed 1992	Iron Age and Roman salt production and the medieval town of Droitwich. London: Council for British Archaeology. (CBA Res Rep **81**)

A Note on the Life of Stephen Penney

Stephen Penney was educated in Norfolk and graduated in archaeology from Queen's University, Belfast in 1974. His first post was as Research Assistant at the Ashmolean Museum, from where he moved north to become Assistant Keeper of Archaeology at Lancaster Museum until 1983. He returned to Oxford, this time as Curator of the Museum of Oxford, and then moved to Cheshire as Curator of the Salt Museum and Stretton Watermill in 1988.

Stephen always maintained a close interest in archaeology, having been Chairman of the Lancaster Archaeological Society, Vice-Chairman of the Lancashire Archaeological Society and a Committee Member CBA North-West Regional Group. In Cheshire he co-directed excavations at Anderton Boat Lift and at Shavington, where a number of Roman lead salt pans have been discovered, and carried out and published research on bog bodies in the region. He also established a finds identification service at the Salt Museum, and in doing so contributed much to the fruitful co-operation which exists today between archaeologists and metal detectorists.

Adrian Tindall MA MIFA
Principal Archaeologist, Cheshire County Council

III: St John's Church

and the Early History of Chester

by S Matthews BA

This speculative paper argues that the reference to Chester being 'waste' in 893, far from indicating its status through the 'Dark Ages', was merely temporary. In the sub-Roman period it was arguably the seat of a secular and religious authority straddling the Dee, supported by an estate at Holt-Farndon and the Cheshire salt industry respectively. After the imposition of Mercian rule the western boundary of this unit was delimited by Wat's Dyke. The traditional foundation date of 685 for St John's is to be accepted — indeed it may represent a re-foundation — and the church became the see of a *chorepiscopus* supported by some of the land west of the Dee. Chester's pre-existing importance led to the creation of the *burh* in 907 rather than *vice versa*.

Introduction

It is fortuitously fifty years since the late Graham Webster published his review of pre-conquest Chester (Webster 1951). Much has been written and excavated since then but, save some inscriptions, the body of written evidence remains the same. I have therefore to start by acknowledging that this paper presents no new evidence but puts together and develops themes considered by other writers whose work is acknowledged in the bibliography. It attempts to describe an historical context for Chester and the area immediately surrounding it from the end of the Roman period up to the foundation of the *burh* in the tenth century. Whilst it is primarily a review of the written evidence the archaeological record has dramatically improved, especially in recent years, but by its nature the latter cannot conclusively answer the questions that we want to ask.

As will become apparent, I believe that the role played by the church of St John was critical in the continuing existence and later development of Chester after the end of the Roman period, and in reviewing the evidence for the city itself we may note the number of recorded events that have involved or been dependent upon that church. This paper therefore falls into two parts. First, observations upon early Chester as a whole; second, a possible role for St John's church in the city's history. Inevitably, its conclusions are beyond proof but lie in that tantalising range of historical possibilities.

Post-Roman Chester and its environs
Written sources
Quality

There is no written record that is anywhere near contemporary, the earliest being Bede, who wrote in the early eighth century. He was a careful scholar with good sources, but he was extremely hostile to the Welsh church, which he saw as having spurned Augustine's mission. If ever there was a Mercian equivalent of the *Anglo-Saxon Chronicle*, it has long since disappeared, though part of what has become known as the *Mercian Register* has been incorporated into the Abingdon MS of the *Chronicle*, covering the early tenth century. For most of the period, the *Chronicle* itself is hardly contemporary: it was first composed in the late ninth century from a variety of sources and was a production for the royal house of Wessex, whose interests it served. 'Florence' of Worcester wrote later still, dying about 1118, although he was a conscientious recorder of his sources and seems to have had access to some material now lost. Goscelin, who died about the same time, was a professional hagiographer, whose works often contain more invention than fact, as we can see if we compare his *Life of St Werburgh* with the more sober record of William of Malmesbury. William, who died about 1143, was another conscientious gatherer of records, many of which are now lost, and his narrative is generally considered reliable.

Nearer to the city itself are the *Chronicles* of Ranulf Higden and the *Annales Cestrienses*, attributed by its editor to Simon of Whitchurch. Both of these were written in the fourteenth century and drew upon earlier writers, not always accurately — the latter, for example, citing William of Malmesbury for probably 'Florence' of Worcester in the entry for 1057. Despite this error, Simon (or whoever) produced a sober and unromantic narrative and showed some critical ability by stating plainly that Harold Godwinson died at Hastings and ignoring the legend of his death as a hermit at St John's, which must have been known to him. He also ignored Goscelin's fanciful *Life of St Werburgh*. I believe that he recorded what he had read or heard rather than invented material to prove a contentious point or make a more interesting story. This becomes important when we consider the foundation of St John's. The story of Ingimund's attack on the city does not emerge until the seventeenth century, when it was claimed to have been copied from an earlier manuscript. This claim can neither be proved nor disproved but even though its details may be fanciful, authorities have accepted its basic truth. (For the most recent discussion of it *see* Cavill *et al* 2000, especially chapters 1 and 4, the latter being a modernised version of Wainwright's 1948 paper). Lastly, we have the Welsh sources, ninth-century in their written form, being incorporated in the text of the historian Nennius, dated to 828/9 (Morris 1973, **1**, 44). We have to consider the strength of the oral traditions that underlie them.

The 'waste Chester' of the *Anglo-Saxon Chronicle*

Paradoxically we need to start at the very end of the period under consideration, to evaluate a statement that has dominated our interpretation of Dark Age Chester. The *Anglo-Saxon Chronicle* for 893 recorded that the Danes, pursued by Alfred, turned west and came to 'a deserted (or 'a waste') Roman site in the Wirral, called Chester' ('*anre westre ceastre on Wirhealum, seo is Legaceaster gehaten*'). This has commonly been taken to mean that Chester was then an empty shell. For example, in their commentary to the *Anglo-Saxon Chronicle*, Earle and Plummer observed:

p88 westre ceastre) Deva was the station of the XX legion 'Victrix' MHB pxxi; hence its name 'legaceater' 'legionis castra'. Its desolation probably dated from the battle of Chester; v BHE II.2 & notes. From this epithet 'west' = 'waste' comes the name Westchester, sometimes given to Deva. It has nothing to do with 'west' as a point of the compass. (Earle & Plummer eds 1892, **2**, 106–7)

This is a harsh observation and invites us to believe that nothing had happened at the desolate site during the intervening 278 years, assuming both that the battle was fought in Chester rather than near it and that the site was totally devastated. However, 'waste' is not a necessary meaning: the context is military not demographic and it could simply mean that the site was deserted and undefended. *Westre*, from *westen*, means 'deserted' as well as 'waste' and is frequently used in a biblical context of people living in remote places. The desertion could be for a number of reasons but the most probable is that in trying to trap the Danes the Saxon armies had left the site unguarded. The narrative suggests that this was so by going on to say that 'the levies were unable to overtake them before they got inside that fort'. It is possible also that the annalist meant no more than that the city was decayed, only a shadow of its former self; *westen* can bear that meaning too. That statement would also be both true and in accord with the Anglo-Saxon tendency to see their ruined towns as a legacy of former greatness.

We return to the itself battle below but in this context we may note that Webster (1951, 40–2) created an elaborate interpretation of its site from Bede's words: *rex Anglorum fortissimus Aedilfrid collecto grandi exercitu ad civitatem legionum* (Colgrave & Mynors eds 1969, 140). However, it is hard to accept a reconstruction based upon the one word *ad*, translated as 'against' or to accept a battle front stretching down to Heronbridge. Neither argument is supported explicitly by the evidence, and battles frequently take their names from the nearest urban site or other feature without actually being at them.

Before leaving this description, one neglected statement of the obvious must be made. Viking raiding parties did not embark upon mystery tours, striking out in the hope that they might find something of value to plunder. They knew exactly where to attack, whether the target was commercially or politically important, and it seems likely that in 893 they were heading for Chester because there was something there worth having, either protection or loot. Equally, the defending army moved swiftly to try to stop them getting there first. Both behaved as if Chester was a significant place, and this is borne out by the fact that it took so long for the invaders to be ejected. The Vikings must have used existing defences, as they had no time to build anything new before they were themselves attacked.

Much of this is supposition, but in the context it provides can we accept Earle and Plummer's commentary? Is there enough evidence for us to believe that Chester did survive in some form and was a seat of local power, if nothing more, in the centuries leading up to the campaign of 893? What post-Roman evidence is there? At this point we must return to the accounts of the events of the early seventh century and review the evidence from the start.

The Battle of Chester and the Synod of 601

We have three accounts of this. The earliest is Bede's. As mentioned above, Bede was hostile to the Welsh church, and rather relished the slaughter of numerous clergy whose prayers were intended to help their army. We do not need his account in full; the relevant part reads:

> For later on, that very powerful king of the English, Aethelfrith, whom we have already spoken of, collected a great army against the city of the legions, which is called *Legacaestir* by the English, and more correctly *Caerlegion* (Chester) by the Britons, and made a great slaughter of that nation of heretics. When he was about to give battle and saw their priests, who had assembled to pray to God on behalf of the soldiers taking part in the fight, standing apart in a safer place, he asked who they were and for what purpose they had gathered there. Most of them were from the monastery of Bangor, where there was said to be so great a number of monks that, when it was divided into seven parts with superiors over each, no division had less than 300 men, all of whom were accustomed to live by the labour of heir hands. After a three days' fast, most of these had come to the battle in order to pray with the others. They had a guard named Brocmail, whose duty it was to protect them against the barbarians' swords while they were praying. When Aethelfrith heard why they had come he said 'If they are praying to their God against us, them, even if they do not bear arms, they are fighting against us, assailing us as they do with prayers for our defeat. So he ordered them to be attacked first and then he destroyed the remainder of their wicked host, though not without heavy losses. (Colgrave & Mynors eds 1969, 141)

Bede's description of Chester as a city, *civitas*, is important, for he reserved that word for places he thought were thriving settlements. It does not necessarily mean that at that date the place was alive and functioning as a town in the fullest sense; it may, and probably does, mean no more than that it was a military strongpoint, probably also the seat of local administration. For our purpose, the most significant fact is that the battle was known, at least from the time of Bede, as the 'Battle of Chester'. This must indicate that the place was of sufficient importance for it to serve as a landmark: nobody names a battle after a place that has so far ceased to exist that its name has no significance.

The next source, chronologically, is the Welsh version. Although the references are much shorter, the *Annales Cambriae* have two mentions of Chester, though under the wrong years. They record a synod there in 601, convened presumably to consider the failed negotiations with Augustine, and the later battle, under 613. There seems to be a consensus that the *Urbs Legion* and *Caerlegion* of the two entries refer to Chester and not the former Roman fortress at Caerleon. The location of the battle is clear, for a Northumbrian campaign in south Wales is most unlikely, but that of the synod a few years before is another matter, and only the apparent absence of activity at Caerleon makes us assume it was at Chester. If that is so, we must consider whether the martyrs Julius and Aaron met their fate at Chester, rather than Caerleon as is generally supposed. We will return to this below, when considering the church itself. The holding of the synod at Chester would support the assertion that the city was a site of some ecclesiastical significance, although it does not confirm that enough buildings still stood for a substantial conference to be housed there.

We know that at the Synod of Austerfield (702) the king was housed in a tent, and presumably others were as well. The site of a synod would presumably need ecclesiastical rather than domestic facilities, and this points to the existence of a significant church in Chester at that date.

J D Bu'Lock speculated that the young and exiled Edwin may have attended the synod with his protector Rhun ap Urien of Anglesey (1962, 50). If this is so, it increases the likelihood of his having later launched his attack on Anglesey and Man from Chester (Bede *Hist Eccles* II.5 and 9), for all the coastline of the Dee and north Wales would then have been familiar to him.

Finally, the battle features in the *Anglo-Saxon Chronicle*. The ninth-century compilers of the *Chronicle* were well aware of the existence of Chester, although the brevity of the entry suggests either that they knew little of the battle, or more probably did not want to give too much prominence to a major victory by a rival kingdom. They simply recorded that in 615 'Aethelfrith led his levies to Chester and there slew a countless number of Welsh.' This short account probably drew on Bede and, as noted above, specifically does not refer to any devastation in or even around the city.

The twenty-eight British cities of Nennius
Nennius also listed Chester (*Cair Legion*) as one of the twenty-eight cities (*civitates*) of Britain, but this probably reflects historical nostalgia rather than economic or military truth. Once more, however, the name lived on, unlike others which simply disappeared, and this simple fact of survival must be significant.

English expansion
We know that north-west England was of considerable importance to the Mercian kings, both as an area for expansion and as one to be protected against Welsh attack. Higham argued that Penda took the opportunity to annex part of Powys and thus separate Cheshire east of the Dee from Welsh territory (1993, 98–101; 1992, 1–15). If he is right, we must consider the implications of this for the city and in particular the foundation of St John's. Penda, a pagan, would not have founded the church. That would have followed later, but as his successors would have had to secure their grasp of the region first, it is quite possible that it took place as the medieval tradition had it, thirty or so years later, under Ethelred, to provide a symbolic Mercian as well as (Roman) Christian presence in the frontier zone.

Unfortunately there is no mention of Chester itself in the narratives, even though campaigns such as those of 796, 816 and 821 (when Gaymer said that King Coenwulf died at Basingwerk) may well have passed through the city or used it as a base (Harris & Thacker eds 1987, 248). Mercian activity on the English–Welsh frontier continued after the expulsion of Burgred by the Danes in 874 and the partition of the kingdom. Speculation is dangerous but military logic suggests that a ruinous Roman fort in the rear would have been put on a campaign footing to serve as a base for these various expeditions, especially if it included a major religious foundation. Whilst we must not overlook the obvious circularity of that argument, it is not automatically invalidated by it.

The translation of St Werburgh

At some date the remains of Saint Werburgh were brought from Hanbury in Staffordshire to what is now the cathedral, formerly St Werburgh's abbey and, if tradition may be trusted, before that a minster church dedicated to SS Peter and Paul, both names frequently being very early dedications. The reason for the move is commonly and probably correctly given as being safety from the Danish raids. We do not know exactly when this was done. The traditional date of *c* 875 was first recorded in the *Annales Cestrienses* and then by Ranulf Higden in the early fourteenth century, and would fit with the great raids of those times. The *Annales* state the fact baldly:

> In the same year, when the Danes made their winter quarters at Repton after the flight of Burgred, king of the Mercians, the men of Hanbury, fearing for themselves, fled to Chester as to a place which was very safe from the butchery of the barbarians, taking with them in a litter the body of S Werburgh, which then for the first time was resolved into dust. (Christie ed 1886, 13)

This assertion could have been based upon records held at the abbey but may alternatively (and we must say no more than that) be based upon long-standing oral tradition. Nevertheless, in 874 the Danes had driven Burgred of Mercia into exile in Rome and installed a puppet king; this could well have provided an occasion for moving to safety the relics of a saint said to be descended from no fewer than four royal houses.

We gain no more from other writers, for neither Florence of Worcester, who wrote a short but sober account of Werburgh's life nor Goscelin, her hagiographer, mention the translation to Chester directly. What they do and do not say is interesting. Nine years after her burial at Hanbury her remains were exhumed, found to be immaculate, and then re-interred in a new and more fitting coffin. She was then venerated for: 'a considerable time, that is, even up to the time of the Danes, the day of evils, when … this country of the Angles was handed over to the swords of the heathen. Then and only then did the living remains choose to yield to the law of mortality and to disintegrate, lest the enemy … should lay impious hands upon her'. (Goscelin's *Life of St Werburgh*: Munday ed 1974, 17)

For this disintegration to have been observed, the coffin must have been opened and the body examined; the occasion could well have been the move to Chester. The other feature of the passage is that neither Goscelin nor William explicitly mention the translation to Chester and this supports the implication in the *Annales* that the translation was an emergency measure. We can be confident that if Aethelflaed had made it as a symbolic political act at the establishment of the *burh* in 907 the monks of St Werburgh's would have publicised the fact widely; we may compare the well publicised removal of the remains of St Oswald to Gloucester by Aethelflaed in 909 (Thacker 1982, 209).

I have dwelt upon the date of the translation because if it was early, and I think the evidence points to its being so, it is an indication that Chester within the walls was regarded as a safe place. It was further from the eastern Danes, well within the rump of Mercia left under independent English rule, but that would not have been enough. It must have been the safest place in the area in 875. This sits badly with its being deserted and waste in 893.

Archbishop Plegmund

Asser stated in his *Life of King Alfred* that amongst the foreign scholars whom Alfred brought to the West Saxon court was Plegmund, a Mercian who became Alfred's archbishop of Canterbury. We know relatively little about his early life other than that he was scholarly, most learned and a reformer. Gervase of Canterbury, writing long afterwards, added more detail but some is plainly wrong and his sources are uncertain. He says, for what it is worth, that Plegmund had been a hermit, living on an island in Cheshire or Chester. An island in what are now the Mersey flats is not impossible, but it is an unlikely site for scholarship of an orderly and academic kind, which is what Plegmund later imposed on Canterbury (Brooks 1984, 173–4). It is more likely that Plegmund had access to a well established scriptorium, which brings us back to Chester. The two most likely places for an island in Cheshire are Ince, which at Domesday belonged to St Werburgh's and, better, Plemstall, which has always been the site associated with the archbishop on the evidence of the place name. I think it more probable that Plegmund was attached to one of the churches in Chester and had access to a retreat in the marshes. His work as archbishop points to a degree of scholastic and calligraphic competence superior to that in contemporary Canterbury — a remarkable tribute to the capacity of the rump of the Mercian church.

The story of Ingimund

Wainwright printed this account of an attack on Chester, which took place about the time of the foundation of the *burh* and therefore marginally within our period. Its description of the city is once more hard to reconcile with its being 'deserted' in 893. I follow Stenton and others in accepting its basic authenticity, though its details may be fanciful. The precise date of the attack is unclear but the story is that the Norse under Ingimund, expelled from Dublin in 902, wished to settle in the Wirral, whereupon:

> Then Edelfrida gave him lands near Chester and he stayed there for a time. The result of this was, when he saw the city full of wealth and the choice land around it, he desired to possess them. He claimed it was 'right for them all to come to seize Chester and to possess it with its wealth and its lands'. (Wainwright ed 1975, 80–1)

They were eventually defeated by the release of all the bees in the city!

This episode must have taken place within twenty years of 893 and possibly even before the foundation of the *burh*, which was undertaken as a defensive measure against Norse aggression; either way it was hardly a long enough time for a deserted and sterile site to have developed into a desirable target. The city's prosperity must have had a longer gestation.

St Germanus

Out of sequence but simply for completeness, we must look at the stories associated with St Germanus of Auxerre and the possibility of the 'Alleluia victory' being fought and won near Chester in 429. There is no credible evidence that St Germanus ever reached the north-west of England, and I follow Higham in dismissing the connection despite the arguments of Morris and the Laings (Higham 1993, 96–7; Morris 1973, 63; Laing &

Laing nd, 27). It is not impossible but, tempting though it is, it strains the evidence too far for us to learn anything certain from it about the state of Chester in the fifth century.

Non-literary evidence

The Viventius salt pans

Higham speculated about the continuation of episcopal authority (1993, 66), and since he wrote some direct evidence for this has emerged in the fragments of two late Roman salt pans recently discovered at Shavington, near Crewe (Penney & Shotter 1996 and this journal). The earlier bears an inscription whose best reading is *Viventi (epis)copi*. The translation could be 'overseer' but is more likely to be 'bishop', even if only because Viventius is an adopted rather than a birth name. The second pan bears the name FL VIVENTIUS, which is presumably a reference to the same individual, here given an additional name Fl(avius). These finds may well indicate not only the existence of a late or post-Roman bishop based in north-west Cheshire but one who was controlling a substantial local industry. There is no need to repeat Shotter and Penney's findings but merely to accept them fully. They inferred from the finding of a sixth- or seventh-century brooch nearby that activity may have continued to that date. The ecclesiastical character of the name is supported by evidence from Kirkmadrine in Galloway. There a chi-rho inscribed pillar, dating from not before the later sixth century, has an inscription: *Hic iacent s(an)c(t)i et praecipui sacerdotes id es(t) Viventius et Mavorius* (Collingwood 1927, 2). The context could not be more clear, and this undoubtedly ecclesiastical example of a very rare name suggests that the Cheshire use is also religious. There is additional evidence for fourth-century Christianity in the north west in the finding of a chi-rho engraved spoon at Biddulph (British Museum, catalogue PRB 1971.5-1.1), and we need not be surprised at the emergence of more artefacts between there and Chester. Finally, Thomas suggested Gaulish influence in the style of script, which throws open the possibility of continuing contact with southern Scotland (Thomas 1994, 201). If there was contact between the continent and southern Scotland, it is unlikely that Chester, in between, would have been excluded.

There is no reason why a late Roman episcopacy should not have survived the departure of whatever Roman military regime existed at the turn of the fifth century, for that would simply mirror Gaulish history, but as unfortunately we do not know for certain that there was a bishop in the city in the imperial period, the proposed continuation of a see in later times must remain speculative. It is nevertheless hard to find any other satisfactory context for such an inscription. Even if the reference is not to a bishop but to an overseer or some other administrator, there can be no escaping the fact that it represents some degree of organisation by someone.

Wat's Dyke

There are reasons for believing that there was an administrative region based upon Chester, whether civil or ecclesiastical, to which we will return below, and I suggest that it ran side-by-side with that presumed by Nash-Williams to exist in north Wales, based upon Caernarfon or Bangor. This region is discussed by Matthews who sketched its bounds (Carrington ed 1994, 55), but I see no reason why the western boundary should not follow Wat's Dyke. The common dating for that is late ninth century, built after Offa's Dyke to the west, but it is impossible to see any military or political context after Offa's time within which it could have been built. It is west-facing, so it is not a Welsh over-running of an earlier English frontier. It may alternatively be pre-Offan, and indeed one recent radio-carbon date puts the construction no later than *c* 600 and very possibly earlier rather than later (Worthington, pers comm). This is not sufficiently precise to be conclusive, and the most practical dating of the dyke is to put it before Offa's Dyke for lack of any reason for later construction. (For a recent general discussion of Wat's and Offa's dykes, *see* Hill 2000, 195–206). It has also been a fiscal boundary, marking the hundredal boundary, and could well record a long-standing division between the territory of Chester and that of the neighbouring Welsh. If we are pushed to giving an historical context, the most likely is the intervention of King Penda of Mercia in the middle seventh century, preceding the traditional date for the foundation of St John's. We may at this point speculate even further that the 'the land that lay beyond the water which is called Dee' considered below in the context of *Domesday* lay between the Dee and this earthwork. If there is any merit in this suggestion, it places both the dyke and the *Domesday* entry in a recognisable context.

Place names and churchyards

A number of British place names survive in north-west Cheshire around the city, and one, Eccleston, clearly indicates a pre-Saxon Christian site. Other sites (like Dodleston) may be indicated by the scattering of curvilinear churchyards (Harris & Thacker eds 1987, 240) though that is not as reliable a guide. We know from Bede and from elsewhere that there was a very large British monastery at Bangor-on-Dee, whose monks were slaughtered at the Battle of Chester. It is possible that this religious cluster had a centre at Chester, which would be consistent with the holding of the synod there; this would conform to the early practice of urban-based episcopacy. Snyder infers from the Llandaff charters that the Welsh church, unlike the Irish, gave a superior role to bishops in relation to monasteries and other churches, playing the same supervisory role as did their medieval counterparts (1998, 122), and although control could have been exercised from some other ancient site, like St Asaph, Chester is a more likely place.

Excavations

Excavations have told us relatively little about the Middle Saxon development of Chester. The artefacts found at Abbey Green have proved to be both later than originally thought and not necessarily ecclesiastical in character, so that no useful inferences may be drawn from them. In the eighth or ninth century there was agricultural activity stretching south-wards towards the river along the line of what is now Lower Bridge Street (Mason 1985, 2–7) and there was pre-Aethelflaedan occupation at the junction of Northgate and Eastgate streets (Matthews *et al* 1995 64–5). The southern agricultural activity is probably more typical of Chester as a whole. On the other hand, we need to recall the silver brooch found during the Lower Bridge Street excavations, which was dated as probably belonging to the second half of the ninth century. Neither that nor the early development of the Chester mint, *c* 890 (*see below*), easily relate to an economically marginal society (Mason 1985, 35, 61). Moreover, more recently and dramatically, excavations in the amphitheatre have suggested that there was an insertion into the east entrance passage for which the best parallels are seventh-century crypts like those at Repton and Ripon (Matthews 2001 and pers comm; Taylor & Taylor 1980, **2**, 510–18).

Coinage

The origins of the Chester mint are obscure, but it seems likely that it was functioning well before the end of the ninth century and certainly before the establishment of the *burh*. Maddicott speculated that it 'may well have been active as early as Alfred's reign, when Chester, already a wealthy city, was probably the unidentified centre in north-west Mercia from which coins were being issued' (1989, 41). This view has recently been reinforced by Stewart Lyon, who has pointed to the presence of a Chester coin in the Cuerdale hoard, deposited about 905. Even if placing the origin of minting in the reign of Alfred is rather too early, the coins point to significant pre-*burh* prosperity. Lyon presumed that the moneyers 'worked in a *wic* outside the walls, as had been the case in London but since there is no archaeological evidence to show whether minting took place within or without the old Roman walls, it is equally possible that any moneyer might have sought whatever protection was available within them'. (Higham & Hill eds 2001, 75). Our conclusion must be that what Aethelflaed did in 907 was strengthen an already-active community by concentrating it within the walls rather than create a new structure from a long-abandoned site. The parallel with the presumed transfer of activity from Aldwych into the walled city of London is most apt.

St John's church

Having reviewed the evidence for Chester as a whole we may now turn to the history of St John's church and a possible role for it in the early history of Chester.

The historical background
Foundation

The traditional foundation date is late seventh century in the reign of King Ethelred *c* 675–704, deriving from Higden and the *Annales Cestrienses*, which state:

> In the year of our Lord six hundred and eighty-nine, Ethelred, king of the Mercians, the uncle of St Werburgh, with the assistance of Wilfric, Bishop of Chester, as Giraldus (Cambrensis) relates, founded (*fundavit*) a collegiate church in the suburbs of Chester in honour of St John the Baptist. (Christie ed 1886, 11)

The problem immediately arises that no Wilfric can be traced in the episcopal lists of Mercia. However, at very much the relevant time Bishop Wilfrid of Northumbria was in exile in Mercia and is known to have been at Leicester (Thacker 1982, 200). *Legrecestra* (Leicester) could have been confused with *Legaceaster* (= Chester) as Thacker suggested, but neither that nor the slight miss-spelling are grounds for dismissing the connection in its entirety. We are told in his *Life* that whilst in exile, 'Wulfhere, King of the Mercians, out of sincere affection for him, invited him into his realm to fulfil various episcopal duties (*ad officia diversa episcopalia in regione sua*). He granted our bishop many pieces of land in various places, on which he forthwith founded monasteries for the servants of God'. (Colgrave ed 1985, 31). Wilfrid's interest in missionary work and the importance of a frontier zone may have drawn him to Chester. His prestige was such that his involvement may have been remembered long afterwards, albeit in garbled form. It is also possible that in the less well structured conditions of the seventh century some episcopal status was given to Chester, but we know far too little about the Mercian church to be sure.

It is nevertheless possible that there was a church on the site before the traditional founda-tion date. Unlike the minster of SS Peter and Paul it is outside the Roman walls and close to the amphitheatre. This proves nothing by itself, for its siting could have been related to a Roman *vicus* outside the east gate, stretching out along Foregate Street. Nevertheless, it is not uncommon in the Roman world for churches to be associated with amphitheatres as sites of martyrdom, one of the most dramatic examples being at Tarragona in Spain where it is in the centre of the arena, and in this connection Matthews' recent speculations become critically important. St John's could be an equally early site, commemorating the death of some long-forgotten martyr in much the same way as the cathedral of St Albans marks the spot where that saint was killed. Although the similarity of the early names makes it tempting to speculate that Julius and Aaron, early martyrs, met their deaths not at Caerleon but at Chester, there is no evidence in support, and two arguments against First, there are a number of dedications to those saints in south Wales, but none near Chester (Farmer 1978, 227–8). Second, Bede was quite clear on the separate identities of the two places. Although he referred to Chester as a *civitas*, his choice of name for the other 'city of the legions', Caerleon, was *urbs* (...*Aaron et Julius legionum urbis cives*...). This not only suggests that he saw Caerleon as a different kind of site from Chester, but indicates that he was not confused between the two sites. However, neither of these objections precludes the existence of another unknown martyr. Any original dedication could have been lost at the time of a putative refoundation by Ethelred or at the next refoundation as a cathedral.

Edgar's triumph

Both the *Anglo-Saxon Chronicle*, Florence and, later, Higden carried another story, later than the period we are considering but relevant to it. In 973 King Edgar was rowed to St John's by seven subject kings. Leaving aside the political significance of this, what was the detail? As the three accounts cannot easily be reconciled it would be as well to quote them all, the *Chronicle* first:

> Soon after this (May) the king led all his fleet to Chester, and there six kings came to him to make their submission, and pledged themselves to be his fellow workers by sea and land. (Swanton ed 2000, 119)

And now Florence:

> Thence, after a short time, he sailed round the north part of Britain with a large fleet, and landed at Chester. Eight petty kings, namely, Kynath, king of the Scots, Malcolm, king of the Cumbrians, Maccus, king of several isles, and five others, named Dufnall, Siferth, Huwall, Jacob, and Juchill, met him there as he had appointed, and swore that they would be faithful to him, and assist him by land and by sea. On a certain day they attended him into a boat, and when he had placed them at the oars, he himself took the helm and skilfully steered it down the river Dee, and thus, followed by the whole company of earls and nobles, in this order went from the palace to the monastery of St John the Baptist. After having prayed there, he returned with the same pomp to the palace. As he was entering it, he is reported to have said to his nobles, that then his successors might boast themselves to be kings of the English, when, attended by so many kings, they should enjoy the pomp of such honours. (Thorpe ed 1848, 85)

Finally, Higden:

> Thus king Edgar, in the twelfth year of his reign after being anointed king and consecrated by the blessed Dunstan and Oswald at Bath, sailed round the north of Britain to the City of the Legions, now called Chester. Eight underkings came to him, who getting into a boat with him on the river Dee, he taking the helm and they rowing downstream with great ceremony, came to the church of St John and coming to his own palace in the same way, observed that any of his successors might be proud to be treated to such service and ceremony. (Lumby ed 1876, **7**, 16–18)

Surprisingly, the *Annales* do not have the story.

To dispose of one point first. This story need not mean that the fleet sailed around the north of Scotland: the 'north of Britain' was a term then commonly applied to Wales in distinction to the south-western peninsula. In addition I think it unlikely that Edgar would have made the voyage in person, as it would have been hazardous in the extreme, with the risk that if he had been forced to put to shore he himself might become the captive. His plight would then have been like that of Harold in Normandy, at William's mercy. It seems more probable that, having been crowned at Bath, he moved north either overland or in part up the Severn to join his fleet at Chester.

The obvious reading of Florence's words is that the trip was downstream to Chester and then back up The latin is: *ipse clavum gubernaculi arripiens, eam per cursam fluminis Deae perite gubernavit* (Thorpe ed 1848). Webster's objection to an upstream journey is sound (1951, 46). We do not know the source for Florence's statement, but he was a sober reporter not given to invention, although he could have been mistaken. If he was correct, this rules out any starting point in Chester, for all known settlement is downstream of St John's. Thacker is surely right in suggesting that the trip was from Farndon, where the river was still navigable in medieval times, and, being a royal estate (Edward the Elder had died there), would have been a logical place for a diplomatic gathering (1982, 201). If so, perhaps the subject kings either rowed one way only, with the current, or did so symbolically with another stronger man on the oars to help (rather like modern symbolic pallbearers).

Why should the West Saxon kings acquire or inherit from their Mercian predecessors a palace near to but not in Chester? Does the answer lie in the survival as an estate of the old Roman industrial base at Holt, on the west side of the river? In the Middle Ages, as we shall see below, Holt 'was linked with the mother church at Farndon, both being annexed time out of mind to the upkeep of the deanery of St John's church Chester'. The combination of Holt and Farndon straddles the river, and this unusual feature supports the likelihood of an early formation, one possibly dating back to late Roman times. Such an estate could have been preserved as a unit after the collapse of imperial authority and exploited to support whatever power had taken over locally. If it was farmed out at the end of the Roman period, whoever had the use of it could easily have taken possession and perpetuated his tenure.

However they acquired it, the Saxon kings had spare land in the area to give away as is evidenced by Edgar's gift in 958 of a number of estates around Chester to the community at St Werburgh's, including, significantly, Hoseley, near Gresford (Hart ed 1975, no 121). We can follow Hart in inferring from the wording that it was not the first such gift. Farndon itself was presumably another such gift, as by 1066 it was held by the bishop of Chester.

The river episode also tells us something about the status of St John's in the middle of the tenth century. If the occasion had been simply religious, there was a minster church at Farndon which could have served the purpose just as well; in addition, Farndon has signs of being a planned *burh* and therefore a site of some importance. Although Florence only refers to the king having prayed at St John's before returning, there must have been something more like a formal ceremony to confirm the oaths of fealty that the kings had sworn before. It seems that after the foundation of the *burh* in 907 St Werburgh's was generally the favoured foundation. However, the fact that this journey was made to St John's strongly suggests that this site must have retained some sacramental or other symbolic importance from an earlier period that gave it primacy over the newer foundation. We will return to this below in considering the church itself.

Domesday and the Bishop
Early ecclesiastical estates

One of the oddities of the Cheshire *Domesday* is that it frequently refers to 'the bishop' or 'the bishop of Chester' as holding land or having rights in 1066. Strictly speaking there was no 'bishop of Chester' in 1066 and it is possible that the *Domesday* commissioners were merely updating the record to reflect the situation in their own time when the see was based at St John's. However, it is also possible that there was someone who in 1066 was known as the bishop of Chester whose lands had, twenty years later, become amalgamated and confused with the lands of the actual bishop of Chester. As it seems that the lands in question were those that subsequently reverted to St John's (*see below*), then the pre-Conquest 'bishop of Chester' was presumably the head of that church, as argued by Thacker (1982, 201–2), following Sawyer. What evidence is there to suggest this idea?

Higden certainly thought that Chester was a see from the time of the foundation of St John's:

> Wilfrid, having fled from Northumbria, succeeded at *Legecestriam*, which is now called Chester. However, within two years, on the death of Alfred, king of Northumbria, Wilfrid returned to his proper seat at Hexham... (Lumby ed 1876, **1**, 130)

Bishop Tanner, writing in the seventeenth century, wrote in far more specific terms:

> It is more certain that before the end of the seventh century, an episcopal see for part of the Mercian dominions was placed in this city. This was sometime under different, but for the most part, under the same bishop with Lichfield and to that at length was united; but, after the Conquest, Bishop Peter and his successor Robert de Limseye removing wholly from Lichfield, fixed their residence for almost thirty years at St John's church where bishop Peter was buried, till AD 1102 when bishop Robert, taking

greater liking to the rich monastery of Coventry, made that one of his cathedrals and left Chester. Though afterwards several of the bishops of Lichfield and Coventry wrote themselves and are styled by others, bishop of Chester. (Caley *et al* eds 1846, 370)

Third, there is the passage in *Domesday Book*, 263a, which reads:

King Edward gave to King Gruffudd all the land that lay beyond the water which is called Dee. But after the same Gruffudd wronged him, he took this land from him and restored it to the Bishop of Chester and to all his men, who had formerly held it. (Morris ed 1978)

I interpret this passage to refer to the *Domesday* hundreds of *Atiscros* and *Exestan* (as shown on the *Domesday* map in the Victoria County History), which Gruffudd would have been eager to control, thus pushing the English frontier back to the Dee. Sawyer noted the ambiguity of the words 'and to all his men, who had formerly held it' (Harris & Thacker eds 1987, 340–1, 344, n 17), observing that the 'men' could have belonged either to the bishop or to the king. If the land in question was both of these hundreds, the second reading is preferable, for it accords with the mixture of Earl Edwin and 'free men' shown to occupy *Atiscros* in 1066. By contrast, in *Exestan* a significant part of the holdings seem to have lain in ecclesiastical hands: at Eyton, Sutton and, at one time, part of Gresford. In addition, the bishop held Farndon nearby on the English side of the Dee. There was one substantial secular 'free' holder, Thored (at Gresford and Allington), while Rhys held a smaller property at Erbistock. However, ecclesiastical control could have been enhanced if the Thored was the same man who was associated with the bishop at Tarvin, Guilden Sutton and, possibly, at Wroxeter. This brings us to the speculation that Thored was in fact an episcopal tenant, who in 1066 held part of an original five-hide estate of some antiquity (Harris & Thacker eds 1987, 271–3). The ambiguity of the Domesday wording, noted above, makes it as possible for an individual to have been a tenant of the bishop as of the king, here more probably the former.

We may also note the careful distinction made in this passage between return of rights to the bishop of Chester (*reddit ep. Cestre*) and the repetitive use in the rest of the section of the simpler '*ipse eps*'. I am sure that the change in wording, here as elsewhere, is deliberate and important. The entry is generally presumed to refer to the head of St John's (Thacker 1982, 201–2). As we have seen, later in the Middle Ages Holt, on the Welsh side, 'was linked with the mother church at Farndon, both being annexed time out of mind to the upkeep of the deanery of St John's Chester'. Holt, of course, was not founded until the late thirteenth century, but its link with Farndon and St John's could derive from that of the Domesday ecclesiastical estates referred to above.

To summarise a tangled story, the proposition is that the 'bishop's' lands in Exestan hundred had originally been held by St John's. It is probable that Gruffudd acquired these and other lands as part of the settlement of 1058, at the instigation of his ally Earl Aelfgar of Mercia, lately in rebellion with him against Edward. Edward may have had no choice but to acquiesce at first in Gruffudd's demands, but was probably able to regain them for their previous owners on his enemy's betrayal and death in 1063. In 1075 the estates of St

John's were merged in the combined episcopal holdings. They remained merged until 1102 when on the removal of the see to Coventry they, and other holdings and interests, were re-allocated to St John's. The attribution of the church at Eyton to St Chad's probably reflected an ancient connection later overlain by possession by 'the bishop of Chester'.

When did St John's first acquire this territory? Can we posit an arrangement by which the church was given control of a block at the southern part of an early buffer zone on the west side of the Dee preceding the *burh* — for once that had been founded there would be no reason to create such a defensive zone. Ownership could indeed date back to the years following Penda's annexation of eastern Powys. On the other hand, the church need not have acquired all its lands at once, as witnessed by the implicit gift to it of royal land at Farndon in the tenth or eleventh centuries and by the parallel of the gift of Hoseley to St Werburgh's in 958.

A chorepiscopus?

Why should the head of St John's be known as 'The bishop'? The answer may lie in the existence of a sub-bishop, a *chorepiscopus*. In canon law there cannot be two bishops in one diocese, but in practice a sub-bishop was sometimes appointed in missionary areas where an existing bishop was too infirm to perform his duties or where a diocese was too big for it to be satisfactorily managed by one person. Finberg suggested that Asser was made *chorepiscopus* in the vast diocese of Sherbourne before becoming full bishop himself and evidenced two other *chorepiscopi* based at North Tawton, whose names are known (1964, 109). Eventually the diocese was divided and the practice ended. Is it possible that a parallel arrangement existed in the over-sized frontier diocese of Lichfield in which Chester lay? The sequence could be that St John's was founded or chosen to become the base for a succession of *chorepiscopi*, appointed to spread the faith, and with it political control, in a strategically important area. To support them ecclesiastical lands would have been separated from the cathedral at Lichfield and allocated to St. John's in exactly the same way as Asser was given the monastery at Exeter to support his activities.

This can only remain a model and a speculation; it is beyond proof, but a succession of assistant bishops on the frontier, with lands to maintain them, would be a logical step to ensure religious and political conformity. Their existence would help to explain the primacy of St John's in matters like Edgar's receipt of submission and later, the choice of the site for the Norman cathedral. We can, unfortunately, go no further than that.

A symbolic site?

I have argued above for the church as being originally a cult site whose local or possibly regional importance was seized upon by successive regimes, and I suggest two possible demonstrations of this after our period. After the Norman Conquest, in 1075, the bishopric was briefly moved to Chester and the present church was constructed for the purpose. At first sight, this foundation would be outside the city and therefore uncanonical, but it may be that the late Saxon area had spread to the east of the Roman fort and included the new building. Nevertheless, it would still be a rare if not unique example of a Norman cathedral being erected outside the defended area of its city, and this can only be because there was some over-riding importance attached to the site. The placing is even more remarkable given Chester's frontier position, which would normally require security for the new building. The second clue is fabulous but no less important for being so. In the *Vita Haroldi*, Harold, a survivor of the battle of Hastings and by now a pious hermit, was called by a divine voice to go to St John's and spend the rest of his life there (Swanton ed 1984, 31–2, 38–40). There were by then other churches that he could have gone to, including St Werburgh's, and the story is not connected to the building being upgraded as a cathedral, so why St John's? It was simply the most prestigious place for the legend to adhere to and so provides another royal connection.

I would very tentatively suggest that St John's was at first a martyrs' church which possessed sufficient symbolic importance by the seventh century for it to be taken over and refounded by the Mercian kings, used for some time as the base for a succession of *chorepiscopi* and then taken over in turn as a symbol of royal power by the West Saxon and finally the Norman monarchies.

Conclusion

What can we say of Chester in these centuries? It most unlikely that the site ever ceased to exist in the sense that that there was no one there, inside or outside the walls. It still had most of its walled circuit intact and was easily defensible in 893. So long as there was political authority in the region it seems unlikely that such a site would be left unguarded, even if its activity simply shrank to maintaining a military presence in or near the circuit. As yet there is no archaeological evidence to suggest that the amphitheatre was adapted as a defensible strong point, as so often happened on the continent. Matthews' speculation that there was a post-Roman church on the site need not affect the issue, for whilst the church could have been built in the amphitheatre because it was defended, equally it could have been placed there precisely because the site was not military.

The possible archaeological evidence for the presence of an early church, supporting the string of documentary references, each weak on its own, builds up a picture of a place which either continued to be a centre of authority after the collapse of Roman rule or had been reinstated as one by the early seventh century and whose economy was more likely centred upon a trading area outside the old walls, as at London and York, before being concentrated again within them in the early tenth century. It may well have exercised spiritual supremacy, if not political control, over an area extending into Cheshire and what is now Flintshire, down perhaps to Bangor-on-Dee. We cannot determine whether the early authority was independent or whether for the whole or part of the period it was subordinate to some neighbouring state, such as Powys. Those questions have been considered elsewhere (Higham 1995, 130–43).

Three highly speculative conclusions are offered. The first is that there was by about AD 600 a British authority centred upon Chester controlling both sides of the River Dee, which was then not a frontier but an internal corridor for traffic and power. Its power probably sprang from inherited control of the former Roman imperial estates and was backed by a religious establishment which was the predecessor of St John's. The second is that after its annexation by Penda this territory was delimited to the west by Wat's Dyke and attributed, at least in part, to the re-founded St John's church. The third is that it was

Chester's economic prosperity, evidenced by the mint, and probably its religious standing by the ninth century which led to the foundation of the *burh* in 907 and its more critical importance in the century to follow. Far from it being 'wasted', its significance led to the foundation of the *burh*, rather than the other way round.

Acknowledgements

I am grateful to Keith Matthews for commenting upon an earlier draft of this paper and to Peter Carrington for editorial improvements; the errors remain firmly mine.

Bibliography

Brooks, N 1984 — The early history of the church of Canterbury. Leicester U P

Bu'Lock, J D 1962 — The Battle of Chester, AD 616. *Trans Lancashire Cheshire Antiq Soc* **72**, 47–56

Caley, J *et al* eds 1846 Dugdale, W. *Monasticon Anglicanum*. London: Bohn

Carrington, P ed 1994 The English Heritage book of Chester. London: Batsford

Cavill, P *et al* 2000 — Wirral and its Viking heritage. Nottingham: English Place-Name Society. (English Place-Name Soc popular ser **2**)

Christie, R C ed 1886 — *Annales Cestrienses*; or Chronicle of the abbey of St Werburgh at Chester. (*Rec Soc Lancashire Cheshire* **14**)

Colgrave, B ed 1985 — The Life of Bishop Wilfrid by Eddius Stephanus. Cambridge U P

Colgrave, B & Mynors, R A B eds 1969 — Bede's ecclesiastical history of the English people. Oxford U P

Collingwood, W G 1927 — Northumbrian crosses of the pre-Norman age. London: Faber

Earle, J & Plummer, C eds 1892 Two of the Anglo-Saxon Chronicles parallel. Oxford U P

Farmer, D H 1978 — The Oxford dictionary of saints. Oxford U P

Finberg, H P R 1964 — *Lucerna*. Oxford U P

Harris, B E & Thacker, A T eds 1987 A history of the county of Chester **1**. Oxford UP for London Institute of Historical Research. (Victoria History of the Counties of England)

Hart, C R ed 1975 — Early charters of northern England and the north midlands. Leicester U P

Higham 1992 — King Cearl, the battle of Chester, and the origins of Mercian 'Overkingship'. *Midland History* **17**, 1–16

Higham, N J 1993 — The origins of Cheshire. Manchester U P

Higham, N J 1995 — An English empire. Manchester U P

Higham, N J & Hill, D eds 2001 — Edward the Elder, 899–924. London: Routledge

Hill, D 2000 — Offa's Dyke: pattern and purpose. *Antiq J* **80**, 195–206

Laing, J & Laing, L nd The Dark Ages of west Cheshire. Cheshire County Council Planning

Lumby, J R ed 1876 — *Polychronicon Ranulphi Higden monachi Cestrensis*. London: Longman

Maddicott, J R 1989 — Trade, industry and the wealth of King Alfred. *Past and Present* **123**, 3–51

Mason, D J P 1985 — Excavations at Chester, 26–42 Lower Bridge Street, the Dark Age and Saxon periods. Chester City Council. (Grosvenor Mus Archaeol Excav Surv Rep **3**)

Matthews, K *et al* 1995 — Excavations at Chester, the evolution of the heart of the city: investigations at 3–15 Eastgate Street 1990/1. Chester City Council. (Archaeol Serv Excav Surv Rep **8**)

Matthews, K 2001 — *The Past Uncovered.* (Chester City Council), Autumn 2001, 1–2

Morris, J 1973 — The Age of Arthur. London: History Book Club

Morris, J ed 1978 — Domesday Book **26**: Cheshire. Chichester: Phillimore. (History from the Sources)

Morris, J ed 1980 — Nennius, British history and the Welsh annals. Chichester: Phillimore

Munday, N J ed 1974 — Goscelin's Life of St Werburgh. Chester Cathedral

Penney, S & Shotter, D C A 1996 — An inscribed Roman salt pan from Shavington, Cheshire. *Britannia* **27**, 360–5

Snyder, CA 1998 — An age of tyrants: Britain and the Britons, AD 400–600. Stroud: Sutton

Swanton, M 1984 — Three Lives of the last Englishmen. London: Garland

Swanton, M ed 2000 — The Anglo-Saxon Chronicles. London: Phoenix

Taylor H M & Taylor J 1980 — Anglo-Saxon architecture. 3 vols. Cambridge U P

Thacker, A T 1982 — Chester and Gloucester: early ecclesiastical organisation in two Mercian *burhs*. *Northern Hist* **18**, 199–211

Thomas, C 1994 — And shall these mute stones speak? University of Wales Press

Thorpe, B ed 1848 — *Florentii Wigorniensis, Chronicon ex Chronicis*. London: English Historical Society

Wainwright, F T 1975 — Scandinavian England. Ed Finberg, H R. Chichester: Phillimore

Webster, G 1951 — Chester in the Dark Ages. *J Chester Archaeol Soc* new ser **38**, 39–48

IV: The Tatton Park Project, Part 3
The Post-Medieval Estate and Halls: Grandeur to Decline

by N J Higham PhD, P Aylett MA, M Phil and J H Smith PhD

Lordship played an influential role in the landscape history of Tatton after *c* 1600, particularly once the estate had devolved to a branch of the Egerton family who established themselves as residents. Initially their management was characterised by improvement and enclosure, and probate records suggest a farming population which was comparatively affluent by regional standards. However, from the 1730s onwards the Egertons progressively emparked Tatton, bringing about a profound but gradual shift from an agricultural to a park landscape, albeit one in which livestock grazing continued.

The Egertons had a new hall constructed on a green field site and then largely rebuilt it early in the nineteenth century, which is the mansion house that still survives. However, the estate was not sufficiently well endowed with land to sustain the social pretensions of its owners, and, prior to it coming into the ownership of the National Trust, the estate in the twentieth century was overshadowed by debt.

Settlement, landscape and community 1600–1750

Prior to emparkment, the seventeenth and early eighteenth centuries make up the best documented period of Tatton's history. It has been possible to examine probate records (wills, inventories and/or bonds) for forty-nine individuals, fifty-three leases or sales and a variety of supplementary sources such as the Rostherne parish registers and hearth tax returns. The relict landscape which survives as earthworks in the parkland is specifically relevant to the early eighteenth century and compares closely with the earliest cartographic evidence from the same period. Archaeological excavation and fieldwork has added further to the record. However, the documentary sources are not spread evenly across the period: of the thirty surviving probate inventories, one is dated 1589 and one 1709: the remainder date to the seventeenth century, with twenty belonging to the last four decades. The surviving tenurial documents are exclusively eighteenth-century, with thirty-two belonging to the first half and the last (a sale) to 1781. The Rostherne parish records are extremely variable in quality during the late sixteenth and seventeenth centuries, with large runs of entries unusable because they contain no township information. The evidence is, therefore, weighted towards the latter part of the period, although the identification of several well established trends at that stage may have continued earlier but less well evidenced developments.

Lordship and tenure

This period witnessed the final abandonment of the Old Hall and its precinct as the capital messuage of the estate. A new mansion house was built in the first two decades of the eighteenth century on the site now occupied by the nineteenth century great house. This was on a 'green field' site in the north-west quarter of the principal manor, within the demesne lands.

The re-appearance of a noble residence in Tatton stemmed directly from re-organisation of the estate of which it formed a part. The estates passed from the Breretons to Sir Thomas Egerton, the long-serving Lord Chancellor, successively Lord Ellesmere and Viscount Brackley, whose death in 1617 deprived him of the chance to become Earl of Bridgewater, a title subsequently granted to his heir by a grateful King James I (Stephen & Lee eds 1908 **6**, 579–81, 574). Sir Thomas had purchased Dodleston Hall (7km south-west of Chester) early in his career, and this continued to serve his needs as an occasional country residence throughout his life. He and his first wife were buried in Dodleston church. Sir Thomas thus had little need of Tatton Old Hall himself, despite its recent extension, particularly since he was normally resident in the London area. Instead, he used it as an asset in his network of patronage. In 1614 the Tatton demesne and capital messuage was occupied by one John Egerton,[1] probably an obscure relation of the Lord Chancellor who was, himself, an illegitimate son of Sir Richard Egerton of Ridley (in central-southern Cheshire). John seems to have enjoyed the major manorial perquisites such as the mill as tenant of the Lord Chancellor's manor, but his was a very subordinate role in a large estate system which was being managed from an office outside the manor by agents of an absentee proprietor.

Sir Thomas's heir disposed of Dodleston Hall and reverted to the residence at Worsley in Lancashire, which was more central to the landed estates of the new earldom.[2] About 1677 the north Cheshire group of lands was detached from the estates of the earldom to provide a marriage settlement for Thomas Egerton, third son of the second earl, to Hester Busby of Buckinghamshire, from whom it thenceforth descended separately and successively to their son John (d 1724) and grandchildren, John (d 1738), Samuel (d Feb1780) and Hester Tatton, widow of William Tatton of Wythenshaw (d July 1780) (Ormerod 1882, **1**, 446). For Tatton and its history this proprietorial change is of major importance and underpins the distinctive development of the township in the subsequent period. It brought to Tatton a cadet branch of a major aristocratic family, who maintained wide social and political contacts among sections of the aristocracy who were better resourced than themselves. They set about the establishment there of a new dynasty and, eventually, a new residence as the focus for their own comparatively localised network of patronage. This new commitment to the locality on the part of Tatton's owners is most eloquently evidenced in the adoption of Rostherne churchyard as their final resting place, in preference to either Dodleston or Eccles (where are the graves of Sir Richard Brereton and his wife Dorothy). Rostherne provided burial for John (senior) and his wife Elizabeth (d 1743), their daughter Elizabeth (d 1763), John (junior) and his wife Christian (d 1777) and Samuel and his wife Beatrix (d 1755). The inheritance of Hester in 1780 caused a hiatus since her son and heir, William Tatton Egerton, preferred his father's family tradition of burial at Northenden church, although he clearly used Tatton Hall as a residence.

The choice of site for the new residence reflects the attitudes of the new owners. Implicit in the decision was a rejection of farming as a life style. The demesne continued to be managed from the messuage centred on the Old Hall, where large farm buildings had already been constructed during the tenure of John Egerton (d 1614). If this large farm had initially to provide accommodation for the new incumbents it was probably considered excessively pastoral and hopelessly inadequate to sustain the social pretensions of the son and daughter-in-law of an earl.

A new hall was therefore commissioned, *c* 1.2km distant from the Old Hall. At minimum, this was the fourth hall to be constructed in the township since the late Saxon period and all seem to have been built on sites which had previously been unoccupied. Structural details concerning this hall are few because it was very largely destroyed in the large-scale rebuilding of the early nineteenth century which resulted in the bulk of the present fabric. On the basis of the elevation incorporated by John Hussey on his estate map of 1733 (*see* below),[3] it seems to have been a double-fronted, two-storey building of brick or stone with two chimney stacks and a hip roof, fronting over Turn Mere to the south (the mere was described by Ormerod as newly drained in 1816, but was recorded on every eighteenth-century estate map).[4] Stables were constructed on the west side, and by 1733 a formal garden had been created to the south; orchards screened the entire complex on the east side, where tenants worked fields partially enclosed from the old town fields. The sole approach to the new mansion that can be clearly identified was a tree-lined road providing access not from the old Rostherne–Knutsford road through the township but from Mere Heath (Ill IV.1). This is now no more than an earthwork, albeit one which is still tree-lined. However, a drawing of a coach and horses on Hussey's map may imply the presence of an unenclosed road from the Rostherne entrance approximately on the line of the modern drive.

The owners and residents of Tatton Hall at this stage were not wealthy men by the standards of the aristocracy, although John senior's marriage to Elizabeth Barbour eventually brought a much-needed cash injection to the family fortune in the shape of the estate of the wealthy Samuel Hill of Shenstone Park in Staffordshire. A family whose principal income came from rural rents, they were keen to maximise their returns from their limited estates. The policies they adopted had a substantial impact on the development of local settlement, land-use and landscape even before their emparkment of Tatton and the slow landscape revolution which that entailed.

In 1733 they owned all but about 10% of Tatton township, the remainder being then in the hands of Philip Clark, a yeoman resident at Birken Green, and Sir Charles Dukinfield (of Dukinfield). In 1738 the latter had lately sold a messuage and land holdings (Ill IV.1) to John Egerton, leaving only the small holding of the Clark family outside his direct control. As lords of both manors, the Egertons held a court baron which had oversight of their tenants in Rostherne and High Legh as well as Tatton, although brief records of such have only survived among the Tatton muniments for 1718, 1736, 1738 and 1756.[5]

Tenure, settlement and landscape

The earliest detailed map of Tatton was made in 1733 by John Hussey, an agent of the Egertons, probably in anticipation of a projected mortgage on, or sale of, the property. This

III IV.1 John Hussey's map of Tatton (1733), redrawn (Not to scale)

document is in poor condition and badly faded, but a copy was made locally for Knutsford Historical Society before much of this deterioration had occurred and this copy is of some assistance in transcribing the original. Although the names of fields and any tenements owned by Philip Clark or Sir Charles Dukinfield are omitted, this map provides a valuable and authoritative starting point for an examination of landscape and settlement in the township prior to emparkment.

Apart from the new hall, a degree of nucleation can be identified at three locations within the township, at the 'village' site in Tatton manor and at two smaller sites in Norshaw.

Tatton Village

This settlement lay adjacent to the Old Hall, now a substantial farmhouse, with a scatter of tenements along the Rostherne–Knutsford road on both sides of Tatton Brook (Ill IV.1). South of the brook tenements were associated with a series of small crofts. One, owned by Philip Clark, may imply that he was a landlord renting to a tenant who was resident there alongside the agricultural tenants of the Egertons. North of the brook, buildings clustered around the edge of what, on a slightly later map (CCRO, DET/1424/31), was described as Tatton Green, where byways from Mobberley and what is now the Knutsford Gate of the park met the principal medieval road from Rostherne to Over Knutsford (Ill IV.1). It is impossible to calculate the total number of holdings in this hamlet. Sir Charles Dukinfield owned about one-third of the frontage along the principal road in 1733 and within his land individual tenements are unmarked. Although the sale of this property to John Egerton refers to only a single messuage, surface traces of at least two small enclosures which might be associated with buildings are clearly visible beside the sunken way (Higham 1998–9, ill V.6) and are respected by narrow ridge and furrow which is confined by field boundaries consistent with Hussey's map. On the Egerton land, that same map indicates that there were something like twenty-one individual buildings, but of these at least four were certainly part of the capital tenement and several others probably represent farm buildings. It seems unlikely that the number of individual tenements on the Egerton estate in this settlement exceeded ten, to which we should probably add at least a further four or five outside his lordship to account for the total community.

The form of this settlement had clearly diverged significantly from the late medieval plan. What had then been ditched fields behind tenements lining a street frontage had by the 1740s become a small green, with structures and perhaps cottages attracted to its edge, the clay floor of one of which was identified on the periphery of the 'village' excavations. The new layout probably reflects the importance of the Old Hall, built since the abandonment of the excavated medieval tofts, which seems to have exerted sufficient influence on the settlement plan to attract new building away from the Rostherne road to its gates, leaving the old messuage as a group of hedged and ditched fields (Ill IV.2).

The sunken road was examined by excavation in 1981 and found to have run between lines of stone or kerbs and been patched with bricks to fill the potholes no earlier than the late seventeenth century (Ill IV.3). Beside it was an area of building debris — nails, bricks and sandstone fragments — associated with a thick clay floor, all dated by pottery to the decades after 1700. From a pit cut into clayey soil immediately adjacent to the clay floor came an empty lead-glazed earthenware jug, already broken around the rim when deposited. From the building debris came an almost intact, green and yellow glazed cup with applied decoration. Given the apparent proximity of major structures recorded on a mid-eighteenth-century (undated) map (*see* note 4), it seems likely that this was part of a tenement of the period. Given the location, it is possible that this was the tenement occupied by John Bayley in 1741.

Norshaw

In Norshaw a small hamlet occupied a shelf of land sheltered from the dominant west winds and adjacent to what had been the Norshaw town field. In 1733 it consisted of about six tenements arranged linearly (Ill IV.1). This settlement may have been the Birken Green named as Philip Clark's place of residence, unless this represents an alternative name for Birken Heath. Access to this hamlet was *via* a single ditched and banked track, still today clearly visible in the parkland, providing a way from Birken Heath and the Salters Way which ran close to the township boundary between Rostherne and Tatton.

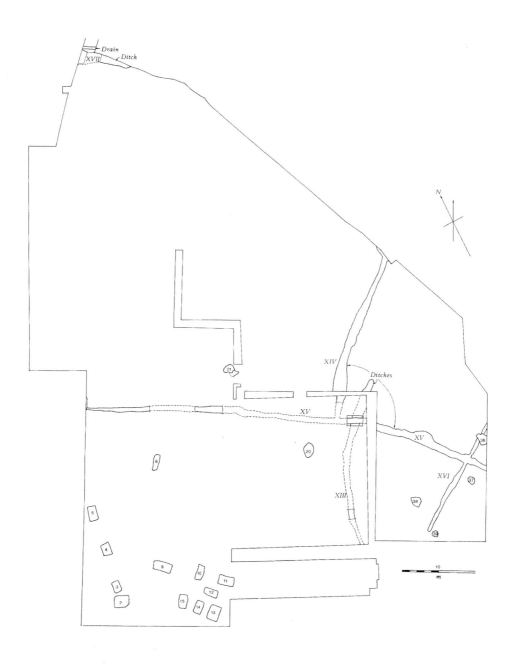

III IV.2 Tatton Village: post-medieval features in the excavated area: plan.
Pits 2–5 and 8–15 were cattle burials. (Scale 1/500)

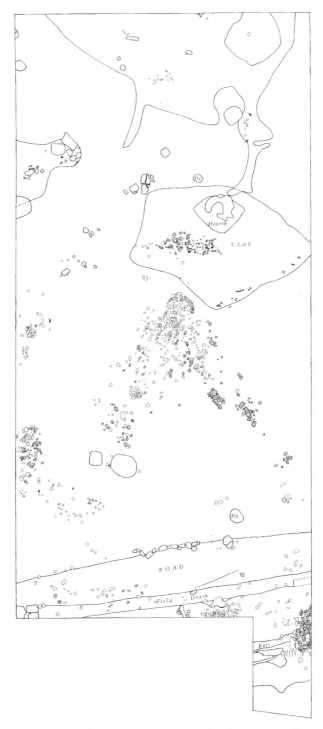

III IV.3 Tatton Village: Trench D across the sunken road: plan of irregular clay floor with hearth dated to *c* 1700. (Scale 1/125)

Norshaw Mill

The third and smallest nucleated settlement lay around the Norshaw mill and dam where three or four tenements can be identified.

All three nucleated groups of tenements had medieval antecedents, as already explained (Higham 1998–9, 68–79). They do, therefore, reflect a degree of continuity in the local settlement record which, but for emparkment, would probably have allowed what was essentially a medieval pattern of settlement to pass down to the present day. Having established that, excavation on the village site demonstrated that beneath this veneer of continuity lay a history of successive occupations and abandonments which severely restrict the extent to which we can identify continuity or usefully employ this much-misused word when referring to the settlement history of this community. Not only were the manorial halls occasionally peripatetic but there were periodic changes in the organisation of settlements of lower status, as individuals adapted to changing economic, technological and social circumstances. In important respects, therefore, the impression of continuity is a serious over- simplification.

Alongside these more or less nucleated groups of tenements, early eighteenth-century Tatton was also characterised by dispersed farms. Not all individual farms are easily identified on John Hussey's map, particularly in its present condition, but field names such as 'House Field', 'House Croft' and 'Well Field', small groups of hemp crofts and similar indications supplement the portrayal of buildings. It is possible to locate the sites of about seventeen tenements, including the flour mill.

These tenements were dispersed in all quarters of Tatton except the north-west, through which the Egertons had cut their principal access from Mere Heath to the hall and where they may have excluded tenant farms from the area west of Tatton Dale. Elsewhere there were tenements fronting Birken Heath and along the road from Tatton to Over Knutsford (in what had probably been medieval Hazelhurst) but not along the (possibly much newer) road towards Nether Knutsford on the west side of the mere. Four farms were sited along the sandy rise west of the mere, one of which was associated with a 'Well Field' and therefore probably a well. A substantial farm with an orchard and an approach road defined by a hedge and ditch occupied the south-eastern quarter of Norshaw (Ill IV.1). A scatter of buildings is also in evidence on the old town field of Tatton along the Rostherne road, where a melee of enclosed and only partially enclosed fields reflect the core of the medieval arable. The manorial flour mill lay close to the boundary between the two old Tatton manors, apparently serving both communities. It was attached to John Egerton's estate in 1614 and the protection of the mill's monopoly was a standard proviso in the early eighteenth-century leases. Several neighbouring fields were probably within the tenement of the miller, hence 'Mill Croft', 'Milly Croft', Milly Croft Nook ' and 'The Mill Field', although these might be no more than indications of location.

In the early eighteenth century the pattern of holdings was dynamic, enclosure was under way and new farms were being established. The estimate of about forty-two tenements in Tatton in 1733 contrasts with the twenty-five recorded in the hearth tax of 1664 and thirty-five in that of 1673/4 (PRO E 179/86/145; PRO E 179/86/155). A marked increase in the number of houses with two, three or four hearths had occurred between those dates, including the house of John Bolton, in which the two hearths were recorded as having increased to four by Lady Day 1674. In all, the evidence suggests a rapid rise both in the number of residences and their size.

Existing holdings were being variously divided or amalgamated, and farms were being improved by tenants acting in conjunction with their landlords. New enclosure is a marked feature of John Hussey's map. Numerous groups of fields have the same name or names which use the same element, implying that they had been subdivided. This is a particular feature of areas which had probably been townfields in the Middle Ages.

Field size and shape was not standard across the township. Numerous strip-shaped fields lay in the core of the principal open field alongside fields such as the two 'Sheper Longs', which arguably originated as medieval furlongs enclosed in totality. Hedge banks and ditches were the standard method of enclosure, giving rise to numerous field names in 'Hey', some of which probably refer to hedges which were already old by 1733. Many holdings contained one or more of these small enclosures along with a scatter of other fields, usually in a single manor. Although some leases imply a move in favour of ring-fenced farms, this was far from being characteristic where farms can be reconstructed, and some holdings were dispersed.

In the south-east corner of the township at Hazelhurst, around the village site and in parts of Norshaw, fields tended to be small and irregular, perhaps indicative of piecemeal enclosure. On the west side of the mere, in the 'Coppy' area and on the Mobberley side of the township, groups of much larger and very regular fields imply the enclosure of sub-stantial areas of the township at specific times under central authority (Ill IV.1). The regularity of enclosure characteristic of the demesne lands in the vicinity of the new mansion house implies that the capital holding had early been removed from whatever strip system had existed and had been consolidated and enclosed.

Birken Heath in Norshaw had clearly shrunk under successive enclosure. The resulting fields betray their origins in their names — 'the Nearer Intack' and 'The Further Intack', 'The Higher Birken Field', 'The Lower Birken Field', 'The Higher Birken Heys', 'The Nearer Birken Heys' and 'The Lower Birken Heys'. Elsewhere groups of field names in 'Coppy' and 'Shrogs' probably indicate recent subdivision of old woodland and there is plentiful evidence that this process continued beyond 1733.

Some instances can be documented. In a lease dated 1731 in favour of Peter Newton, the Coney Greave (a total of ten acres) is described as lately divided into three. By 1756 the 'Conecre' was in four parcels (JRULM, bundle 31). In 1739 'a certain moss in Tatton … called the Barron Coneygree … to be divided according to the meers already fixed for that purpose' was part of a tenement leased by Matthew Lowndes (CCRO, bundle DET/302).

In 1738 Joseph Hough surrendered his existing holdings in the vicinity of Tatton Dale in return for:

> All that messuage or cottage with the croft or parcell of land thereunto belonging… in Tatton… called Hunt's Cottage and also that Field or close lately inclosed from Birkin

Heath in Tatton or known by the names of the two pipers heys and the Birkin field and lately parcell of a certain tenement there lately called Steel's and now Twemlow's tenement … (*ibid*).

The Piper's Heys and the Birken Field can be identified and Hunt's Cottage was probably one of the several unnamed tenements fringing Birken Heath in 1733. The terms of the lease continue:

> And that said Samuel Egerton shall… before 5th May now next at his… expense erect and build 2 bays of good and sufficient outbuilding on the said demised premises convenient of a barn and shippon and make and hang a new gate to the South end thereof and convert the present barn now adjoining to the said messuage or cottage into a convenient kitchen or parlour with a chamber over it and also at his or their own expence do 60 roods of ditching in such places on the said premises as the same shall be most necessary …

In February 1739 a memorandum recorded overleaf a further addition to Hough's tenement of 'that parcell of ground lately meered out from Birkin Heath and marled by the said Joseph Hough being half an acre of ground or thereabouts …'.

Further 'new Intacks…lately taken in…from Birketts Heath' measuring 1a 3r 17p (Cheshire large measure) were leased by Philip Clarke in 1756 (*ibid*).

New buildings were also common. A new dwelling house which had lately been erected by Samuel Egerton was let to Samuel Siddely in 1739 (*ibid*). A nominal entry fine probably reflects the scale and expected cost of Siddely's commitment to finish the dwelling, build a barn, stable, cowhouses, carthouse, swinestoats and house of ease, erect gates and marl the 'heathy unimproved land' which formed part of his tenement.

In the same year Egerton committed himself to build for his new tenant Matthew Lowndes at Salter's Dale:

> a convenient dwelling house to consist of two ground rooms with chambers over them instead of the house already situate thereon and two bays and a half or three bays if necessary and required of outbuilding to be joined to the present barn and to be the height and width thereof. (*Ibid*. Salter's Dale was later known as Tatton Dale).

Even more expensive, a major refurbishment of the Old Hall led to the total replacement of the timber-framed walls erected in the sixteenth century with brick in the decades around 1700 (Higham 1998–9, 125). Bricks were being made in Tatton. Brick-making probably gave rise to the field name 'Kiln Croft' at Norshaw hamlet — bricks on the ground surface would support this. Such works represent a major investment in buildings, largely, though not necessarily exclusively, resourced by the Egertons themselves.

Within this increasingly enclosed and managed landscape there were widespread attempts to improve yields. References to marling are commonplace in the leases, sometimes to be undertaken by the landlord but more normally by the tenant. The practice seems to have been seen as an essential part of improvement. Pits were dug and subsoil extracted and spread on the surface in an attempt to lower the acidity of the soil. The ratio agreed in 1739 between Samuel Egerton and Matthew Lowndes was five roods to the acre (CCRO, bundle DET/302). The area between the hamlet of Norshaw and the Walkmill is pockmarked with pits which were presumably dug for this purpose. Elsewhere they were dug into the edges of the valley of the stream or on the hedgelines: such were commonplace among the 'Coppy' group of fields south of the Old Hall. Pits are scarce or entirely absent in the areas thought to be old arable, much of which lie on sands and gravels. Marling was largely confined to clayland, mossland and heathland such as occurred widely on the periphery of the township. John Hussey's map identifies a group of 'Marl'd Fields' adjacent to Mereheath, where a series of field names also contain the term 'Heath'. Jackson's or Furnivall's Park in the same quarter was scheduled along with the 'Coney Greave' group of enclosures for improvement by marling in 1739, being described as a 'certain parcell of warren or unimproved land' (ibid).

A standard condition of the leases is a prohibition on the sale of either marl or manure. However, although muck-spreading was probably a regular seasonal activity, marling was less commonly undertaken. Only one Tatton probate inventory referred to a marl cart while three had muck carts and five corn carts.

In the early eighteenth century the Tatton estate was a progressive, improving one and there are signs that this process had already been under way for a considerable period under the careful scrutiny of two generations of Egerton landlords. This probably had a marked effect on both settlement and landscape. The mansion house provided a new focus within the township which significantly altered the existing pattern of settlement ranking. An active style of estate management led to the construction of new farms and the overhaul of existing units. While dispersal in hamlets and individual farms had been a long-established characteristic of the settlement pattern of Tatton, the late seventeenth and early eighteenth centuries witnessed an expansion in the number of dispersed farms. These were established in a landscape of hedged fields which exhibited a tendency to group as regards size and regularity of shape.

It was a standard requirement of tenancies of the period to plant small numbers of new standards annually, the timber belonging to the estate and not the tenant. This helped to offset the loss of woodland, only one large stand of which had survived to 1733, on the steep stream banks near the flour mill. Elsewhere areas which had previously been wooded were now agricultural land. Heath and moss rapidly became extinct at the hands of im- proving tenant farmers. Turves stored for fuel were mentioned in probate inventories dated 1623 and 1648 and in 1709 Benjamin Hobson had two flay turf spades and a deep turf spade, which imply that some residents still dug turf as fuel at that time. However, 'coles and cannel' appear in inventories dated 1690 and 1695, which may imply a gradual switch in the mid-seventeenth century from local but increasingly scarce deposits of peat moss to imported coal (see note 1). A 'Gig Hole Field' in Norshaw may imply an attempt to locate and mine coal in Tatton; if so, it was presumably a failure.

The identification of the tenements of specific individuals is not a simple matter. Leases often convey land described by reference to the previous possessor rather than specific fields. To give an example, in 1721 Samuel Harrison leased a parcel of the Tatton Park lately held by William Antrobus, Pownall's cottage and messuage, and a further field, all then in the occupancy of William Hurlburt (CCRO, bundle DET/302). The names of all three of the earlier tenants survived to 1733 in field names in the same area of Tatton — viz Antrobus Park, Pownall's Moss and Hurlbutt's Moss — which may imply that these were the properties which Samuel Harrison was leasing. However, this is a matter of speculation and we cannot be sure of the precise area conveyed under this lease. Many others are far less explicit, conveying title to, for example, 'Norbury's Tenement', leased to John Blease in 1747. In a few instances, holdings are specified by their several field names, most or all of which can be identified. This occurs in the cases of leases in favour of Richard Shaw (1705; transferred to John Bayley 1741), Richard Clark (1731), Peter Newton (1731), Joseph Blease (1739; hitherto Broadhurst's tenement), Joseph Hough (1738), Francis Falkner (1739), Ralph Pickering (1739) and Joseph Brown (1748), which have where possible been mapped (Ill IV.1). However a proportion of the field names as stipulated in the leases do not occur on Hussey's map. In areas of recent enclosure, fields in 1733 tend to carry names derived from seventeenth-century tenants and some of these were apparently being replaced in consequence of changing tenancies. These and other field names were comparatively unstable and some fields may have been referred to by two or more names in tandem. In contrast, a minority within the old open field area were apparently at least four centuries old by this period.

Others of the leases provide an estimate of acreage in large Cheshire measure, as follows:

Table IV.1 Tatton: size of tenant holdings in large Cheshire measure

Date	Tenant	Holding size	
		Area (Cheshire)	Area (statutory)
1718	Higson	14	c 34
1721	Antrobus	13 + cott + mess	c 31
1731	Clarke	8	c 19
1735	Harrison (Street ten.)	12+ mess+ tenement	c 29
1739	Lowndes	22	c 53
1739	Pickering	18	c 43
1739	Siddeley	50 impr+ 10 unimpr	c 144
1748	Brown	22	c 53

Although it is rarely certain that the lease covered the entirety of the lands farmed by an individual (in Harrison's case clearly none did), these figures probably represent the middle range of Tatton farms, below which were cottagers, often artisans or labourers, with only a tenement and perhaps a croft. At the other extreme was the substantial acreage of the total Harrison tenement, parts of which were presumably sub-let, after which the Siddeley farm was the largest documented, passing entire to Thomas Egerton, youngest of the Egerton brothers, in 1747.

Almost all the surviving leases were for three lives and forbade unlicensed sub-letting. However, this practice was clearly widespread, with or without permission, often for a term of years. To give just one example, when the wealthy Richard Bower died in 1648 (*see* note 1), he enjoyed the keeping of ten sheep annually in Tatton Park for three lives, a 'tack' of John Bentley with fourteen years to run, a 'tack' called the Milne Field for one year and a 'tack' called the New Haye of John Cartwright for two years. These were disposed of through testamentary bequest. Leases might alternatively be used as collateral against a loan or sold, a strategy adopted by widow Allen of Rostherne whose lease of 'acres in the Coneygreave' (part of the Tatton Hall demesne) was purchased by John Higson before 1683 (CCRO, bundle DET/302).

Wealth, occupation and income

The inventories of possessions which were made on the death of local individuals provide evidence of a high level of personal wealth among the husbandmen and yeomen of the Tatton community, compared, for example, with those of the upland fringe of the North-West, at Glossop or Disley.[6] They compare with but are perhaps marginally higher than those of Stockport (Phillips & Smith 1985) and are comparable with southern communities, such as those of King's Langley (Hertfordshire) (Munby 1981).

Table IV.2 Tatton: value of personal estate as totalled in probate inventories, 1600–1700

£ 0–10	1 husbandman
£10–25	3 husbandmen, 1 yeoman, 1 widow, 1 tailor
£25–100	2 husbandmen, 3 yeoman, 3 widows
£100–200	2 husbandmen, 3 yeoman, 1 widow
£200–300	1 yeoman
£300–500	1 husbandman, 1 yeoman
£500–750	2 yeoman, 1 gentleman (John Egerton, 1614)
£750 +	1 yeoman (Richard Bower, 1648)

As a rough guide, the wage for a journeyman weaver or shearman in 1673 was assessed by the Lancashire justices at £2 10s 0d pa, or £3 if he was very skilled (Wadsworth & Mann 1931, 49). In 1695 John Bower, yeoman of Tatton, left his wife £4 pa as agreed in the terms of their marriage contract, so that this was clearly an adequate if not comfortable annual income. This sample of Tatton residents is clearly biased towards the more affluent end of the social spectrum. It does, however, imply that the local economy was a successful one, perhaps even an outstandingly successful one.

As the leases and landscape clearly imply, the wealth of this community derived principally from agriculture. Of the thirty individuals evidenced in the inventories, twenty-two were certainly engaged in arable husbandry and this cultivation was presumably responsible for the widespread narrow ridge and furrow still visible on much of the parkland. Hussey's map records field names which indicate that rye, French wheat, wheat and hemp were grown. Crops were mentioned in probate inventories as follows:

Table IV.3 Tatton: frequency of crops mentioned in probate inventories

Oats	7
Barley	6
Wheat	5
French wheat	4
Blended corn	3
Rye	3
Beans	3
Peas	2
Hemp	3
Flax	2
Hay	16

Evidence of ploughs was confined to the seven ox yokes, six ploughs and assorted accoutrements listed among the goods of John Egerton (1614). It is possible that the bullocks listed in the same inventory were used as plough beasts, but later seventeenth-century farmers probably abandoned ox ploughing in favour of horses. Thirteen individuals had horses, five with only one but several with two to four, two with five and one with ten. Horses also feature in field names. There is clear evidence of joint sowing of closes, which may mean that co-aration was practised with ploughteams made up of beasts from more than one farm.

The value of stored crops varied considerably. The most valuable recorded were those of John Egerton, who had over £83 in corn apart from £17 in corn sowed. Edmund Harrison, also probably resident in the 'Old Hall', had £76 worth of corn in 1676 and Richard Bower £60 in 1648 but others had comparatively little — Jane Johnson in 1625 had £6 in corn and hay and this was typical of the remainder.

Stock

Of the thirty people listed in the inventories, nineteen had cattle, fifteen of whom kept substantial numbers. Again, they were led by John Egerton (forty-one) and Edmund Harrison (thirty-nine). At some stage after 1700, at least one of the farmers at Tatton village killed and buried in individual pits dug for the purpose the complete carcasses of a herd of at least twelve cattle, since these pits were identified archaeologically on the edge of Tatton Green only marginally within the area excavated in 1982 (Ill IV.2). These may have been victims of the widespread cattle murrains which affected the region during the eighteenth century.

Ten had sheep, with five holding flocks of more than forty head, among whom John Egerton had 120. Five had fewer than twenty. Sheep also appear in field names. Thirteen had swine, of whom seven had only one, four had two, one had eight and John Egerton had twenty-three. Ten inventories recorded pullen (hens, ducks, geese) and John Egerton's total of forty-three included peacocks. Two had bees, one worth 2s, one with eight hives worth £1 10s 0d.

Eleven had cheese presses, a further two cheese tubs, and three had butter churns. Seven had cheese in commercial quantities, varying in value from 7s to £60 — the latter being the property of Edmund Harrison, yeoman, whose inventory in 1676 itemised £25 10s 0d in old cheese and £35 in new. Three inventories recorded cows out at hire, one with three, one with eight and one with twelve beasts. These would have been hired to members of the local community without cows of their own to provide their households with dairy produce and a saleable surplus in cheese.

The textile connection

Hemp appears as a crop in three inventories and flax in two, while others left hemp seed. Small closes named 'Hemp Yard' and 'Hemp Croft' occur on Hussey's map adjacent to tenements at Norshaw Walkmill, a barn and settlement on the Mobberley road, beside Tatton Green, at Hazelhurst and beside the Antrobus Park (Ill IV.1). Hemp was, therefore, clearly being grown in Tatton. It seems probable that much, if not all, of this hemp and flax was retted, heckled, scutched and spun locally.

Two individuals had heckles and twelve had spinning wheels, of whom six had one, four had two and two had three. Four had cards. Eleven had hemp, flax or towe (or a combination) in value ranging from 3s to £1; in weight 5lb and 12lb are mentioned. Eight individuals had yarn, four in combination with flax, hemp or towe. Yarn was valued variously from 8s 2d to £1 10s 0d.

Probate records exist for only a single webster, Richard Lea, who died in 1648. He left goods to the value of £42 5s 4d and was a linen webster, leaving looms and their furniture to the value of £2, a table, shearboard and trestles worth 12s and yarn to the value of £1. He also had two kine and perhaps £25 on loan, as well as a bible and turves for his fire.

Only two persons had much cloth, excluding normal bedding, table and dress clothes. John Broadhurst had new flaxen cloth worth £4 2s 0d in 1667 and Richard Jackson had woollen cloth worth £1 10s 0d in 1673. In 1614 John Egerton had a loom in his Great Parlour. In 1686, Ralph Percival was described as a tailor. He left a personal estate worth £20 12s 9d which included some hemp and flax, two pairs of cards, a cheese press, some hens and £1 6s 0d worth of growing corn.

Between 1724 and 1737 Samuel Albinson was repeatedly described in the parish records as a walker or fuller, making his last appearance therein as the father of an illegitimate child in 1747. In 1748 a tenement described as the walkmill tenement was leased to Joseph Brown, a tailor late of the City of London, upon surrender of a lease of his father's dated 1742, without any indication that it was at this stage other than an ordinary farm. If this holding had been in the family for several generations, it may be significant that John Brown, who died in 1681, was described as a yeoman rather than a walker. It seems likely, therefore that the Walkmill Tenement was so named not because it included the walkmill but because it was adjacent to it, in the tiny hamlet already noted there. As such, the fields listed in the lease confirm the general position of the walkmill. Given this information, it seems clear that the mill, its leet and dam are all represented on Hussey's map alongside the 'Tentry Croft'

Table IV.4 Tatton: status and occupation to 1750

(All dates refer to the first mention of an individual in this context; L= information from a lease, W= information from a will).

Servant (8)

1722 William Austin; 1732 James Brierley; 1733 Philip Buckley; 1737 Samuel Groves; 1738 James Falkner; 1742 Joseph Orford; 1747 John Walker; 1752 Griff Dale

Labourer (14)

1721 Tristram Stafford; 1723 Isaac Falkner; 1723 James Austin; 1724 Joseph Mills; 1727 William Austin; 1730 Jasper Worth; 1730 Joseph Blease; 1732 Samuel Leigh; 1732 John Davenport; 1737 Charles Brandon; 1738 William Smith; 1747 John Falkner; 1749 John Bebbington; 1749 William Irlam

Chapman (1)

1739 Ralph Pickering (of Nether Knutsford (L))

Carrier (4)

1721 Andrew Whitchurch; 1723 James Bentley; 1738 James Gandy; 1741 George Tabley

Carpenter (4)

1723 James Domville; 1739 Francis Falkner (L); 1749 John Falkner; 1750 William Falkner.

Sawyer (1)

1722 Robert Bancroft

Slater (3)

1726 Richard Rilstone; 1734 William Leigh; 1739 Joseph Blease (L)

Blacksmith (4)

1722 Peter Newton; 1732 Samuel Moult; 1739 John Bailey; 1748 John Moult

Farrier (1)

1722 George Twemlow

Miller (4)

1736 Samuel Oughton; 1745 Peter Newton; 1750 John Bebbington; 1773 Thomas Jackson (W)

Walker/ Fuller (1)

1723 Samuel Albinson

Webster (1)

1648 Richard Lea (W)

Taylor (4)

1686 Ralph Percival (W); 1728 Hugh Brodey; 1741 George Tabley; 1748 Joseph Brown (of London (L))

Hatter (1).

1736 Henry Orrell (deceased (L); 'of Knutsford' 1705 when he married a Tatton bride).

Innholder (2)

1739 Ralph Domville; 1746 John Newton

Shoemaker (1)

1724 Joseph Millington

Butcher (2)

1747 Thomas Shelmardine; 1752 Richard Higginson (L)

Schoolmaster (1)

1739 Matthew Lowndes.

Husbandman (19)

1588 John Chorlton (W); 1588 Robert Edge (W); 1623 Jeffrey Kell (W); 1626 Robert Bower (W); 1661 Roger Street (W); 1673 John Bearsley (W); 1676 Edmund Harrison (W); 1684 Hugh Die (W); 1694 Thomas Renshall (W); 1695 John Ashpole (W); 1731 Charles Brandon (of Gawsworth (L)); 1732 Joseph Sigerley; 1740 Joseph Heyes; 1741 Isaac Falkner; 1741 Philip Buckley (W); 1744 John Beighton (W); 1745 John Walker, George Jones; 1747 Peter Toft

Farmer (13)

1722 William Austin; 1724 Andrew Whittaker, John Alcock; 1726 George Twamlow; 1734 William Allen; 1738 John Hobson; 1739 Peter Barrow; 1741 Joseph Heyes; 1743 George Johnson; 1744 Joseph Orford; 1745 George Brown; 1747 George Jones; 1750 James Clark

Yeoman (29)

1648 Richard Bower (W); 1667 John Broadhurst (W); 1671 William Hough (W); 1673 Richard Jackson (W); 1678 William Bancroft (W); 1681 John Brown (W); 1683 John Higson (W); 1689 William Hough (W); Geoffrey Dickens (W); 1695 John Bower (W); 1718 Richard Higson (of Mobberley (L)); 1721 Samuel Harrison (L); 1722 Richard Clark; 1727 Henry Tatton (W); 1728 Edmund Harrison (W); 1730 Thomas Starkie; 1731 Samuel Albinson (L); 1734 George Twamlow, Peter Newton, Joseph Bowen; 1736 Thomas Street (L); 1737 William Clark; 1737 Samuel Harrison (W); 1738 Joseph Hough (L); 1739 Samuel Siddeley (of Ollerton (L)); 1744 John Newton; 1745 Francis Hough

Gentleman (9)

1614 John Egerton (W); 1651 Charles Whitcott, Armiger; 1703 Peter Crosby; 1722 Samuel Harrison; 1724 John Egerton (W); 1732 Hugh Johnson (of Nether Knutsford (L)); 1738 Thomas Starkey (of Ashley (W)); 1744 John James; 1749 Thomas Ascheton Esq

---

(Higham 1998–9, ill V.2, 303) where fulled cloth was tentered or dried; the leet and dam remain today as visible relics in the landscape.

The evidence does, therefore, imply the presence of an operative walkmill at Norshaw in the early eighteenth century. The presence of fullers in the same manor in the fourteenth century may, but need not, imply the continuous presence of wool processing on the site over four centuries.

Other trades

Probate records provide little indication of other trades. Nathaniel Hobson in 1686 was an arable and dairy farmer but he also left bark and leather worth £20 and thatching tools. In 1709 Benjamin Hobson also had a thatcher's scythe and in 1761 William Leigh mentioned his clogging tools in his will, despite being described as a yeoman. By bringing together information from the parish and probate records with the leases it is possible to identify a wider range of employment and professions undertaken by Tatton residents.

As a caution, it is important to realise that several individuals are recorded at least twice as the description of their occupation varied through time: for example, George Twamlow appears as farrier, farmer and yeoman. In other instances the profession given is that of the individual before settling in Tatton, as is clear in the cases of Matthew Lowndes and Joseph Brown. Both were thenceforth yeomen or similar. With these provisos, the husbandmen, farmers and yeomen (total sixty-one) outnumber all other occupations (fifty-seven), if gentlemen be excluded. Since the statistics are weighted against this result, it seems reasonable to argue that the majority of Tatton's residents throughout the seventeenth and the first half of the eighteenth centuries obtained the bulk of their income from farming. On the evidence of probate inventories it would appear that corn and cheese were the main revenue-earners, at least in the seventeenth century, with the growing and spinning of wool, hemp and flax providing a valuable ancillary source of income which would fit into the farming year and way of life.

The inflow of cash from these market activities was clearly more than was needed to pay entry fines, rents, taxes and leys. Those who had holdings of land represented in the records could feed, and, to a large extent clothe, warm and shelter, themselves from their own resources. Most had a favourable balance of income over expenditure and the probate inventories help to explain to what use they put this surplus.

Only eight probate inventories included money worth more than £1. Most had less than £12, but one wealthy yeoman, Richard Bower, left the large sum of £214 cash among assets valued in excess of £790. Nor did Tatton residents hold substantial sums in plate or jewellery — the most valuable recorded being John Egerton's silver salt gilt and five silver spoons, worth £3. However, sixteen of the thirty individuals whose inventories have survived were owed money, some in large amounts.

Table IV.5 Tatton: money on loan at death

£1–10	2 individuals
£11–50	4 "
£51–100	2 "
£101–200	4 "
£201–300	1 "
£301–400	1 "
£401–500	1 "
Over £500	1 "

Much of this was on bond or by speciality and the borrowers were not necessarily poor men. John Egerton (1614) was, *inter alia*, owed money by Sir Uriah Leigh (£66) and Sir Alexander Barlow (£12). Richard Jackson, a yeoman, was owed a total of £466 by more than fifty individuals when he died in old age in 1673. William Hough died in 1689 with £505 out in loans.

Many of the eighteenth-century leases carried substantial entry fines. Figures of £50–£150 were commonly attached to leases on modest farms, let for three lives. There was an approximate balance maintained between entry fine and rent; where the former was low or non-existent, the latter was proportionately higher. For example, Ann Harrison's lease of the Old Hall tenement and demesne attracted no entry fine but an annual rent of £200, whereas John Blease, described as a slater, in 1747 paid the vast sum of £286 as an entry fine for a farm on which he was to pay an annual rent of £1 16s 0d.

Outside the gentry few individuals would have had the means to pay such large entry fines and begin farming. Considerable sums were presumably raised on loan and the indications are that the facilities by which this could be achieved were available among the neighbours of a new lessee. Others may have borrowed to purchase freeholds, to build, to restock, to apprentice their sons or marry off their daughters.

Community and continuity

In 1662 John Brown of Tatton, Edward Hewett of Mobberley and Edward Allen of Rostherne were described as charterers of Tatton (Ormerod 1882, **1**, 440), from the second of whom the status passed to his son-in-law Richard Parker. The Hewett family were already present in the township in the years around 1600. John Brown, however, had only recently purchased his holding from John Bentley of the Hole in Mere, but both families retained a connection with the township until the changes of the mid-eighteenth century. In contrast, widow Allen had sold her lease in Tatton to John Higson before his death in 1683. These three separate cases are representative of the balance of continuity and discontinuity in land tenure and family structure at Tatton throughout the period.

The practice of leasing for three lives provided an opportunity for tenants to provide for their widows and children, although some stipulated the lives of young people apparently unrelated to themselves. Several of the leases for lives seem to have been effective for no more than a handful of years. Several contracts were with men who were not previously long domiciled in the township, if at all. It is possible to identify what amounts to two communities: one of families long established in the township or entering and establishing themselves over generations, and the other of individuals or families who entered and left the township relatively quickly. A group of fifteen family names can be identified from the parish records in the period 1595–1606 and can be treated as an impromptu sample. Of these, nine were named in the 1673/4 hearth tax[7] and eight were still resident as late as the 1690s. The Hewitt and Street families retained links even after emparkment. The names of Pickering and Newton seemed to have been re-introduced after gaps in the seventeenth century, during the 1730s and 1720s respectively. The Hunt family obtained a lease of a Tatton farm as late as 1742. Of the remainder, some may be represented by families living outside the township but retaining an interest in land within it. Higson is a name which recurs in leases as the common title of a tenement and in field names. The name occurs in Tatton in 1600–1605; probate records exist for 1683 and 1718, and in that same year a Richard Higson of Mobberley took out a new lease. The constant re-appearance of such familiar names is orchestrated by the occasional disappearance of one and the introduction of new names in a continuous process of gradual change.

The occasional re-establishnent of individuals from Tatton in other townships was generally a very local phenomenon — the emigration of the son and heir of Brown at the Walkmill tenement to a new career as a London tailor is almost unique, but it is worth noting that it is only evidenced from the fact that he returned when he inherited his father's lease: more emigration probably went unrecorded. There was, however a distinct parochialism evidenced in the choice of marriage partners for the daughters of Tatton residents. Between 1703 and 1752, fifty-two of the possible fifty-three brides recorded for the township found grooms within the parish of Rostherne or in townships directly bordering it. Twenty-four marriages involved two partners from Tatton itself, although this may include those who were temporarily resident as co-habitees or pending marriage.

Those who were least sedentary were at opposite ends of the social spectrum — the poor and the better off, including the gentry. For the peripatetics among the former we have little more than a host of single entries in the parish records. Servants and labourers were often able to move freely, yet even in these categories several families like the Falkners and Brandons stayed for decades and made some progress up the social ladder. Of the latter, many had assets spread across several townships. In 1678, Sibbell Brooks, a widow, had a house in Nether Knutsford as well as one in Tatton. In 1737 Samuel Harrison had houses in Mobberley, Baguley and Cranage, the last called the Manor House, while maintaining his principal residence at Tatton Old Hall. John Egerton senior held at his death in 1724 an estate in Lancashire from the Duke of Bridgewater. Of all the individuals variously described as gentry across the whole period, it is unlikely that any except the Egertons and the Harrisons regularly resided in Tatton, the remainder probably being absentees, letting or sub-letting what lands they held in the township to resident farmers.

For those with a stake in the land there was an incentive for generations to follow one another, barring only the failure of families to produce heirs. If we can isolate a Tatton community in the seventeenth and early eighteenth centuries, it consisted of these families — the Clarks, Streets, Higsons, Bowers, Dickens, Newtons, Twamlows and their kind, farming beside or under the lordship of several generations of the Egertons. In the employ of both the Egertons and the better endowed of their tenants were servants and labourers, many of whom were occasionally itinerant. Some farmers also had by-occupations such as slating or thatching. Other men had cottages but were virtually landless, maintaining themselves and their families by craft skills or trade. Few such stayed within the township over many generations. Social contacts for those below the level of the local gentry reached no further than the periphery of the parish, within which they found marriage partners for their children, lives for their leases and witnesses for their legal documents. At Knutsford they attended market and at Rostherne they prayed, baptised their children and were themselves at the last committed to the earth. The last could be an elaborate event. In his will (made in 1648), Richard Bower, yeoman, directed that the vast sum of £27 14s 8d of his £790 fortune should be spent on his funeral. This must have been a lavish affair, the subject of conversation in Rostherne parish for years to come.

Tatton and its emparkment 1750–1800

During the second half of the eighteenth century Tatton was transformed from the mainly agricultural landscape described in the previous chapter to a parkland where deer and cattle roamed almost unrestrained. This section will examine how the Egerton family esta-blished its park, garden and mansion over five decades of fundamental if gradual change.

It is clear that, in broad outline, at least, the eighteenth-century emparkment at Tatton followed a similar pattern to that seen at other country seats. Many large parks grew out of small beginnings, areas that might be only a few acres in extent.[8]

Tatton in 1733 already contained some areas known as 'parks' — the Nearer and Further Antrobus Parks close to the boundary with Knutsford, and Furnivall Park along the drive leading from the gate at Mere. Their proximity to main entrances might suggest, perhaps, that they were used to house some especially fine cattle for display purposes; it is very unlikely that deer, with their destructive athleticism, could have been kept so close to farmland in such small enclosures. In 1739 the Furnivall Park appears to have been leased in part to Mathew Lowndes of Sythington (Siddington), a schoolmaster.[9] It therefore seems unlikely that Samuel Egerton was at this time using his parks for anything other than cattle.

There were clear impediments to the expansion of the Antrobus Parks. In 1733, and indeed until the 1750s, they were surrounded by smaller fields in agricultural use and leased to tenants. Just to the north lay a house, hempyard and several small enclosures leased to Ralph Pickering,[10] and the marshy area between Pickering's holding and Turn Mere was divided into several fields. These were given names such as Newhall's Croft and the Barn Croft, which confirm the impression of agricultural activity.

But by 1739 there is clear evidence that Samuel Egerton was seeking to give his estate a more gracious appearance. Ralph Pickering's lease refers to a 'way or vista' that had been laid out recently along the western sides of the Antrobus parks, also splitting the Nearer and Further Heath Field. This avenue survives to this day, having weathered the criticism of Repton (*see below*). Egerton's wish to extend his park is indicated in his lease to the executors of Samuel Harrison of demesne lands and the Old Hall, drawn up in 1739. This allows Egerton to:

> take and inclose any part of the said demesne lands adjacent to the said Turn Meir (in case he or they shall think proper) to convert the same into a Park but not otherwise.

The lease also makes provision for Egerton to pay financial compensation to the lessees if he should convert the land into a park.[11] It is not easy to say what sort of physical changes would have been necessary — perhaps the erection of higher fences or hedges to prevent the escape of deer. In any case, nothing was done to the lands around Turn Mere until the 1750s. The parks at Tatton remained a minor feature of the landscape and Samuel Egerton lacked either the resources or the motivation to extend them into a really impressive estate.

Hoskins gives some examples of the ways in which eighteenth-century parks were created (1955, 170–1). There is a fair amount of evidence of drastic change to the landscape on estates across England. In Normanton in Rutland, for example, Sir Gilbert Heathcote created his park in the mid-1760s after demolishing the medieval church and village. He rebuilt the village elsewhere and the church in the park. Burton Constable in Yorkshire saw the complete loss of a village as the park was extended. The Cambridgeshire village of Wimpole was removed to make way for improvements, while the somewhat decayed Dorset market town of Milton Abbas was demolished in the late eighteenth century to allow the building of a new mansion. Both were rebuilt elsewhere as model villages.

Nothing as drastic had to happen at Tatton. The farming population was small and scattered, with some holdings in absentee hands and no church to act as a very visible obstruction to change. On the other hand, agriculture was widely established across the township and there were several fixtures that would need to be removed to create the complete park landscape. Among other things, as we shall see, there were two mills, a number of houses and established hedgerows in profusion.

In understanding the eighteenth-century emparkment of Tatton, it is important to recognise that some areas were more significant than others. In particular, the section of the township lying between the Knutsford boundary and the new hall would be the focus of special interest: it was clearly important that visitors coming through the nearby market town should have a good early impression of the estate. So it was logical that when, around 1750, Samuel Egerton came to consider emparkment, he should look first at that area.

But why did Egerton begin to take action to empark at that time? What made him turn his latent intention into reality? No one piece of evidence is conclusive, but there are several straws in the wind. During the 1740s the Egerton finances seem to have stabilised after the traumas of the 1730s. The correspondence gives little clue to the state of finances at that time, but there are no anxious letters as there had been in the previous decade. Certainly there seems to have been no financial problem in 1747 when his cousin Francis, the eleven-year-old Duke of Bridgewater, became Samuel's ward.[12]

In addition to this apparent improvement in his resources, there was in all likelihood a more subtle influence at work. Although Egerton had a wide acquaintance of Cheshire squires, his contact with such an exalted personage as the duke must have made a strong and unaccustomed impression. Malet suggests that Samuel had a fair amount of influence on his cousin Francis, but there must also have been some influence the other way. Accustomed to the company of Cheshire squires, Egerton may well have been given more expansive notions about his estate by his contacts with a member of the country's highest order of nobility. Outside the township of Tatton, Egerton was by the mid-1750s purchasing large tracts of land in south Lancashire.[13] Assisted by his uncle Samuel Hill, Egerton was intent on establishing an important presence in an area that was beginning to see increasing industrial development.

Nor was Egerton only concerning himself with his own estate. A letter from William Tomkinson, solicitor to both Bridgewater and Egerton, dated 18 July 1752,[14] shows how he was turning his mind to the wider affairs of his Bridgewater ward. Tomkinson writes thanking Egerton for writing to him from Dunstable, not far from Woburn, where Samuel had clearly been consulting the Duke of Bedford, Bridgewater's uncle. The subject was the young Bridgewater's future: 'I hope the measures intended for his Grace to pursue will answer your Designs, and am very certain, yt. if they do, they will turn out to his Honour and Advantage and your Credit and Satisfaction'. Egerton's important role in the planning of Bridgewater's affairs is clear, and it is significant that the letter turns immediately to the arrangements for change in Egerton's own estate of Tatton: 'I will take care of making up ye Waste at Turn Meir properly which Geo. Potter will begin upon Tuesday morning next.' What exactly is entailed by 'making up ye Waste' is by no means clear, but Turn Mere, right in front of the hall, would be a prime target for landscaping aimed at producing an attractive approach.

More significant is a reference to land transactions in the letter's next section: 'I … will endeavour to compleat the Purchase of Dolly's Share and Mr. Vernon's before your return as I have wrote to Mr. Fairclough abt. the former and will do all I can to effect it.' 'Dolly' here refers to Dorothy Heatley, who jointly with her husband Thomas held a fifth share in the Old Hall and Tatton demesne previously held by Samuel Harrison, while 'Mr. Vernon' is Ralph Vernon, husband of Harrison's daughter Hannah, who held important shares in a very significant area of Tatton township, taking in land around Turn Mere as well as large holdings to the east of Tatton Mere. It is notable that this sign of intent to buy up leases is combined in this letter with a description of the steps being taken towards an 'ejectment' affecting 'the Parks' presumably the Antrobus parks, whose lessee is not known. This 'ejectment' was a legal procedure by which the question of title to land could be tried, and the fact that it was being used shows the seriousness with which, for the first time for many years, the Egerton family were considering the future shape of their Tatton estate.

All these signs of activity — albeit contained in the letter of one enthusiastic attorney — were bound to result in action eventually, and the 1750s saw a wide range of leases bought up as Samuel Egerton took parts of his estate in hand. Apart from the Heatley and Vernon holdings, other shares in the demesne were purchased during that decade: the one-fifth held by John Egerton of Chester, beerbrewer and probably no close relation; another daughter of Samuel Harrison, Ann; and the fifth belonging to Samuel Harrison junior. These were bought in a series of transactions starting in 1753 and continuing to 1757.[15] Although the cost to Samuel Egerton of these deals is not in every case known, he paid £250 for the John Egerton share and it seems likely that he spent similar sums on the others. Considering the large amounts he was laying out at exactly the same time for land in south Lancashire,[16] the expenses of the Tatton purchases do not seem excessive, but they were complex transactions that took time to arrange. That Samuel saw them through demonstrates his determination to 'improve' his township.

In 1755, Ralph Pickering surrendered his lease to the small farm close to the Antrobus Parks,[17] releasing a significant part of the estate for Egerton's own use. Then, in 1760, the Knutsford attorney Samuel Wright surrendered his lease of the Merefields on the banks of Tatton Mere, giving Egerton access to both sides of the drive or track that led from Knutsford to the Old Hall.[18]

Thus, by the end of the 1750s the fields that lay between the township boundary with Knutsford and both halls were in Egerton's complete control. Most of the landscape changes at Tatton centred on that area, but leases on other sections of the township were also purchased during the 1750s. Among them was a lease on land in the north of the township, partly taken out of the Barren Coneygreave and adjoining a parcel of Glebeland, where a track entered Tatton from the direction of Rostherne.[19] This had been held since 1738 by the Massey family of Dunham Massey — an example, like the attorney Wright's lease on the Merefields, of land held by absentees of high or fairly high social standing. The tenants of Tatton, then, were varied — not all of them would suffer loss of livelihood on emparkment. The lack of drama in the changes at Tatton was no doubt emphasised by this broad social base — there is no sense that Egerton was forcibly sweeping small farmers out of his way to gratify his aesthetic sensibilities and impress visiting gentry.

Further away from approaches to the hall, land leased by John Babbington near the Old Hall — known as Cartwright's New Hey — along with a house was transferred to Samuel Egerton on 3 May 1757.[20]

These purchases were by no means the only sign that Samuel Egerton was adopting a more expansive attitude to Tatton during the 1750s. Another letter from William Tomkinson, written in 1756,[21] discusses what appears to have been extensive work on rooms in the new hall, including a sitting room. A new staircase is seen as promising to provide 'a very handsome entrance' to a room. In the gardens, meanwhile, Samuel sought more professional advice than was available locally. During 1757 he wrote to Lancelot 'Capability' Brown, seeking his views on a gardener. Brown obliged, writing from Hammersmith on 22 September 1757 to say: 'I have found a gardener that will answer your Purpose; he is ready and waits for your Orders, when and in what manner you wou'd have him come to Tatton Park'.[22] Although we do not know the name of the gardener selected, this letter shows clearly Egerton's growing enthusiasm for a more stylish quality of life.

The 1760s saw the purchase of more leases. In May 1762 John Bayley, a blacksmith, surrendered his lease on some important fields once held by Samuel Harrison and his heirs, including the Wain Loons and the Sheperlongs in what had been the medieval open field, on the fringes of the direct 'route' between Knutsford and the new hall.[23] The sensitivity of Samuel Egerton to the danger of social disruption from emparkment is illustrated by the clause in the surrender deed that allows Bayley to retain the house he used in the Smithy Croft free of rent during the term of the original lease. Perhaps Bayley was especially useful as a blacksmith who was on the spot in Tatton. Excavation in 1981 revealed what was presumably his home and smithy, defined by a thick clay floor and brick scatter. A broken lead-glazed earthenware jug was still buried in a small pit in the floor and a decorated cup or tyg of the early eighteenth century, which may have been Bayley's, was recovered almost intact from demolition.

If the Bayley deed illustrated that Egerton was inclined to be patient about entering into full possession of the Tatton landscape, it also shows something of what was intended when the buying-out process had been completed. It allows Samuel and his heirs to 'take down and convert and dispose of said Barns fields closes or parcels of Land in such manner as he or they shall or may think proper or necessary.' For the first time since the 1739 Turn Mere lease, Egerton was setting out his intentions for the township in some detail.

More arrangements to smooth the process of change are contained in a deed of October 1763 by which Phillip Clarke sold his lease on a messuage and land.[24] This purchase probably related to a holding identified as 'Phillip Clarke's' on Hussey's map of 1733, to the east of Tatton Mere. Clarke was now apparently short of somewhere to live in Tatton, for Samuel Egerton agreed to the house being held by Clarke for the next year on an annual rent of £72. If this did not suit Clarke, he could hold Higginson's house and the 'Little croft behind it' for two or three years, rent free 'untill he can accommodate himself'. Egerton would not force removal, especially of someone with a long history of residence in Tatton. The area of Clarke's holding was no doubt sufficiently out of the way for Egerton to be relaxed about its remaining temporarily in fields.

Another six years passed before a more distant part of the township — the land near Birkin Heath in the north-east held by William Falkner — was bought out. Once again an arrangement was made to help accommodate the departing tenant. The deed of 1769,[25] for the transfer of fields such as the Nearer Intack, the Further Intack (both taken from the margins of Birkin Heath, probably not long before 1733) and the Nearer Birkin Heys, also allowed William Falkner to hold Statham's Tenement in Rostherne rent-free for an unspecified period. A number of other transactions in similar vein, with no special distinguishing mark, helped to complete the process by which Samuel Egerton was able to hand over at his death a Tatton township that had for the first time become Tatton Park. The evidence of the landholding shows that Egerton's way with change was slow but sure. Despite his willingness to accommodate, in every sense, his departing tenants, he never appears to have wavered in his determination to create his own landscape out of the agricultural hotch-potch he had inherited in 1738.

How did these changes in the landscape affect Tatton's society? The Rostherne parish registers give a few clues. In the 1740s baptisms of Tatton children recorded at Rostherne numbered forty, with twenty-nine different sets of parents. Fortunately occupations of parents were noted in the registers at the time and these give the impression of a small but fairly widely based community, with a number of retail traders and craftsmen resident in Tatton township itself. Apart from the inn-holders Ralph Domville and John Newton, there was a tailor (George Tabley), a butcher (Thomas Shelmerdine) and a drysalter (William Irlam). John Faulkner the carpenter, Samuel Albinson the fuller and Francis Hough the carrier appear as fathers during the 1740s, along with Peter Newton the miller. Given that these were all in the limited category of fathers, it seems very likely that there were some more retail traders and craftsmen in Tatton during the decade, too young or too old to sire children. It is unfortunate that no occupations are given in the Rostherne registers for those whose burials are recorded.

In the 1750s the registers offer rather less evidence of retail activity in Tatton, although comparisons are difficult because recording of occupations ceases in 1757. John Newton still kept an inn in the 1750s, while William (*sic*) Falkner appears as a carpenter, with John Bebbington as a miller, John Blease as a slater and Robert Haltridge as a gardener. Blease, Haltridge and Falkner might well have been kept in work mainly by Egerton, and only Newton and Bebbington seem likely to have been employed largely by the township's ordinary inhabitants. However, it is dangerous to conclude too much from such a small sample, especially when the total of baptisms actually rose during the 1750s to fifty-four. After 1760, as the gradual buying-up of leases continued, numbers of births in Tatton held up well — thirty-five of them between 1760 and 1769. Most parents, to judge by other evidence, were farmers or labourers. There were twenty-three different sets of parents, hardly changed from the 1750s total of twenty-seven and not far off the 1740s figure of twenty-nine.

It was not until the 1770s, with only nine sets of parents producing ten children (of whom two were illegitimate) that a sharp fall is noticeable in Tatton baptisms. The patient, modest buying up of leases finally seems to have cleared the township of all, or almost all, of its farmers. As far as can be seen from the Rostherne registers, the occupations of those fathering children in Tatton during the 1770s were associated with the house or gardens, with only a handful of the old Tatton community — the Clarkes, Bleases and Masseys — still represented. A brief tally of Tatton people during the second half of the century does, however, confirm that change was gradual. The total of Tatton burials in the Rostherne registers in the 1750s was twenty-five, a rise of seven on the previous decade and an interesting parallel with the figures for baptisms. The 1760s saw a more rapid decrease, with only ten Tatton burials being recorded, but, as with baptisms, it was not until the 1770s that activity — if that is the right word — really fell off. Between 1770 and 1779 there were just five burials of Tatton men and women. Thus Tatton only features in the Rostherne baptism and burial registers fifteen times during that decade, compared with forty-five times in the previous decade. But the 1770s, the last ten years of Samuel Egerton's life, was to prove a low point in the demographic history of Tatton.

It is impossible to avoid the conclusion that it was the arrival of the thirty-one-year-old William Tatton Egerton, who inherited Tatton from his mother Hester, Samuel Egerton's sister, in 1780, that finally established Tatton as a country estate with agriculture restricted almost entirely to the home farm at the Dale (*see below*). A good idea of the way Samuel changed things at Tatton can be gleaned from the number and nature of the receipts for work in the house, park and gardens. Amid a group of receipts for garden work is one for as many as 3,600 young trees and seedlings purchased in March 1781, and including 2000 beech seedlings, 100 Portugal laurels and 100 Balm Gilead Fir.[26] That suggests a level of planting far in excess of anything seen before 1780. In 1781, one James Duesberry submitted bills for about £46 of brick-making, and during the next two years continued to provide bricks in amounts worth up to £20.[27] Although it is impossible to say precisely where these bricks were used, it is conceivable that they went into the massive perimeter wall that now surrounds Tatton Park. In August 1782, labourers were employed in making new roads in the park,[28] a task that was still being completed in November that year.

While Samuel Wyatt, as we shall see, prepared plans for the new hall that foreshadowed the eventual face of the stately centrepiece of Tatton, the other parts of the estate were undergoing rapid changes.

A new community began to appear in Tatton in the 1780s, much of it probably housed in the offices surrounding the new hall. After the lull of the 1770s, which saw the final demise of the varied agricultural society of the pre-1750 era, the period from 1780 to 1790 saw an influx of labourers and servants whose lives centred on the Egerton family. There were twenty births, to eleven different sets of parents, in the decade following William Tatton Egerton's arrival at Tatton. New names such as Bracegirdle (from 1779) and Hackney (also from 1779, and a miller) appear on the Rostherne registers, and almost all of them can be identified as garden or park labourers or servants. Even when an old name is seen — Street — it belongs to Hannah Street, who worked as a garden labourer and had the misfortune in 1781 to give birth to a 'base' son, James, fathered by Richard Leech, also of Tatton.

This is not the place to go into the detailed architectural history of the hall, but it is interesting to look at the mood of William Tatton Egerton as he contemplated the changes he was to make to his house during the early 1780s. In one sense at least, his attitude to improvements mirrors that of Samuel Egerton: both show a reluctance to undertake hasty and expensive work to either house or estate. In a letter to his brother-in-law Christopher Sykes on 23 February 1783, Egerton outlined his ideas for alterations to Tatton (Sykes was to become the owner of the splendid Sledmere in Yorkshire).[29] Egerton's letter was pre-occupied with his own problems with his 'thin, cold house'. The alterations under consideration would drive Egerton and his family out of Tatton for a time, he says. His intention is to 'run a passage before the present North Front which will make a much handsomer approach both to the Dining and Drawing Rooms, and by adding the part of the present passage to the little drawing room, I shall get a very good Library below stairs, this addition which I am going to make is but to be one Story, and merely as a Convenience and not intended to cost much Money'.

For all his ambition in the park improvements, Egerton was clearly unwilling to stretch his resources too greatly in changes to the house. He is almost coy about his plans, stressing that they are aimed at convenience rather than show. It is significant that Samuel Wyatt, who had already prepared plans for Samuel Egerton in 1774 and whose ideas were to form the basis for the rebuilt Tatton Hall, does not rate a mention in this letter. The dates of Wyatt's involvement at Tatton are not certain, but one recent writer hazards a guess at c 1785–90.[30] It is possible that no thought had been given by early 1783 to the employment of an architect, and that Egerton, ignoring the earlier plans by Wyatt, was doing his own thinking about the planning of the house.

Whatever Egerton's hesitations and reservations, by the last years of the 1780s extensive work was in train around Tatton Hall, with the neo-classical designs of Samuel Wyatt being followed. Egerton was, however, still disinclined to be extravagant. Although Wyatt's 'Grand Design' prescribed for Tatton a large house with eleven bays to the south or garden front, it was built in stages, with the old house being removed almost brick by brick as the new house took its place. As we shall see, the house was to remain half-old and half-new for many years during the 1790s, red brick sharing the facade with yellowish sandstone in uneasy combination. That Egerton should be content with such a curious piebald compromise shows that, despite his engagement of a fashionable architect and his extensive work in the park, he was not able to spend all he would have liked on improving his estate.

How was Egerton's work seen by his more humble neighbours in the Knutsford area? A glimpse of the local attitude to the changes in park and house is given in the diaries of John Byng, Viscount Torrington, who passed through in June 1790. Visiting Knutsford, 'a clean, well-built, well-placed town where the cotton trade brings plenty', Byng sauntered into Tatton 'by an avenue' — the beech avenue that still exists. He got good information ('a rare thing') from an 'honest-looking intelligent fellow' who told him that Squire Egerton was the park's owner. Egerton, the fellow says, has 'a vast estate' and 'this vast park, ten miles round; and deserves it all: for he is a noble, well spoken-of gentleman'.[31]

This comment may not, of course, be representative of Knutsford opinion — the man may have been an employee or tenant, anxious to say the right thing to a traveller who might find himself talking to Egerton. But it does suggest that Egerton had won good opinions for his behaviour towards the people of the area and that his achievement in obtaining a splendid landed estate, both in Tatton and beyond, had not caused resentment. There is no sign that people thought him arrogant or haughty. That both Samuel and William Tatton Egerton had a gradual approach and a modest attitude to change may have won admiration from a wide range of local people.

In November 1791, the renowned landscape designer Humphry Repton passed through Tatton and delivered his professional verdict on what improvements he deemed to be necessary for the park. The Tatton work was part of a group of commissions by gentlemen in the North-West, which began in July 1790 with a visit to Rode Hall, a seat of Wilbraham Bootle. There, Repton had, as usual, given his views on changes to the park, contained in a '*Red Book*' (bound in a red or brown cover), costing, in Bootle's case, £55 13s 0d (Stroud 1962, 51). Bootle was Egerton's brother-in-law, and it was almost inevitable that Tatton would feature among the other North-West commissions for Repton. Another Bootle property, Lathom near Ormskirk, Hooton (Sir Thomas Stanley), Crewe Hall (John Crewe) and High Legh (Henry Cornwall Legh) were all the subject of Repton's *Red Books* in the early 1790s. But Tatton was the most famous of the north-western group and was to cause more controversy than almost any of his commissions.

An important point about the *Red Book* that Repton produced for Tatton (it seems to have taken him until February 1792 to finish the plans) is that its proposals are largely concerned with views down one axis of the park only — the approach from Knutsford and the scene looking back down that approach. As with all the changes in the landholding since the 1730s — since the planting of the 'way or vista' of beeches towards Knutsford and the hint in 1739 that the Turn Mere demesne lands could be imparked — the prime intention was to provide a suitable approach for visitors entering via Knutsford. The area to the north of the house was much less important. Indeed, despite his dislike of strict formality in landscape features, Repton was quite content to allow a formal double avenue of trees to remain to the north of the house, leading towards Mere and Rostherne. No view of or from the north front appears in the *Red Book* for Tatton.

Such tolerance would not do at all when Repton came to consider the approach from Knutsford. Scorning all plantations in 'any regular form' as 'unnatural', he directed particular criticism at the Tatton beech avenue, the 'way or vista' planted sixty years earlier and now containing sizeable trees. What particularly piqued him was that it consisted at that time of alternate plantings of Scotch Fir and beech which were seen during the autumn when the beech wore its orange tints. 'It is a caricature of Nature's colouring, for if she paints in the warmest glow of Autumn, her tints are still in harmony, she never mixes green and orange in such equal quantities that we are undecided how to look at them, but one or other prevails thro' the whole scene' is his comment in the *Red Book*. Instead of this, Repton advocated that there should be smaller clumps of trees (some of them formed out of the original avenue) through which the approach from Knutsford would wind. This would give (after many years, as Repton acknowledges) the typical Repton landscape, with trees and drives mingling to give a natural — but never wild — approach.

The proposals for the management of the water in the park were shrewd and imaginative. For one thing, they would be capable of bearing fruit much sooner than the suggestions for planting. They entailed the digging-out of bays in both Tatton and Turn meres to give the impression that they ran into each other. Viewed from the house, using the hillocks that were present to hide the artificiality of the bays, the impression of a free-flowing river, lively and satisfying, would be presented to the eye. It was a neat and ironically artificial way of lending a natural look to the Tatton landscape. But the labour involved would have been great and the Egertons never managed to carry out the work. In another irony, nature did something very similar itself. Although Turn Mere was drained in 1816, the early years of the twentieth century saw serious subsidence, caused by the huge expansion in brine extraction for the Northwich area salt industry. The result was Melchett Mere, which was to give anyone looking out of the south front windows the strong impression that it was linked physically to Tatton Mere. Thus the effect intended by Repton to be achieved by careful artifice was brought about by brute industrial processes at work several miles away. Repton would also have approved of later planting and felling policies, which have followed his suggestions, just as other estates have Reptonised their own landscapes. The chief irritant to the Reptonian eye would, of course, have been the beech avenue, still surviving after 250 years and nearly 200 years after he suggested its removal.

One incident, though, was to resonate more than the fate of the beech avenue or any suggested alteration to Tatton Park itself. One of the keys to Repton's success — apart from his brilliant eye for detail and his stamina in travelling the length and breadth of the country to view landscapes — was his understanding of the ambitious gentleman, the man with substantial but perhaps not gigantic estates who was keen to see his inheritance expanded. The country estate of people like William Tatton Egerton was an important symbol of their power and prosperity, and Repton was adept at suggesting ways to establish greatness in the minds of others through the landscape. In the Tatton *Red Book*, Repton says, in characteristically grandiose terms: 'The first essential of greatness in a place, is the appearance of united and uninterrupted property, and it is in vain that this is studied within the pale, if it is too visibly contradicted on the outside'. Thus, he implies, whatever is done to prettify the park, the splendour of the owner's name is diminished if the surrounding area does not reflect his influence. What he calls 'a large manufacturing town, like Knutsford' cannot be expected to be the property of a single individual, but 'the proportion of interest belonging to the adjoining great Family, should impress the mind with a sense of its influence'. Suggestions for impressing the mind included building the church in the same style as the great house, or putting the family coat of arms on a market house or public edifice. But Repton, as it turned out, over-reached himself in suggesting, in a passing hint, that the coat of arms of the Egertons should appear on the local milestones.

Apart from being impractical and unsuitable for a county where gentry abounded and where Tatton was only one among many great houses, this was snobbish enough to earn Repton notoriety; he was widely criticised for giving airs to owners. Richard Payne Knight attacked him for it in his book *Landscape* in 1794, and, in 1816, Thomas Love Peacock satirised Repton in his novel *Headlong Hall*. Egerton must have regretted showing the *Red Book* to anyone outside his family circle (Stroud 1962, 13, 79).

Despite the grandiose ideas of the *Red Book*, Egerton never seems to have nursed extra-vagant concepts of his place in the world. The half-brick, half-stone Tatton Hall of the early 1790s bears witness to his caution. In a countryside like north Cheshire, with its plethora of gentry, no one man could dream of total dominance. The Egerton approach throughout the late eighteenth century was to recognise the limitations of their power while gradually improving house and park. The nineteenth century was to see further success, achieved with a gradualism that mirrored that of the eighteenth century.

Tatton 1800–1958: Rising status, rising debt

The gradual rise of the Egertons continued in the nineteenth century. Starting the century as prominent but not dominant members of Cheshire society, they slowly but surely attained higher status in the county, the region and the country. Without ever achieving national fame, the Egertons proved a solid and respectable aristocratic family for a century after the ennoblement of William Egerton as the first Baron Egerton of Tatton in 1859.

But these social advances were not matched by any very significant changes to the fabric of the Tatton estate after 1820. The major alterations to the house, for example, were completed by 1813 by Lewis Wyatt, nephew of Samuel. Neither did the landscape of the park change radically, apart from planting which clearly reflected the influence of Repton's *Red Book*.

Yet, as this section will show, the estate had by the early twentieth century encountered severe and apparently intractable financial troubles. Long before the death of the last Lord Egerton in 1958, the survival of the estate was under threat. This chapter will try to explain why the estate suffered such a shortage of cash, but the reasons are difficult to find. Firstly, as we have noted, the Egertons were not overstretched in the building of their house; the mansion was added to gradually as funds became available. Secondly, the Egerton estates were relatively compact. Management was easier than on many aristocratic estates. Although they owned 8,876 acres in Cheshire and 1,870 in Lancashire by 1873 (Local Government Board 1875), their holdings did not compare in extent and complexity with those of, say, the Duke of Rutland, who held many thousands of acres in the counties of Derbyshire, Leicestershire, Lincolnshire, Cambridgeshire and Wiltshire. Separate stewards were needed to oversee each county section of the Rutland estate.[32]

How did the Egertons fare in the administration of their estates? A good idea of how their affairs were ordered in the early nineteenth century can be obtained from the abstract books kept for Wilbraham Egerton in the period 1817 to 1833.[33] They show that repairs on the estates comprised the largest single category of expenditure in all but five years in that period. In ten of those years, more was spent on estate repairs than on the house and garden combined. Spending on building activities inside the park does not seem to have been included in the total for repairs on estates. For instance, in 1828, Joseph Worthington was paid £97 3s 4d for bricks under 'repairs on estates', while on the same day he was paid an unusually large £205 8s 2d for bricks under the heading 'park and plantations'.[34]

The totals spent on repairs were erratic as well as high. They varied from £1685 in 1829 up to £3410 in 1833. This must have caused problems of budgeting that added to the burden on the Egerton finances.

Spending on Tatton Dale home farm could also be erratic, although it was generally modest. In 1818, for example, it was a mere £680, while in 1819 it suddenly rose to £2425. But a major part of the rise could be attributed to spending on stock, and that of course could be more than offset by skilful sales. In addition, the sums raised by 'leying', the practice of allowing other farmers to graze their cattle on Tatton land, were an important part of the economy of the estate. The £1172 6s 0d transferred to the accounts from 'Dale ley book' on 12 October 1819 was not untypical of the money that could be made from the rich grassland of the township. Even the landscape of Repton could be made to yield a decent financial return.

The gardens demanded a substantial but not huge financial commitment. Between 1817, when they cost £647 to run, and 1833, when the total was £597, they fluctuated considerably. These variations may have had something to do with improvements by the owners, especially the building of an orangery, designed by Lewis Wyatt in 1818. The Abstract Books give hints of the impact of this work, including a record of £128 4s 6d paid to a tradesman called Heap for work in the 'conservatory', which could refer to the Wyatt addition on 19 August 1819. On 31 December of that year a man named Hughes was paid £54 8s 0d for painting the conservatory, and the glazier Barlow received £69 17s 2d for plumbing and glazing the same day.[35] In addition to these amounts paid for construction or repair, the labour bill rose from a monthly £24 in June 1817 to £36 3s 4d in June 1822. This was an important factor in the rising trend of spending on the gardens from 1818 to the mid-1820s, when the totals fell again. In June 1833, the four-week labour bill there was down to £27 6s 0d.

Some capital spending affecting the gardens was not recorded as being laid out there. This happened in the case of the Golden Brook, now an integral part of the garden, but in the first part of the nineteenth century simply old marl pits in the parkland. On 29 October 1819 Samuel and Henry Worsley, drainers, were paid for twenty-four days' work each 'at soughs from the Golden Brow pits to Birch Island'.[36]

The house was equally a less than onerous burden on the estate's purse. Spending ranged from £1041 in 1829 to £2671 in 1819. Only occasionally did it rise above £1500 a year. The fact that little was being added to the Wyatt family's work in the house after 1813 meant that there was little pressure on capital spending. But staff costs were also controlled well. The column showing 'Men Servants' Wages and Clothes', which must be assumed to represent mainly the cost of house staff, ranged from £666 in 1818 to an exceptionally high £1118 in 1820 but only twice exceeded £1000. Although the increasing numbers and more elevated social status of house guests in the later nineteenth century may have pushed spending on this category higher, there is no sign of great extravagance.

Casual expenses were of their nature a more variable part of the pattern of spending. They fluctuated between £205 in 1822 and £2064 in 1830. The latter figure was affected by two £500 cash sums, one paid to Wilbraham Egerton's own use on 27 July and the other received by a Mr Carter on 30 September. Another large and important sum was the £477 0s 10d paid over by Egerton to a William Tomlinson, a solicitor, for the county election on 27 September. Although politics still revolved around the polls taking place in Cheshire, it was to the growing town of Manchester, close to the family's Lancashire lands, that the Egerton interests were now increasingly turning. Evidence of this is found for example in the ten-guinea subscription paid to the Manchester Infirmary on 6 May 1819,[37] and the five guineas for the 'Agriculture Society Manchester' on 28 September 1830.[38] These were recorded in the category of 'Donations', a more stable figure ranging from £255 to £583 annually between 1817 and 1833.

What about the income needed to sustain this expenditure? Apart from sales of livestock and sundries like farm and garden produce (not a large sum), the main income was from rents. The account books show regular half-yearly payments from the Cheshire estate, with the example from 12 January 1832 being typical: 'Rec'd from Mr Lingard half a yr. rents of my Cheshire property paid at Tatton £3,348 13s 4d'. This was followed on January 14 by a similar entry revealing that Mr Lingard (probably either Roger Rowson Lingard or Alexander Lingard, attorneys of Stockport) paid a year's rents of Knutsford property (separated here from the rest of the Cheshire estate, and considerably more urban in character), amounting to £489 after deduction of payments of £63 11s 0d. This suggests that the whole of the Cheshire estate of Wilbraham Egerton raised about £8000 a year in rents at this time. If, as seems likely, the sums paid for repairs on estates related only to the Cheshire property, then the repairs took up between 20 per cent and 37 per cent of the income from rents in the 1817–1833 period. Other income, such as the £1237 10s 0d dividend for the first half of 1832 paid to Wilbraham Egerton on 28 July 1832, was not balanced by such considerable costs.

Those who have studied the levels of rent and other aspects of the financial relationships between landlords and tenants in the difficult years following the end of the Napoleonic Wars have seen reduction in some rents as a means of the landlord's assisting the tenant and preserving the flow of income.[39] C S Davies sees little agricultural distress in Cheshire and no signs of a widespread reduction in rural rents (1960, 47). There is nothing in the limited material we have about the Egerton estates to suggest that any reduction took place there. There was, however, one other method of helping tenants — by increasing spending on repairs, thereby releasing more of tenants' capital to enable them to invest and survive the hard times. The Tatton figures suggest that a large proportion of spending went on repairs, as high as the highest figures collected from other estates by Thompson. So, although there was no evidence of a fall in rents, this may in some years at least have been because the Egerton estate was in effect subsidising tenants.

There is no sign that such expenditures caused financial embarrassment, during the nineteenth century at all events. Building continued, though at a slower pace than in the very first years of the century. The octagonal Mere Lodge was built by Lewis Wyatt in 1822, while in 1833 the Rostherne Lodge was erected, to the design of James Hakewill. Later in the century there were some significant additions to the house: a second storey to the west or family wing by Paxton's son-in-law, G H Stokes, in 1860; in 1884, walls and arches around the entrance forecourt, a chapel, a smoking room and a study to the south front.[40]

Spending on entertainment increased considerably too, if the exalted invitation lists of the second half of the century are any evidence. The death of Wilbraham Egerton in 1856 ended a long and successful period at Tatton, a half-century in which the house had been completed in most respects, gardens had been extended and the farm had become established. Ironically, we know more of the management of the estate by the eighteenth century Egertons than by Wilbraham and his nineteenth-century successors, but the family's stock clearly rose in this period and in 1859, three years after coming into ownership of Tatton, William Egerton was created Baron Egerton of Tatton. An active politician, he had followed his father's footsteps by sitting as MP for Cheshire. A long period of service to political life — not distinguished on the national stage, but consistent — was rewarded with a peerage for this Tory family, recommended by a Whig Prime Minister, Lord Palmerston. The fact that recognition came from across the political divide shows the solid reputation of the family.

The 1860s saw invitations sent to a much wider circle of people than had been the case early in the century — dukes and viscounts were now on the lists. By the 1870s, letters were coming in from the Archbishop of Canterbury, Mr Gladstone in Downing Street, the French and Italian ambassadors and — to reflect a greater interest in things intellectual — the editor of the *Edinburgh Review*.[41] Many of the paintings that now hang in the house were bought in the latter half of the nineteenth century by the much-travelled Wilbraham Egerton, who succeeded William in 1883. Wilbraham's travels took him to Asia as well as Europe and there are lively accounts of forests and waterfalls in Ceylon, along with sensitive descriptions of churches in Belgium, in his journals.[42] Among other things, Wilbraham could write with a pleasing wit. On a boat in Germany, he played a minor role in a romantic interlude: 'There was a pretty Russian lady on board, with whom the Captain fell desperately in love, and seeing that she was talking to my Mother, applied to me repeatedly for her name, which I did not know any more than he did. He confided to me that her eyebrows were as fine as if they had been traced with a pencil, which they probably were'.

The able young Wilbraham was to become the second Lord Egerton, and in 1887 he welcomed to Tatton its most distinguished visitor, the Prince of Wales. With his princess he stayed at Tatton during the Royal Jubilee Exhibition held at Manchester, and planted a tree in the gardens.

While we have reasonable documentation for the activities of the Egerton family itself, we know less about the social and economic life of the people who lived in the township of Tatton. For instance, we have few names of servants and those who looked after the horses and gardens in the nineteenth century. But it is clear that people still lived in the parkland.

An account of leasehold rents (CCRO Egerton Papers, DET 1424/8) dating from the 1840s shows that there were eighteen cottages or lodges in the township of Tatton, almost all of them held rent-free by employees or their widows. The Old Hall, known as Old Tatton at this time, was divided into three sections and housed George Birch, John Havelock and a 'Miss Hodges', all living rent-free. Another cottage is described as being near Old Tatton, and it accommodated Davenport Mere, while also nearby was a cottage at Tatton Mill occupied by William Toft. There is still a low building used for housing cattle near the site of Tatton Mill and within a few hundred yards of the Old Hall. This may have been the mill cottage of William Toft.

New Tatton, conveniently close to the house, garden and Dale Farm, contained seven dwellings. Originally built in the 1730s, New Tatton was the park's most important centre of population. William Warburton, Thomas Edgerley, Fanny Edgerley, Thomas Hulme, George Hewitt, James Heywood senior and George Pennington lived there. In the Mere Lodge lived Joseph Bowler, while first William Higginson and then his widow were housed in the Birken Lodge at the far northern tip of the township. The important Knutsford Lodge was not in the township at all and its occupier is not listed here.

Because we know so little of the staffing of Tatton in the nineteenth century it is impossible to obtain a full impression of the running of the estate, even in the second half of the period. The first indication of the number of servants comes in a wages book for 1916 (CCRO Egerton Papers, DET 3229/116). This shows how many staff were needed inside Tatton Hall at the height of the First World War. In September of that year there were twelve indoor servants at Tatton, only one, Ernest Mather, being male. It is impossible to say whether the modesty of this figure was caused by the usual restraint of the Egertons in expenditure in the house — seen 100 years before — or by the special circumstances of war.

In October 1927, Lord (Maurice) Egerton, considering the bequests he might include in his will,[43] asked for a breakdown of the staff of the estate, with their pay, job and length of service set out. Perquisites such as free coal (from the Bridgewater mines), milk and butter were also mentioned. There were 120 employees in all, ranging from estate office staff to farm labourers. By far the biggest single section was the Building Department, based at the Tatton Dale Home Farm and employing fifty men. The Building Department served not only Tatton but the whole of the Cheshire estate. At its head was the twenty-eight-year-old Clerk of Works, James Anderson, appointed in 1927 and making £200 per annum, along with rent-free accommodation, coal, light and milk. Assistant Clerk of Works was fifty-one-year-old James Vernon who had entered Egerton service in 1914 and received sixty-five shillings weekly along with rent-free accommodation. The estate was clearly not tied to the principle of 'Buggin's turn' for promotion, being prepared to bring in youthful employees, even when a long-serving man was available.

On the other hand, the Building Department did have its share of men with records of long service. Of the fifty it employed, twenty had been there for more than ten years. They included the seventy-four-year-old yardman Edwin Wragg and the seventy-one-year-old Samuel Cash, both of whom had entered service with the Egertons in 1876, making them the longest-serving employees of all. But they were not the oldest people in the employ of the estate, for the bricklayer Henry Jervis, who began working there in 1879, was eighty-one years old — and also on the staff of the Building Department. It is worth pointing out that the average age of the Building Department was, at forty-five years six months, lower than that of the farm workers (fifty years) or the drainers (fifty-five years).

It is also notable that very few even of the oldest men in the Building Department had been with the Egertons 'man and boy'. Samuel Cash joined in 1876 at the age of twenty, while Edwin Wragg was twenty-three. Other long-serving employees who joined several years after their working lives began included Samuel Vost the well-sinker, who came to Tatton aged twenty in 1880: Henry Jervis, thirty-three when he started in 1879: and John

Murphy, a slater, born around 1857 and thus aged twenty-nine when he was taken on in 1886. These were all in the Building Department, but others on the Tatton strength were also appointed when they had acquired some experience: George Davies, a farm labourer, who must have been about thirty when he came to Tatton in 1886; John Bailey, another farm labourer, who was aged about thirty-one on appointment in 1894. The general policy of going for experience continued in the twentieth century. In the Building Department, the plumber James Berwick was first employed in 1919 at the age of fifty-two, while Charles Blake the electrician was twenty-eight or so when he began to work at Tatton in 1910. Other tradesmen who were employed at relatively or very advanced ages included Arthur Sibbald (appointed in 1927, aged forty-five). James Gathercole the wheelwright (sixty-three when he began with the estate in 1925), John Davies, Blake's assistant, who was forty-eight on first employment in 1926 and Thomas Johnson, a plasterer who joined in 1919 aged fifty-one. Even among labourers, the Egerton policy of employing mature men was maintained in the early years of the twentieth century. Several of the Building Department labourers joined in their mid-twenties or slightly later: Peter Foy (in 1924 aged twenty-three), David Hillkirk (in 1926 aged twenty-four) and Samuel Ainscoe (in 1927 aged twenty-nine). Even older on joining was Wilfred Stead, the labourer to carpenter Arthur J Russell. Stead had just been appointed at the age of forty-one.

Tatton demanded experienced men no doubt partly at least because it was in a position to do so, as one of the district's most important houses and estates, but such a policy would undoubtedly have increased staff costs as compared to one which brought in and trained up young men. It was therefore not only the numbers but also the quality of staff that made the Building Department in particular so costly.

Another area where works staff were expensive was in draining. Quite apart from the Building Department, the drainers numbered nine, with the high average age in the mid-fifties already noted. Two men in their mid-twenties, Samuel Clayton and Ernest Slater, had been taken on in 1927 to add to the staff. Tatton itself was not without its damp and mossy spots, and some of their time must have been spent in the park but much of it must have been spent in the outlying parts of the estate. Did this large force of drainers bring a return on the investment? It seems unlikely that it did. Although drainage formed a very large proportion of capital expenditure by landlords in the latter part of the nineteenth century, there seems little doubt that in general drainage did not pay. Between 1847 and 1878, for instance, on eight of the largest English estates, returns on drainage were just 2.36% in the form of improved rent (Beckett 1986, 178). Thus the £850 or so spent each year on drainage staff alone may not have been a good investment. The havoc caused in the 1920s and 1930s by the subsidence which caused Melchett Mere to form may have forced Egerton in those years to employ drainers to repair rather then build.

The finances of Dale Farm are not entirely clear, but it certainly did not require as many staff as the Building Department and represented less of a drain on resources. The farm had nineteen workers, including the farm bailiff, John Pollock and the park shepherd, Edward Kirkham. There were fourteen gardeners, including one, Henry Bell, at Rostherne Manor, nine gamekeepers, seven foresters and three office staff.

All the office staff were salaried, although twenty-one-year-old Rupert Baker received just £91 annually after six years' service, a sum which made him less well paid than his contemporary, the dairymaid Edith Badrock, who made £84 a year but also received coal, rent, light, butter and milk free. The twenty-two-year-old 'motor lurry driver', Henry Spilsbury, was better off then either, on forty-five shillings a week (although there may have been seasonal variations in his wage).

What of the house staff? Surprisingly, their numbers had decreased since the wartime figure of twelve. There were only seven indoor staff, with one more at Rostherne Manor. Even taking into account Maurice Egerton's bachelor status, this is a very small number for a large and beautiful house. Egerton was, of course a great traveller who spent much of his time away from Tatton but he did take an interest in his house and he did spend some time there each year. However, the employment of a French cook (*sic*) Albert Joubert, aged 37, suggests that the standards were kept high. On the other hand, Joubert was paid 5/6d daily, which indicates that he was only employed when necessary, when there was company. The house staff had undergone a rapid turnover since 1916 with only one person, Matilda Burton, staying over the eleven years. She had been employed first in 1916, at an annual rate of £32. By 1927, as the laundrymaid, she was earning £43 pa, with milk, butter and vegetables free. There was a butler valet, H Laflin, who received £120 a year, along with board, lodging and washing. He had first been employed at Tatton in 1923. Joubert had first been employed at Tatton in 1920, but all other house staff were recent entrants. Mrs Parker, the housekeeper aged fifty-six, was appointed in 1924 while the under-laundrymaid, Annie Cullister, now aged seventeen, came in 1926 and the housemaids Frances Pawley (twenty-five) and Hilda Wilding (twenty-one) entered Tatton service in 1926 and 1927 respectively.

This establishment was financed by a diminishing income base as the estate adjusted to the difficulties of the post-war world. In the early 1920s land was sold to raise ready cash. On 26 December 1922 a list was drawn up of property sold in recent times. Seven plots of land in Marthall, just south and east of Knutsford, and one in Ollerton, had been sold for a total of £31,690 (CCRO Egerton Papers, DET 3229/107). The period just after the First World War was a very active one in the land market, with the landowners stricken by high taxation and keen to sell, and tenants benefitting from high prices and controls on rents (Beard 1989, 39–40). There is, however, a feeling that this was a forced sale, perhaps prompted by the recent death of Alan de Tatton Egerton, the third baron; death duties had been raised to 40% on estates of £2 million in 1919. Certainly the sale did not do much to help the overdraft that had accumulated in the Cheshire estate. Accounts for the year to 31 December 1923 show that at the end of the year the estate's overdraft was £21,930 19s 4d, against an overdraft on 31 December 1922 of £15,370 16s 9d (CCRO Egerton Papers, DET 3229/107). Rents for 1923 were £21,722 5s 11d, a huge proportion of the estate's income of £25,772 15s 4d. Spending was £31,332 17s 11d. With no quarrying or substantial commercial interests, the Egertons were very reliant on rents to make ends meet. Even drastic measures failed to make much difference to the financial weakness of the estate. The size and expense of the estate workforce were supported on flimsy foundations.

The situation did not improve as the 1930s succeeded the 1920s. Egerton's accountant Norman Cowell drew up a very damning *General Report on Staff and Finance for Lord*

Egerton's Cheshire Estate in April 1936 (CCRO Egerton Papers, DET 3229/107). In it, Cowell reminded Lord Egerton of some of the problems being encountered. He says that, when in 1932 'the outlying portions of the Estate'[44] were sold to Mr Baker, the rent roll was reduced by £5,500 'after crediting the consequential reductions in rates, taxes, tithe etc'. The capital this yielded was used to reduce an overdraft in 1931 of £46,609 to one of just £15,115 in 1932 but the benefit was short-lived. In 1933 the overdraft rose again to £27,129 and in 1934 it had mounted to £34,320. By 1935 the overdraft was £44,293 — almost back where it had started in 1931. The loss on the year's working was just over £12,000 in each of the years 1933, 1934 and 1935. Land sales could not cure the estate's malaise.

But what caused that malaise? Cowell had no doubts. The problem was staff. He concludes his report by saying that: 'the bulk of the expenditure on the Estate is in respect of salaries and wages and whilst the total number of persons employed on the estate remains at its present level of 102, it seems evident that a large debit balance on the year's working is inevitable. If it is to be seriously reduced, there is no doubt that a reduction in the staff is the first essential'. He goes on to note that the Building Department 'carries the largest proportion of the staff'. Despite the land sales, and a 15% reduction in staff, there had been no improvement in the profit and loss account.

The most prominent expense continued to be in the Building Department. Virtually no reduction in staff had taken place in nine years to April 1936, with a total of forty-eight, including five based at Tatton Hall, against the 1927 figure of fifty. This was despite the loss of such a large part of the rent roll in 1932. The department, which was there to sustain income from rents, had maintained its size despite a sharp fall in the income from that source.

While the Building Department was little changed, other outdoor sections suffered cuts, notably the farm, which decreased its staff complement from nineteen in 1927 to just nine in 1936. Drainers were reduced in number from nine to five, and there were eight game-keepers instead of nine and twelve gardeners against fourteen. But foresters had increased from seven to eight and house servants from seven to eight as well.

We do not know whether Cowell's suggestions were taken up, but the fact that they were made indicates that Egerton's advisers were seriously worried about his finances.

As the 1930s came to a close, of course, another and more drastic threat to the estate was to emerge. The first hint of the problems ahead is contained in an inventory of the works of art at Tatton, made on 11 November 1938 by Capes, Dunn and Company, valuers, of 23 King Street West, Manchester (CCRO Egerton Papers, DET 3229/107). It was intended that these works of art should be 'removed to the basement in the case of aerial attack'.

When war came in September 1939, Tatton, like many other estates, found itself in a very different environment.[45] Troops used it for training, including, most importantly, for parachute drops. Large areas — at least 300 acres of the township's 2000 — were ploughed up for food production and planes were parked in the avenue of beeches which leads from the gardens down to Knutsford. Lord Egerton was far from pleased at the dis-

ruption caused by his military visitors and kept up a flow of sometimes amusing correspondence with senior officers.

The first contact with the social changes wrought by war came in October 1939, when
Lord Egerton hosted four poor boys evacuated from London. The visit was recorded by his
agent, Reginald Wiglesworth who picked up the boys and brought them in at the Knutsford
Entrance (CCRO Egerton Papers, DET 3229/85). The account shows the impact of the
country on children with no experience of it. They were impressed by the red and fallow
deer, and by the black St Kilda sheep that were and are such a feature of the park. Wiglesworth goes on: 'L.E. met us at the Gate and, after saying 'how do' we wandered around
the lawns, Italian Gardens, swing, Maze, Temple (gathered chestnuts). Goldenbrook pits,
African dugout, Canadian canoe. We split into two parties and L.E. took the dugout and I
the canoe after teaching the boys how to sit in the canoe, how to hold the paddle we started
off round the island...'. The Golden Brook water feature in the gardens became the
inspiration for a typical piece of adventure by the imaginative Lord Egerton; sometimes it
seems as if he was as much of a child as his young guests. Lord Egerton's interest in boys'
activities led him to found the Egerton Boys' Club, which still flourishes in Knutsford.

The tour then moved to the Rose Gardens, where 'one boy looking into the blue pool said
can we bathe. LE said yes, and before you could count 10, they were stripped and were
chasing gold fish (I had to run to the house for towels).'

But not every guest was as welcome as the evacuee children. The Cheshire War Agricultural Committee visited Tatton on 16 January 1941. They asked Egerton to plough up and
fence about 200 acres of the estate within the park. One area was on the far eastern side
of the park, where it abuts Mobberley, and another patch was in the north-eastern corner,
close to Ward's Plantation. Neither were in the central area of the park, and Egerton seems
to have made very little complaint about this news. But, as he told the Major General in
Charge of Administration at Western Command in Chester in a letter the same day, two
other areas were mentioned as likely to feature on the list of areas to be ploughed in
future.[46] One was the section between Albemarle Clump, a group of trees just to the east
of the house and the brook which runs between Tatton Mere and the Mill Pool; the other
adjoined Saddleback Covert, a piece of woodland lying halfway between the House and
Rostherne Lodge. He makes it clear in his letter that he felt these areas to be capable of a
better use than arable: 'All this part seems to me to be very vital from a military training
point of view and was continuously used by the Military during last Summer and Autumn'
is his way of putting it. 'It would therefore be a crime to plough it up'. To amplify his
remarks he pointed out that, on the Home Farm itself, he had already ploughed a good deal
more than his quota.

By April 1942, Lord Egerton had seen 300 acres ploughed up, and was writing to Sir
Charles Portal of the RAF to complain of the damage done by parked planes being moved.
Portal was also the target of a generalised complaint against military men.[47] The RAF plane-
parkers were to blame, he said, for 'unnecessary cutting down of trees, the removing of turf
or soil and suchlike things'. He continues: 'The War Agricultural Committee have made me
plough up about 300 acres inside the Park alone; so it is not too easy trying to run a good-

sized farm holding a couple of thousand sheep and a considerable amount of other stock, with the pasturage steadily diminishing, and strangers trapezing (*sic*) all over it.'

Included among the strangers were the South Staffordshire Regiment, about whom Lord Egerton felt impelled to write in April 1941. Addressing his remarks to the long-suffering Colonel Fraser of Western Command in Chester,[48] Lord Egerton said of that regiment's stay at the Old Hall: 'I was one day just in time to stop the last lot from digging a deep hole into the headwaters of the Tatton Spring-Water Supply. Into this hole they were planning to empty the contents of their latrine-buckets'. It is clear that the sixty-seven-year-old peer was active in his park, ensuring that the depredations of the various military invaders did not get out of hand — and complaining bitterly to Western Command or the RAF when they did.

The parking of aircraft reached a climax in May 1942, when thirty-five Wellingtons were in Tatton, many of them in the beech avenue leading to Knutsford. Lord Egerton took a photograph of one of the tracks used by the aircraft at the time, probably to emphasise the damage being done to his park. The Parachute Training School was, however, the chief military feature: between September 1940 and 27 March 1946 there were 425,636 drops in Tatton (Smith 1981, 187–8). Based at Ringway nearby, the school became very closely associated with Tatton. There were inevitably deaths, the first during an experimental drop on 25 July 1940. The cause of that was a failed parachute, but there was at least one drowning in a pond. Overall, more than 60,000 soldiers trained at the school, almost all of them at Tatton.

Parachutists made less impact on the Tatton landscape than either the ploughman, or, more permanently, the planting of rhododendrons by Lord Egerton. Nowadays, rhododendrons and azaleas are a major feature of the gardens and one of the estate's great attractions. On the other hand, many of the acres ploughed up in the 'Dig for Victory' drive were returned to grassland after the war, albeit that much reverted to plough land during the 1980s.

Tatton found it much less easy to shrug off the financial difficulties that had beset it since the early 1920s. Lord Egerton spent a great deal of his time in Kenya, either on safari (one of the largest of his personal files was devoted to correspondence with the taxidermists Rowland Ward Ltd, 'Naturalists by Appointment to HM the King') or developing his estates. We do not know how much all this cost (presumably the tea, coffee and sisal estates were supposed to be commercial propositions), but there is no doubt that the financial position of Tatton continued to deteriorate.

We have seen that, before the Second World War, Lord Egerton had failed to reverse the trend towards debt. The war itself would not have helped, although there is no documentation which would allow us to examine the direct effects. We do know, however, that by 1953 the alarm bells were ringing loud and clear. A letter from the appropriately named Mr F W Hardstone, Joint General Manager of the Westminster Bank, in July of that year drew Lord Egerton's attention to his overdraft, which had now reached over £250,000.[49] A reply from Lord Egerton makes clear that he was 'inquiring as to the possibility of the National Trust taking over this House'. Egerton also suggested the familiar expedient of land sales, but this time he thought that they should be carried out in Kenya as well as in Cheshire. The bankers were not impressed. The Westminster's Assistant General Manager, Mr N Bennett, wrote back a few days later regretting the fact that 'the proposals [to give the House to the Trust] are in the nature of a long-term solution needing considerable time before they can be brought to fruition … In these circumstances I should be grateful if you would give further consideration to the position with a view to ascertaining some more immediate sources of reduction which could be utilised'.[50]

On the very day this bleak missive was being penned by the money man, Lord Derby was writing from his house at Knowsley.[51] The owner of large parts of Lancashire replied candidly to what he described as a 'gloomy' letter from Egerton of 3 August. Derby clearly reveals the sort of options being considered at Tatton: 'I think it is worth while opening your house to the public if it so lends itself, but to get the full benefit you would have to do it three times a week.' This was the very beginning of the period of commercialism of the English country house.[52] The very same year as Egerton outlined his problems to his more illustrious neighbour, the new Duke of Bedford was returning to England to his decayed home at Woburn. The duke decided that 'there was something in this Duke business after all', but Egerton was not so sure about the pulling power of nobility. Indeed, it is clear that Egerton was also looking at another and more drastic way of making ends meet. Derby's letter continues: 'Demolishing a house is a very expensive business, unless there is a quantity of valuable things to dispose of in that portion of the house, or that the final saving in income is going to make the capital outlay worthwhile'.

Thus the demolition of Tatton Hall was actively under discussion, certainly by Derby and perhaps also by Egerton. In this summer of 1953 — while the country celebrated in the afterglow of the coronation — Lord Egerton contemplated the sale not only of his land and demolition of his house in England, but also the loss of his property in Kenya.

Matters did not improve in the next year. On 14 July 1954, forty-seven lots of property in Knutsford, the biggest town in the Cheshire estate area, were sold, raising £30,750.[53] This sale of urban property at the heart of the Egerton lands must have been prompted by a desperate financial situation and a stubborn level of debt. The chartered accountants, Astbury, Mitcheson and Miller, of Spring Gardens, Manchester, drew up the accounts for the half-year ended 30 June 1954.[54] These showed that the overdraft for the Cheshire estate was, at £243,349 3s 0d, somewhat down from the figure of £247,390 17s 7d recorded at the end of 1953.

The breakdown of expenditure and income for the first half of 1954 shows once again the strong influence of the Building Department on the debit side of the balance. Whereas the Building Department took in £597 12s 11d in income — perhaps for some contracting for others — it spent £5758 19s 3d. The farm, on the other hand, had a surplus of over £4000 — £13,858 5s 2d income against spending of £9,693 3s 11d. The house and garage together cost only £2939 13s 8d, though with no balancing income while the gardens cost £1383 4s 4d, with less than £10 coming in. Even the park did quite well, expending £404 12s 9d but bringing in £320.

Right to the end, then, the Egertons found it comparatively easy to fund spending on Tatton itself but difficult to maintain the outlying estates. Neither do we know how much it cost to collect arrears of rent if and when they were incurred.

The spring before the July sale of Knutsford property there had been correspondence between Lord Egerton and the secretary of the National Trust, Mr J Rathbone. On 12 April, Mr Rathbone had written to explain that the Trust would 'need a capital endowment of £191,600 to enable us to accept Tatton Park and to preserve it worthily in perpetuity. I am afraid this is a large sum of money but if given to the Trust with Tatton Park its income would be free from income and supertax and with the property it would be exempt from death duties on your death'.[55]

Only large land sales would have made this possible. Another letter in the same bundle suggests that Egerton was discussing with his solicitors, Ellis Piers and Co of 17 Albemarle St W1, the possibility of an endowment from either Cheshire County Council or Manchester Corporation to keep the estate running during his lifetime.[56]

Four years later, the questions had become irrelevant. Lord Egerton died in Kenya in 1958, leaving the house and gardens to the National Trust, while the parkland was accepted by the Treasury in lieu of estate duty and then put into the hands of the Trust. Now, as fore-shadowed in 1954, the property was to be financed and indeed managed by Cheshire County Council.

Thus the whole of Tatton fell into the hands of bureaucrats with whom in the 1940s Lord Egerton had spent so much time in combat. The Council and Trust run it very much as 'Lordy' might have wished, with care and consideration for its history. But Tatton was lucky: many great houses were demolished during the 1950s.

Only investment income and other outside sources of funds kept many other houses in existence. Yet the history of Tatton Park suggests that it was not the house, garden and parkland that were the downfall of so many estates during the twentieth century, but the outlying lands. No doubt the house was an obvious symbol of waste and extravagance, a tempting target for the accountants' attack, but the figures suggest that, once built, it could be run cheaply and that its immediate surroundings could also be viable. If landowners had realised this, perhaps some of the houses might have been saved. However, it is true that purely financial considerations may have been much less important a factor in the destruction of country houses than social change: the twenty-room mansion was simply too grand for post-1920 landed society.

It was perhaps a failure of nerve rather than a failure of finance that led to the loss of so many fine houses. In the face of the egalitarian pressures symbolised by estate duty, the landed classes panicked and destroyed their heritage.

Notes

[1] CRO ws 1614, dated April 4. Probate records were identified from the 'Index of Wills' at Chester, LCRS ii, iv, xv, xviii, xx, xxii, xxv, xxxvii and photocopies were very kindly provided by the staff of the former Chester Record Office.

[2] Stephen & Lee eds 1908 **6**, 574. He confirmed his interests in Lancashire by his marriage to Frances, daughter of the Earl of Derby, but both he and his heir were buried at Little Gaddesden (near Whipsnade) and the family was probably often to be found in or near London.

[3] Uncatalogued MS at Tatton Hall during the lifetime of the project, since removed to CCRO. My thanks to Mr Redwood who provided me with a photographic copy.

[4] Ormerod 1882 **1**, 444; undated MS map of part of Tatton: CRO, DET/1424/31

[5] John Rylands University Library of Manchester (hereafter JRULM) Egerton Muniments, 2/2/8

[6] For Glossop the comparison is based on unpublished research by J Powell; that at Disley on unpublished group work in the custody of J H Smith.

[7] See PRO E 179/86/145; PRO E 179/86/155. The Rostherne parish register was consulted *via* the copies made for the Cheshire Parish Register Project at Manchester University by courtesy of C B Phillips.

[8] In the sixteenth, seventeenth and eighteenth centuries the addition of arable or pasture land, sometimes in small parcels, to an already-existing park, was commonplace.

The needs of large deer herds for covert and the demand to frame impressive houses in an appropriate setting impelled owners to purchase and exchange on a wide scale. Apethorpe, Althorp and Deene in Northamptonshire all underwent such changes in the sixteenth and seventeenth centuries: Hoskins 1955, 170

[9] CCRO Egerton Papers, DET 302/332. Lease to Matthew Lowndes, 1739

[10] CCRO Egerton Papers, DET 302/332. Lease to Ralph Pickering, 1739

[11] CCRO Egerton Papers. Lease of Old Hall and demesne to executors of Samuel Harrison, 1739. Even if the Turn Mere land had been imparked it would still have meant that the Tatton parks would have been scattered across the township as separate enclosures, in keeping with Egerton's policy of gradual change.

[12] Unfortunately we know very little about the personal relations between Egerton and the young duke, although Hugh Malet (1977, 5–6) speculates that they were close.

[13] These purchases were to leave the Egerton lands stretching intermittently from mid-Cheshire to the southern outskirts of Manchester and Salford. Clearly Egerton would feel the need for a more worthy park to match his grander estates: Aylett 1987, 348–9.

[14] JRULM Egerton Muniments 2/1/135. Letter from William Tomkinson to Samuel Egerton, 18 July 1752.

[15] CCRO Egerton Papers, DET 302/332 and 302/333. Surrender of leases to Samuel Egerton: by Thomas and Dorothy Heatley, 19 May 1753; by John and Ann Egerton, 16 November 1754; by Samuel Harrison junior, 11 April 1757.

[16] Land in Withington, Heaton Norris and other parts of south Lancashire was purchased in the summer of 1755 for £34,500: Aylett 1987, 347

[17] CCRO Egerton Papers, DET 302/333. Surrender of lease, Ralph Pickering to Samuel Egerton, 28 October 1755. Hannah Tabley and William Baxter had held subtenancies of parts of the land surrendered.

[18] CCRO Egerton Papers, DET 302/333. Surrender of lease, Samuel Wright to Samuel Egerton, 24 March 1760. Wright acted as Egerton's agent in the 1740s, collecting arrears of rent: Aylett 1987, 332–3. The authors are grateful to Mrs Joan Leach for some details of Samuel Wright's connections.

[19] CCRO Egerton Papers, DET 302/333. Surrender of lease, George Massey to Samuel Egerton, 24 March 1757

[20] CCRO Egerton Papers, DET 302/332. Surrender of lease, John Babbington to Samuel Egerton, 3 May 1757

[21] JRULM Egerton Muniments, 2/1/137. Letter from William Tomkinson to Samuel Egerton, 8 December 1756

[22] JRULM Egerton Muniments, 2/1/62. Letter from Lancelot Brown to Samuel Egerton, 22 September 1757. This shows that Brown was prepared to act as an intermediary for clients as well as in his better known role of landscape gardener. There is no sign that he put forward any proposals for the design of Tatton's landscape.

[23] CCRO Egerton Papers, DET 302/332. Surrender of lease, John Bayley to Samuel Egerton, 1 May, 1762

[24] CCRO Egerton Papers, DET 302/333. Surrender of lease, Phillip Clarke to Samuel Egerton, 6 October 1763

[25] CCRO Egerton Papers, DET 302/333. Surrender of lease, William Falkner to Samuel Egerton, 25 March 1769

[26] JRULM Egerton Muniments, 2/3/1239. Bill to Samuel Egerton, 24 March 1781

[27] For example there is JRULM Egerton Muniments, 2/3/1330. Bill from James Duesberry to Samuel Egerton, 24 May 1781 for £14 14s

[28] JRULM Egerton Muniments. 2/3/1609. Labourers' Accounts, 3 August 1782

[29] This letter is among the Sykes family papers, Sledmere

[30] This seems about right, because, in his *Red Book* of late 1791, Repton refers in some detail to work being proposed by Samuel Wyatt (*see below*). The guess is made in Robinson 1979, 259.

[31] Tatton's proximity to Knutsford, as well as its large size and the wide spread of the Egerton land around the town, probably added to its significance for the inhabitants, despite the nearby presence of such sizeable estates as those at Tabley and High Legh: Andrews ed 1934, 243–4

[32] In the very large estate of the Marquess of Bath, an official glorying in the title of Receiver-General supervised the work of a variety of stewards and bailiffs spread across Wiltshire, Shropshire, Gloucestershire, Herefordshire and Ireland: Thompson 1963, 165–6.

[33] CCRO Egerton Papers, DET 3229/3 and DET 3229/4

[34] CCRO Egerton Papers, DET 3229/4. Entry for 31 December 1828

[35] CCRO Egerton Papers, DET 3229/3. Entry for 31 December 1819

[36] CCRO Egerton Papers, DET 3229/10. Account Book, entry for 29 October 1819

[37] CCRO Egerton Papers, DET 3229/10. Account Book, entry for 6 May 1819

[38] CCRO Egerton Papers, DET 3229/11. Account Book, entry for 28 September 1830

[39] In counties as far apart as the North Riding and Wiltshire there were strong reports in 1833, for instance, that it was nearly impossible to find a tenant willing to take a farm on lease: Thompson 1963, 230

[40] Much of the building work carried out in 1884 used terracotta. Whether cost was the consideration or there was a shortage of suitable stone is not known.

[41] CCRO Egerton Papers, DET 3229/80. Correspondence 1866–86

[42] CCRO Egerton Papers, DET 3229/78 and 79. Travel Journals of Wilbraham Egerton, 1852–4

[43] CCRO Egerton Papers, DET 3229/107 contain an analysis of Lord Egerton's will dated 27 January 1941. This records that in a will dated 3 November 1927 he made bequests of 'a sum equal to one year's wages free of duty if they have been in continuous service for the five years prior to the Testator's death' to, among others, Mrs Parker the Housekeeper, Thompson Flood the Head House Carpenter and Albert Joubert the Head Cook.

[44] It is not known whether this was part of a planned strategic move to concentrate the Egerton estate in a manageable core, but considering the poor management of the estate it is likely that the main aim was to maximise the sum realised, whatever the effects on the organisation of the whole.

[45] Beard 1989, 77 describes the impact of the conversion to a military hospital of Hatfield House in Hertfordshire, with the smell of beeswax replaced by that of disinfectant. Tatton Hall itself escaped any such radical change of use.

[46] CRO Egerton Papers, DET 3229/107. Letter to Major General in Charge of Administration, Western Command, 16 January 1941

[47] CCRO Egerton Papers, DET 3229/107. Letter to Sir Charles Portal, 13 April 1942. Portal (later Viscount Portal of Hungerford) was at that time Chief of Air Staff.

[48] CCRO Egerton Papers, DET 3229/107. Letter to Colonel P Fraser, Western Command, 23 April 1941

[49] CCRO Egerton Papers, DET 3229/107. Letter from J W Hardstone, 28 July 1953

[50] CCRO Egerton Papers, DET 3229/107. Letter from N Bennett, 7 August 1953

[51] CCRO Egerton Papers, DET 3229/107. Letter from Lord Derby, 7 August 1953

[52] The thirteenth Duke of Bedford succeeded his father in 1953 and proceeded to make Woburn into the first truly commercialised English great house.

[53] CCRO Egerton Papers, DET 3229/107. Press cutting from *Knutsford Guardian*, July 1954

[54] CCRO Egerton Papers, DET 3229/107. Accounts for half-year to 30 June 1954

[55] CCRO Egerton Papers, DET 3229/107. Letter from J Rathbone, 12 April 1954

[56] CCRO Egerton Papers, DET 3229/107. Letter from N Hudson, 12 July 1954

Bibliography

Andrews, C B ed 1934 The Torrington diaries: containing the tours through England and Wales of the Hon John Byng ... between the years 1781 and 1794. 4 vols. London: Eyre & Spottiswoode

Aylett, P 1987 Attorneys and clients in eighteenth-century Cheshire: a study in relationships, 1740–1785. *Bull John Rylands Univ Lib Manchester* **69**, 326–58

Beard, M 1989 English landed society in the twentieth century. London: Routledge

Beckett, J V 1986 The aristocracy in England, 1660–1914

Davies, C S 1960 The agricultural history of Cheshire, 1750-1850. Manchester: Chetham Society. (Remains Historical and Literary Connected with the Palatine Counties of Lancaster and Chester **10**)

Higham, N, 1988–9 V: The Tatton Park project, part 2. The medieval estates, settlements and halls. *J Chester Archaeological Soc* new ser **75**, 61–133

Hoskins, W G 1955 The making of the English landscape. London: Hodder & Stoughton

Local Government Board 1875 England and Wales. (Exclusive of the metropolis.): Return of owners of land, 1873. London: Eyre & Spottiswoode for HMSO

Malet, H 1977 Bridgewater: the canal duke, 1736–1803. Manchester U P

Munby, L M 1981 Life and death in King's Langley, 1498–1659. King's Langley Local Hist & Mus Soc

Ormerod, G 1882 History of the County Palatine and City of Chester. Ed 2, rev Helsby, T. 3 vols. London: Routledge

Phillips, C B & Smith J H 1985 Stockport probate records 1578–1619. (*Rec Soc Lancashire Cheshire* **124**)

Robinson, J M 1979 The Wyatts: an architectural dynasty. Oxford U P

Smith, D J 1981 Action stations **3**. Military airfield of Wales and the north-west. Cambridge: Stephens

Stephen, L & Lee S eds 1908 Dictionary of national biography. London: Smith, Elder & Co

Stroud, D 1962 Humphry Repton. London: Country Life

Thompson, F M L 1963 English landed society in the nineteenth century. London: Routledge & K P. (Studies in Social History)

Wadsworth, A P & Mann, J de L 1931 The cotton trade and industrial Lancashire, 1600–1780. Manchester U P

V: New Bridge, New Road, New Church
The Building of Grosvenor Street in Chester

by G K Barnes MA

The construction of Grosvenor Bridge and Grosvenor Street was the first major disruption to Chester's street plan since the Middle Ages. The story of Thomas Harrison's bridge has been examined in a previous volume of this *Journal.* However, had he not been pre-occupied with the difficulties of the Rotherhithe tunnel under the Thames, it is possible that a different design might have been successfully put forward by Marc Isambard Brunel. The paper also examines the process of land acquisition for the construction of Grosvenor Street and the relocation of St Bridget's church.

Introduction

On 10 June 1825 Royal Assent was given to the Act providing for:

> … the erection of an additional bridge over the River Dee in the City of Chester; for the making convenient Roads and Approaches thereto and for taking down and rebuilding the parish church of St Bridget and for repairing the present bridge.[1]

This marked the successful culmination of a campaign launched some seven years earlier, following a public meeting in Chester Town Hall on 28 September 1818. This had passed a resolution to the effect that:

> … the existing mediaeval bridge [at Handbridge] and the avenues thereto, which are the principal communication between the great manufacturing counties of Lancaster and York and the whole of the North of England, with the West of England, and with Wales and Ireland, are not only highly inconvenient but absolutely dangerous to passengers in carriages, on horseback and on foot.

It further resolved that it was expedient to apply to Parliament for leave to bring in a bill for the erection of another bridge, and a committee — the Dee Bridge Committee — was appointed: 'to receive and consider plans, surveys and estimates, and the most expedient mode of providing funds for carrying out these resolutions into effect'.

In reaching such a decision it is likely that its proponents would have taken into account not only the problems and delays to traffic endeavouring to use the existing bridge but would also have been aware that Telford's current surveys of the proposed London–Holyhead road were favouring a route through Betws y Coed to the detriment of Chester. They could have been influenced, too, in the timing of the move by the knowledge that finance for such public works was available from the Exchequer Bill Loans Commission.

However, there was also opposition to having a new bridge rather than improving the existing one at Handbridge, and this centred largely on the expected cost to the city. Letters were published in the *Chronicle* and the *Courant*. William Harrison, brother of Alderman George Harrison (of whom more below), was one to have serious doubts and reservations. Writing to George on 23 December, he congratulated him on attempting:

> to lessen what always appeared to me the enormous and prodigal estimate of your intended bridge. The absolute utility of the bridge is to me problematical ... and such as Lord Grosvenor who would be more accommodated ought to come down with a very handsome subscription. Forgetting you have not Roman means and resources, you are ambitious to vie with Roman magnificence. [Thomas] Harrison ought to know that he has not that bottomless purse of the country to draw upon from which he has pulled so hard for so many years, ... I am glad you have had some misgivings and are endeavouring to economise. This is really patriotic. (CCALSS Z G/HS 199)

Grosvenor Bridge

A full and detailed account of the subsequent discussions, decisions and the progress of the work which led to the eventual construction of the Grosvenor Bridge in the form and place in which it now stands is given in the article by J W Clarke in this *Journal* (1958), 43–55.

However, at one time there was a real possibility that the bridge could have been built to a different design and in a different material. This came about following a meeting between George Harrison and Marc Isambard Brunel (1769–1849; father of Isambard Kingdom Brunel). With the passing of the act the Dee Bridge Commissioners had come into existence and, taking over from the Dee Bridge Committee elected at the meeting in 1818, were charged with the responsibility for getting the new bridge built. At their first meeting on 27 June 1825 the Commissioners appointed a sub-committee to consider the various schemes which Thomas Harrison had put forward over the intervening years. These had included designs for iron, single-arch and triple-arch stone constructions with estimated costs in the region of £30,000 (CCALSS Z TRB 57 fo 7v). Subsequently, on 8 November the Commissioners agreed that he should make working drawings and provide detailed specifications for a stone bridge of one arch (CCALSS Z TRB 57 fo 12v). This would cross the river on a line from the Castle portico to what is now known as Old Wrexham Road in Handbridge, being the middle of the three routes shown in Ill V.1.

George Harrison (no relation of Thomas), who was owner of the Roodee Foundry and Paper Mills and had been mayor of the city in 1824/5, was the chairman of this sub-committee. He was in London from 14 to 26 November 1825 and visited Rotherhithe, where Brunel was completing the shaft from which the tunnel under the Thames to Wapping

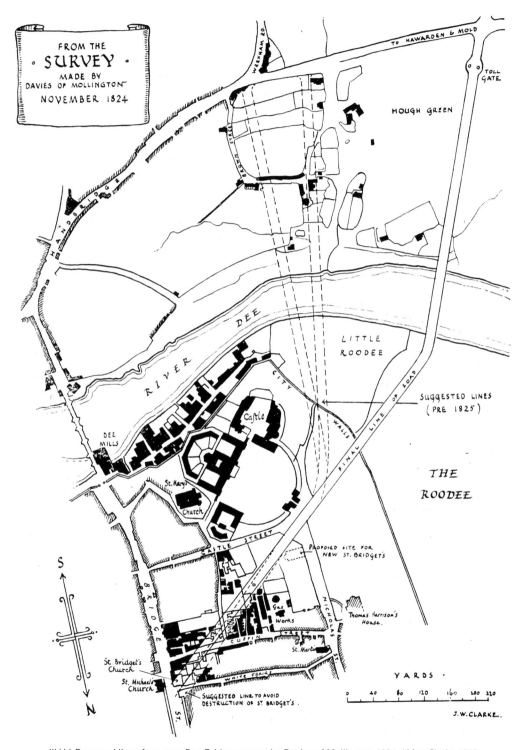

Ill V.1 Proposed lines for a new Dee Bridge: survey by Davies of Mollington 1824. (After Clarke 1958. Reproduced by permission of Chester Archaeological Society)

would be driven.[2] Whether Harrison went with the intention of getting advice from him on the bridge or simply out of curiosity to view this ambitious new project is not clear, but in the event the bridge was discussed.

Brunel's idea was to construct it of rubble — by which he meant brick or stone set in mortar and reinforced with iron — with a facing of solid masonry. Since he said that he could make it in this way with a single arch span of 200 feet at a cost of £10,000, Harrison got very excited and wrote to him the day after their meeting, whilst still in London at the King's Arms Tavern in Kensington. In his letter he asked Brunel to provide more information, for: 'if we can appear with £10,000 work thought to cost £30,000, there is little doubt that it will carry great weight with those who have the disposal of public money'.[3]

Brunel responded to Harrison's letter with a request for information on the height of the arch, an indication perhaps that his estimate of £10,000 was made without knowing fully the dimensions and specifications of the bridge. However, even when given these details, his reply of 23 November was devoted mainly to general comments on the use of rubble stone for the arch instead of granite, the method of construction which he proposed to adopt. Pointing out that the pyramids were not constructed of granite and that the Romans had made extensive use of bricks, he pronounced that employing granite was paying too dear simply to make a monument that might last for ever (CCALSS Z TRB 57, fo 16r, 17v and 17r).

It is not really surprising that he did not focus his thoughts too rigorously on Harrison's request. On 21 November the shaft for the Rotherhithe tunnel had been finished, and Brunel, who had been working seven days a week under extreme pressure, not unnaturally suffered a reaction. As his journal for 22 November records: 'on getting out of bed, I was taken with giddiness and sickness … Dr. Morris was sent for. He ordered ten leeches'. The following day, the date of his letter to Harrison, he wrote: 'Very ill, though much relieved by the leeches. I could not attend the meeting of the South London Docks' (Clements 1970).

During the next few weeks letters were exchanged at frequent intervals, as Harrison, who had been given authority by the sub-committee to proceed on a official basis (CCALSS Z TRB 1, fo 50), tried to get Brunel to commit himself to a definite figure for the cost and satisfy the concerns which had been raised about the practicability, appearance and durability of what was a new and 'problematical' method of building. He was also trying to persuade him to visit Chester and view the site (CCALSS Z TRB 57, fo 18v).

Brunel, although continuing to prevaricate concerning the probable cost, did address himself to these concerns. Thus in a letter of 14 December he said he had shown the proposition to be a practical one:

> … having just prepared a plan for a bridge using Rubble stone across a river 210 feet in breadth, where no more than £10,000 or £12,000 could be obtained in one of our most admired spots in West England. The plan gives satisfaction, but the [money was] not raised.

As for appearance:

> ... the most striking feature of the [Thomas] Harrison bridge is the magnitude of its proportions. A structure of this character must be to the eye what the Parthenon is to the Spectator, an insulated mass set off to the most advantage by a background that tends to magnify the object. When we see an arch of cast iron of 210 feet span we are struck with admiration but if it was of stone or of that imposing character we should view it with something more than admiration, it is the sublime and beyond the powers of description!

The question of costs, however, he dismissed in a sentence as: 'depending on the nature of the ground for the abutments'. He made no commitment about coming to Chester but said that if he were to make the journey, his charges would be 10 guineas per day, plus travelling expenses by public conveyance and 2 guineas daily expenses (CCALSS Z TRB 57, fo 19v).

Harrison, not surprisingly, was somewhat exasperated, complaining in his letter of 17 December that Brunel had not dealt with the important points. The whole affair hinged on whether he would undertake to carry out the work for a given sum and guarantee it. He must answer these questions to the satisfaction of the sub-committee (CCALSS Z TRB 57, fo 20r).

At last, in a letter dated 20 December 1825, Brunel did give some at least of the required information, but even then he was unable to provide a full, comprehensive costing. Having said that for a bridge of 200 feet span, 36 feet in width and a rise of 40 feet with abutments, 'if done with rubble stone or Stucco [he] would have no objection to undertaking it for £15,000' and comparing this to his estimate of £36,900 for one in solid stone with its ornamental parts, roadworks and centreing, he refrained from giving an estimate for the foundations and work below the line 'not being acquainted with the ground'. He did say, however, that the cost of pilings for the foundations of a rubble bridge would be considerably less than that for a stone bridge and he undertook to 'insure the durability of the foundations for a certain number of years'. (CCALSS Z TRB 57, fo 21v)

This letter was placed before the sub-committee on 22 December but, as Harrison told him on 29 December, 'the information did not come up to expectations'. Brunel had, of course, not helped his case by specifically excluding the cost of the foundations from his estimate, so that the sub-committee were not given the full picture. However, the overriding factor which must have influenced their judgement arose from a stupid misunderstanding on their part. Brunel had illustrated his proposal for the arch with a sketch which only showed one half of the bridge. Inexplicably the sub-committee linked his estimate to this sketch and assumed that the figure of £15,000 was for the construction of half a bridge! Consequently they were led to believe that a complete rubble bridge would cost £30,000, plus an unknown sum for the foundations, which would be little less than the estimates for a stone bridge (CCALSS Z TRB 57, fo 22r).

Brunel replied to Harrison on 3 January 1826, correcting the misconception and producing a figure of £9,000 for the foundations and abutments of a rubble bridge, a saving of £3,000 over the £12,000 which he estimated would be required for a stone bridge. For the super-structure his estimate of £15,000 for a rubble bridge would mean a saving of £17,000 over a stone bridge, since he now considered the lowest possible figure for a bridge of that material to be £32,000. He acknowledged, however, that if someone was prepared to build a stone bridge together with its foundations etc for £35,000 — an eventuality which he himself could not conceive as possible — then he accepted that with his rubble bridge costing in total £24,000, a saving of £11,000 would be unlikely to be sufficient to persuade the sub-committee to agree to his scheme (CCALSS Z TRB 57, fo 23r).

So it turned out. The Dee Bridge Commissioners met on 5 January and decided that the saving in expense from the rubble bridge 'was not commensurate with the risks run in applying [this] new mode of construction'. It was therefore resolved that 'consideration of Mr Brunel's plan be abandoned' and that he be informed accordingly (CCALSS Z TRB 57, fo 15r).

On 7 January Harrison wrote to Brunel, relaying the Commissioners' resolution. However, in the light of the friendly relationship which seems to have grown up between the two, the burden of his letter was written on a personal, unofficial basis. Thus, he said that their estimates for a stone bridge had been revised upwards, approaching the figure that Brunel had envisaged and therefore might prove to be more than they could afford. Accordingly he felt that the committee would now be thinking of an iron or chain bridge and suggested that Brunel should come to Chester on his own account. 'By mail up and down it would not cost [him] £10' and Harrison would put him up in his own house. Brunel could then speak to the Commissioners in person at their next meeting, which was set for 26 January 1826. 'He almost owed it to [his] great reputation … to combat the objections which were raised against his mode of constructing bridges'. (CCALSS Z CR 810/1)

In his reply Brunel took the abandonment of his plans philosophically, since 'all my work having been original, I have had naturally to overcome prejudices and struggle with diffi-culties … and I should not risk the loss of the reputation I have acquired by proposing a plan uncertain in its execution'. He admitted, however, that he had changed the form of the arch from that designed by Harrison and approved by the Commissioners, and that if no deviation from that was to be allowed, 'I would give up at once the idea of convincing others of the practicability of executing the same in rubble stone, since although it might be done, it would be too bold for a first step on so large a scale'. As to visiting Chester, the only justification for this would be to offer his services for an iron or suspension bridge. Nevertheless, he was prepared to consider making the journey, but work on the tunnel was at a crucial stage and he did not feel able to leave it for the next few weeks, especially as there was the risk of being detained in Chester by bad weather (CCALSS Z CR 810/2).

There is no record of Brunel having actually attended this meeting. However, as it is known that he did visit Chester and stay with Harrison sometime in January, this would seem to have been the most likely occasion. At all events, following the meeting the Com-missioners wrote requesting him 'to furnish an Estimate with the proper specification of the expense of a bridge cased in white stone to be constructed substantially upon Mr Thomas Harrison's plans together with full observations and explanations'. (CCALSS Z TRB 57, fo 24)

Brunel responded by requesting the driving of piles in order to ascertain the nature of the ground on the north side of the river and offering the loan of a pile engine, which could be sent by coastal vessel. The sub-committee, however, considered that this would cause unnecessary delay and advised him to prepare his estimates on the assumption that 25 feet of piling would be required (CCALSS Z TRB 1, fo 52v).

The Commissioners met again on 9 February, when they considered Brunel's submission. He estimated a cost of £30,520 for a bridge substantially built in brick but cased in white stone and constructed according to Thomas Harrison's plans. In arriving at this figure he had assumed 35 feet of piling from the present site surface but had not included the cost of the columns with their entablature and pediments. He explained that the casing would be of Manley stone from 12 to 24 inches thick. The arch would be of the hardest and best bricks, and the filling of the abutments would be of rubble stonework with substantial bands of wrought iron. He quoted examples of brick structures sufficiently strong to resist the greatest pressure to which they would be subjected, citing St Paul's, the dome of the Pantheon in Rome and the tower of Strasbourg. He himself could not be present at the meeting but, as he advised in his letter, his son, Isambard, 'would be found competent to represent me on this business ... Young as he is, [he was 20 at the time] his powers are those of a maturer age'. (CCALSS Z TRB 72)[4]

Writing at the same time to Harrison, however, he conceded that, if funds would have allowed, a bridge of stone or granite would be best. In the circumstances brick offered the cheapest alternative, dismissing iron as a poor substitute (CCALSS Z CR810/6).

Following the meeting the Commissioners ordered that this estimate and one for a stone bridge from James Trubshaw, a Staffordshire contractor, should be adopted as the basis for an application to the Exchequer Loan Commission for 'a loan of such money as may be wanting' (CCALSS Z TRB 57, fo 25r). However, when Brunel learnt that Trubshaw's estimate was for £31,000, he wrote to Harrison on 3 March, resignedly pointing out that his brick bridge at £30,520 stood no chance of being approved. Harrison replied, suggesting that he should prepare an estimate for a stone bridge (CCALSS Z CR 810/7).

Whilst the Loan Commissioners were considering the application — a procedure which involved a visit to Chester by their engineer Thomas Telford — Harrison and Brunel kept in touch. Harrison, looking to the possibility of Trubshaw's plan being thrown out, on 30 March again encouraged Brunel to produce an estimate for a stone bridge (CCALSS Z CR 810/7). Brunel, however, said that he did not want to appear over-anxious and preferred to wait until he was asked. For Harrison's own private information he told him that he would not undertake a stone bridge for less than £45,000 (CCALSS Z CR 810/8).

On 1 July 1826 the Loan Commissioners announced their refusal to advance any money for the bridge. This decision was based on Telford's report, a copy of which the Bridge Commissioners were able to secure and consider at their meeting on 27 July. The report rejected the site which Thomas Harrison had proposed for the bridge and which had been adopted by both Brunel and Trubshaw as the basis for their estimates, on the grounds that it had no rock for the foundations nearer than 50 feet below the waterline. Telford suggested an alternative position 110 yards downstream (Ill V.1), where the rock was 2–3 feet below the surface and where, since the breadth of the river was only 160 feet, a span of only 175 feet would be required. He estimated the cost of a stone bridge at £31,080 and of an iron one at £25,662. The total cost of the project with a stone bridge would be £50,698. This sum was made up of, in addition to the bridge itself, the embankments, roadway and fencing at £9,388, the purchase of property for the new avenue at £2,480, toll house at £250, new church at £4,000, repairs to the old bridge at £1,500 and other costs £2,000 (CCALSS Z TRB 57, fo 28r).

The Bridge Commissioners decided to advertise for an engineer for the bridge and Alderman Harrison, still seeking to involve Brunel in its construction, suggested that he apply (CCALSS Z CR 810/9). The latter, however, in a letter of 5 July declined, pleading the absolute necessity of his continual presence at the tunnel, 'where every inch of this subterranean labour requires a vigilant eye'. He could not refrain from pointing out that the pressure to which the tunnel was subjected considerably exceeded the greatest that a bridge with a brick arch of 200 feet span would have to bear (CCALSS Z CR 810/10).

On 22 August Brunel wrote to Harrison asking his opinion on charging the Commissioners for his professional services, 'since the business of the bridge [was] now quite at an end'. He wondered whether to put forward a specific fee or 'leave it to the liberality of the Committee'. Harrison replied on 9 September, advising the former course and at the same time telling him that the construction of the bridge had been awarded to Trubshaw. It was to be built in accordance with Thomas Harrison's plans with a 200 feet span, but at the site recommended by Telford (CCALSS Z CR 810/11).

Brunel followed Harrison's advice and on 22 September sent off his account:

> ... for statements and estimates relating to the mode of constructing a bridge over the Dee and for professional communications with the Commissioners between 9 December 1825 and the middle of February 1826; also for subsequent communications at the end of February with Mr Finchett Maddock [Town Clerk of Chester] for the purpose of laying plans and other papers before the Loan Commissioners in London — £63. (CCALSS Z CR 810/12)

The articles of agreement between Trubshaw and the Commissioners for building the bridge were signed on 1 February 1827. Although still incomplete, the opening ceremony was performed by Princess Victoria on 15 October 1832, when it was named Grosvenor Bridge. The certificate of completion was delivered to the Commissioners on 20 November 1833 and a balance sheet presented two weeks later. This put the cost at £49,824 12s 9d but did not include the cost of the toll houses, the new church of St Bridget, making Grosvenor Street and other ancillary works.

The time when the Bridge Commissioners and their sub-committee were deciding about the bridge crucially coincided with Brunel's pioneering work on the Thames tunnel. This undoubtedly in his eyes was pre-eminent, demanding and dominating his attention first and foremost. Although Alderman Harrison tried very hard to have his plan for a rubble bridge accepted, the impression left in the letters is that Brunel was not especially enthused about getting involved and in consequence not overly disappointed when he was turned down.

Grosvenor Street and St Bridget's Church

The Dee Bridge Committee appointed at the public meeting in 1818 was alive from the outset to the necessity of ensuring that there were would be adequate access to the new bridge, and at its meeting of 9 October 1818 ordered that the notice of the intended application to Parliament for the Bill: 'should embrace avenues to the Bridge from the two Churches (sc St Michael's and St Bridget's) to its Wrexham Lane end in Handbridge'. As noted in the minute book of its sub-committee, there was a meeting on 30 May 1821, for example, between the Magistrates of the County and City of Chester and a deputation from the Commissioners of Police to consider 'making a new street to the castle starting from Lamb Row'. At this meeting it was decided that the proprietors of the premises between Lamb Row and Bunce Lane, namely Earl Grosvenor, Sir John Williams, Mr Seller and Mrs Blower, should be asked for their concurrence and assistance in this scheme.

Lamb Row itself had recently collapsed[5] and the site had been bought by a Mr Roberts. He had begun to build there and an earlier meeting of the Commissioners of Police on 15 May had been told that 'he was disposed to give to the Public that portion of the frontage of these premises to Bridge Street and Cuppin Street and to make these linable with Mr Brown's shop in Cuppin Street, receiving for the same £200'. The meeting of 30 May therefore agreed that Mr Roberts should be asked to suspend building and to have a further meeting with the Commissioners. This took place on the following day. Then in reply to the question of what he would want for the ground which fell within the area required for the plans prepared by Harrison, he said he would make up his mind by 19 June, 'provided he had completed the purchase and felt disposed to accommodate the County'. There is no record as to whether he did come to such a decision and, if so, what price he placed on the piece of land. Since he appears amongst the owners and was involved in the valuations which were negotiated when work on the new street finally got under way in 1827, it seems clear that no deal was struck at this time.

The old church of St Bridget or St Bride stood on the west side of Bridge Street at the angle formed by its junction with Whitefriars and, as indicated by the Dee Bridge Committee in October 1818, was the favoured starting point for the new road. According to Ormerod (1882, 1, 341), the church, an etching of which was made by G Batenham in 1816 (Ill V.2), had a neat body with side aisles and a tower holding four bells. It had been repaired in 1785, when it was cased externally with stone. However on 12 May 1823 the vestry had noted that the steeple was in a very dangerous condition and agreed that the tower should be immediately taken down level with the roof.[6] On 24 July, therefore, having considered various options such as repairing the church, rebuilding the steeple or tower, and uniting with another parish and in that case demolishing the church and erecting a new one conjointly with the parishioners of such other parish, it had resolved that removal to a new site would be the most expedient course 'provided the removal could be effected with the consent and co-operation of the city so as to entail upon the parish only the same proportion to expenses, which shall attach to every other parish'.

Ill V.2 St Bride's church: etching by G Batenham, 1816.
(Reproduced by permission of the Chester Archaeological Society)

The vestry appointed a committee to confer with the bishop, the magistrates and the commissioners of police regarding the expenses both of removal and repairs to the church, and it was resolved that the church should be temporarily protected from the weather in a way suitable for divine worship and that no part of it should be taken down until a new one had been built.

At the public meeting held on 17 August 1824, which endorsed the Dee Bridge Committee's plans for the proposed Parliamentary Bill, a resolution was passed that 'the present dilapidated state of St Bridget's and the consent of the parishioners to its removal, as expressed on 24 July 1823, afforded an opportunity of opening the best possible avenue from the heart of the City to a new bridge'.

The meeting had appointed a committee to take matters forward, and this in its turn had appointed a sub-committee to obtain plans etc. On 31 August 1824 it commissioned Mr Davies of Mollington 'to survey and draw a plan, of not less than two inches to a chain, of the land and property affected by the proposed works' and on 12 October ordered him to prepare estimates 'for a new road between Castle Gates and St Bridget's church'. Davies in his estimates valued the premises that would have to be demolished at £3,020, and the expense in taking down St Bridget's, removing the materials and building a new church on county land near the Castle at £4,500. If, however, the road were to be routed on the west side of St Bridget's, the valuation of the premises to be demolished would be £6,200. Ill V.1 shows these alternative routes and the proposed site for the new church.

On 22 November it was decided to ask Thomas Harrison to provide estimates for removing St Bridget's and rebuilding in stone on the site which the county were offering. It was to be capable of accommodating 600 persons, for although the population of the parish numbered 900, the present church held only 350 and the parish clerk, who had been there for thirty-four years, said that he had never known there to be a shortage of room.

Harrison presented his estimates to the sub-committee on 4 December. The church was to be 55' x 45', with the 600 persons accommodated by a gallery around three sides. Cased in red stone, the cost would be £4,100; if white stone was used the cost would rise by £300. Against these sums there could be offset £400 for materials reused from the old church and stone given by the Corporation, but the inclusion of 15% 'poundage' would bring the respective totals to £4,155 and £4,600.

The sub-committee in a meeting with the bishop on 21 December 1824 'minutely examined' Harrison's plans and estimates. It was agreed that the costs should be revised so as not to exceed £4,000 and that 'the Bridge Trustees, being empowered to take down the church and lay the site together with the burial ground to a public street, would pay to the Commissioners of the Church Building Accounts that sum of money to be applied to erecting a new church on a site to be granted by the County Magistrates to the Church Building Commissioners'.

On 22 November the sub-committee had raised the question as to whether it was necessary to obtain the consent of the parishioners, the owners and the occupiers of property on the line of the new avenue, as was the case with turnpike roads. The town clerk was instructed to consult the parliamentary agents; he returned with the answer that as regards the property owners and occupiers, the agents' opinion was that their consent was not required and a notice to the effect that the houses and premises would be wanted would suffice. 'The improvement would be a public benefit and private interests must always give way to the public convenience'. As far as the parishioners were concerned, the resolution of St Bridget's vestry of 24 July 1823 was sufficient. However, in view of the fact that there had been changes in the intended place and mode of building the new church, the sub-committee thought it would be best to convene another meeting of the vestry to ascertain their feelings.

The bishop was consulted and he also recommended the convening of the vestry. He was of the opinion that the rebuilding should be under the direction of the Dee Bridge Committee and that the parish should contribute to the rebuilding a sum to be agreed between it and the sub-committee. If agreement could not be reached, then the parish would be called upon to repair the existing church and rebuild the steeple.

On 11 January 1825 the sub-committee submitted a memorial to the city magistrates on the subject of the new bridge. Referring to the road, which would be the first significant change to the Chester's street layout within the City Walls, certainly since that depicted in

NICHOLAS St.

St Martins Church

NUNS St.

County Land

Gas works

John Hinchcs Esq.

Rev. T. M. Davies.

Dean and Chapter of Chester Cathedral.

Soapery

Rev. T. N. Davies

County Land

BUNCE St.

Sold according to the Court

Mr Daniel Dobb

John Wall Sen

Mr Scott the Poor

Mr Edwards

R. Roberts

UNION COURT.

Mrs Humphreys

Mrs Oaks

Mr John Barnes

Earl Grosvenor

Mrs Blower

Sir Jno Williams Bart

Miss Ratcliffe

Mrs Minnick

Mr Roberts

Mr Goodman

Goodhelser

Earl

Mr F. Roberts

Mr John Massey

Church Yard

Parish St Bridges Church

CUPPIN STREET

WHITE FRIARS

LOWER BRIDGE STREET.

PEPPER STREET.

St Bridgets Church

John Speed's map of the early seventeenth century and probably even earlier, the hope was expressed that:

> ... nothing will impede an improvement so long and so anxiously anticipated as combining utility and ornament in the most eminent degree, opening a handsome street from the center (sic) of the City to the Castle, giving additional and well merited display to that most magnificent specimen of modern architecture, and placing in its neighbourhood a church of simple and beautiful construction with a Bridge that will do honor (sic) to its venerable architect, forming an assemblage of fine buildings alike interesting to the man of taste and honorable (sic) to the district.

The sub-committee, holding that the removal of the church from its present site would be less expensive than re-routing the line of the new road also:

> ... presumed to hope that the Magistrates will assist by empowering [them] to complete the proposed grant of a site for the new church on unoccupied ground to the north east of the Castle Gates (see Ill V.1) and £1,200 out of the County rate with such part of the south end of the Nuns Gardens as may be necessary for forming the road'.

The Dee Bridge General Committee met on 17 January 1825 to receive the sub-committee's report on the revised estimated costs for the undertaking. These included £2,760 'for the formation of a new street from the two churches [St Michael's and St Bridget's] to the Castle Gates'. This sum was exclusive of the property given freely by Earl Grosvenor, but took into account the expenses of the work of making the actual roadway, estimated at £400. The report was accepted and it was agreed that a bill should be drawn up for presentation before Parliament.

This then became the act quoted above, and in it there was included a schedule listing in detail the houses and other premises, which it was proposed to purchase in order to make the new road (Appendix 1). Under the act the Dee Bridge Committee was replaced by the Dee Bridge Commissioners and it was the sub-committee of the latter that on 26 November recommended that the approach to the bridge should be as delineated in Mr Davies's plan. As shown on the attached plan (Ill V.3), this (the continuous line) differed slightly from the Parliamentary one (the broken line).

Subsequently, further adjustments were made in consequence of an order made by the Commissioners on 3 May 1827, extending the width of the road by 12' and authorising the purchase of the additional land required. A considerable part of the extension lay within the boundaries of the county and was granted by the magistrates gratuitously. Of the remainder, which was in private ownership, Earl Grosvenor also gave his land without charge, whilst the others agreed to their property's inclusion at a price of 2s per yard. The total cost of the extension was estimated at £588 (CCALSS Z TRB 57, fo 37).

left: Ill V.3 Plan of properties to be cut through by the new street in Chester. 6 December 1826. (CCALSS Z TRB 192. Reproduced by permission of Chester City Council)

As detailed in Appendix 1, the premises affected in addition to St Bridget's church and churchyard included businesses, such as a counting house, coachmaker's shop, public house, kelp mill and currier's workshop. There were also two shops, fifty-four dwelling houses and a garden house, plus several pieces of unoccupied land and gardens together with portions of the City Walls and the River Dee. These last were for the most part owned by public bodies such as the Chester Corporation, the Crown, the Custos Rotulorum for the county and the Dean and Chapter of the Diocese of Chester. Private owners numbered twenty-eight. These were mostly multiple owners, such as Earl Grosvenor, Joseph Jones and John Edwards, with the properties occupied by tenants. Most of the owners of a single property also had let them to tenants and there were only a handful of houses actually owner-occupied.

Payments of compensation to the owners of the premises were the responsibility of the sub-committee, but the minutes of their meetings contain no systematic or comprehensive account of their management of this task. Details of the negotiations which took place with some of the individuals are recorded and give some indication of the way the process was conducted. Thus, in the case of Mr C W Leadbeater, whose property consisted of parts of a dwelling house, outbuildings and yard, it was agreed that this should be assessed by two competent persons. One of these would be nominated by Leadbeater, the other by the sub-committee and if they could not agree the matter was to be referred to an umpire. In the event an award of £410 was made and accepted. Mr John Brown accepted £575 for his shop and counting house next door to St Bridget's in Bridge Street. The kelp mill owned by the Dean and Chapter and occupied by Messrs Hodson & Winter was to be taken down and rebuilt on a new site under the direction of Messrs Cole & Royle, who seemed to have acted as the sub-committee's assessors in many of the cases. For the land the Dean and Chapter received £170 8s 0d. Mr Edward Roberts, who owned the currier's workshop and two houses, agreed to accept £1,210, plus £32 for loss of rent. It was also agreed that any of his land which was taken but not used should be sold to him for an equitable sum within a reasonable time after the formation of the street.

Agreement was reached with Sir John Williams Bart, whose garden and garden house were to be taken, on the purchase of the land at 5s per sq yard and the rebuilding of the garden house and restoration of the surrounding wall at the expense of the Commissioners. Sir John had expressed a preference to have a piece of land given him in exchange for what he would lose, and the Commissioners also agreed to try to obtain part of Earl Grosvenor's land for him. If they were successful, the payment to Sir John would be reduced in proportion by 5s per sq yard. However, although this agreement is recorded in the sub-committee minutes for 25 April 1827, it is reported in the same minutes nearly twelve months later that Sir John was complaining that he could not enter into negotiations about the land without giving notice to his tenant, which he had not done because of the uncertainty over when the work would be carried out (CCALSS Z TRB 83–5).

Calculations for the valuation of some of the properties between Bridge Street and Bunce Street are to be found on a separate loose sheet (see Appendix 2). Undated and unsigned, it has the appearance of a preliminary draft, prepared in advance of the negotiations, since in those instances where the agreed figures are known through the sub-committee minutes there are significant differences. Mr Leadbeater, whose property was valued at £200 gross, received £410 and Mr Brown accepted £575 as against the valuation of £430 gross. The valuation of £270 gross for Mr Roberts was in respect of 'part of a house, poor shippon and very small cottage' with no provision for the currier's workshop and his other property which went towards his receiving £1,210.

As well as specifically excluding St Bridget's, there are other omissions from the list and properties west of Bunce Street are also ignored. Inevitably the total of £1440 for the property falls short of the original estimates and must be discounted as a pointer to the actual cost. What this eventually proved to be is not known, since although a balance sheet for the cost of the bridge itself was in due course presented to the Commissioners, no comparable accounts exist for making Grosvenor Street.

From June 1827 onwards the sub-committee minutes from time to time recorded the demolition of houses and the sale of materials from them for sums of £50 or so. However, little or no information is given about the progress of the work on the new road, the first reference in the minutes occurring on 25 September 1828, by which it would appear that the footpaths were about to be constructed. The sub-committee ordered that these were to be of the width of 9' 6" inches on each side; the water table was to be paved to a width of one yard; and the centre of the channel to be 1' from the curb stone. Twelve months then elapsed before the sub-committee became involved again, when it ordered that three gas lamps should be placed between Bunce Street and the Castle.

The only direct indication in the minutes that the road had been completed came on 13 January 1834, when it was ordered that the portion of Grosvenor Street — the first direct reference to it by name — between Bunce Street and Bridge Street, 'which it was incumbent on the parishes of St Mary on the Hill and St Bridget's to repair, should be surrendered to them with the requirement to repair it'. They also ordered the placing of gas lamps along the new road and embankment, with oil lamps from where the gas mains ceased to the bridge.

However, building along the line of the new street had clearly begun some time before. The Commissioners had sold a plot of land to Mr Leadbeater on 7 April 1828 on the east side of his existing premises and between them and the new road for £20. This, in effect, was behind the site of the demolished church, and the sale was made on condition that the building he erected there would not be used 'as a gin and spirit shop or be attached to his present house for the purpose of selling liquor'. Despite this, the building would seem to have been what became The King's Head (Ill V.4), as shown on John Wood's 1833 map under number 29 (Ill V.5). It had been purchased some time before November 1831 by Thomas Onslow, who on 23 November obtained the Commissioners' approval to purchase the adjoining plot of waste land for £1, provided he built on the plot, retired part of his front in Whitefriars and agreed not to build stables on the Grosvenor Street front.

Wood's map does not appear to indicate that much other new development had taken place by 1833. The Commissioners' minutes are silent in this regard, other than on 16 December 1836 allowing the City Corporation to erect a weighing machine opposite to the plot of land adjoining Mr Withers's unoccupied soapery (CCALSS Z TRB 57, fo 61).

Ill V.4 King's Head Hotel, Grosvenor Street, c 1935. (From Goulbourne & Jackson 1987)

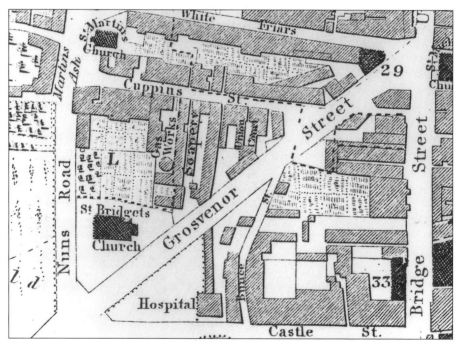

Ill V.5 John Wood's map of Chester, 1833: detail

The census of 1841 also suggests that developments along the street proceeded slowly. The only inhabitants returned for St Bridget's parish were Onslow and his family at the King's Head, and there was one uninhabited house; in St Mary's there were seven households, including Thomas Ellis, who was the Machine Keeper. By 1851, however, the situation would seem to have improved quite significantly in that new houses had been built and these were occupied by members of the middle class. Although the census shows little change in St Bridget's, with the King's Head the only occupied premises and the number of uninhabited houses having risen to four, the households in St Mary's had increased to ten and there were nine occupied houses in St Michael's. Many of the occupants in St Mary's were master tradesmen, whilst the heads of households in St Michael's include a 'Lady', a 'Gentleman' and two army officers on half pay.

Information on the progress of the work of rebuilding St Bridget's is also scanty. Notwithstanding the grant of £4,000 the vestry must have come to an early decision that this was not going to be enough, for on 16 December 1825 it resolved to raise £500 to be used for 'casing the North and East sides of the new church in a style corresponding with the South and West sides and also for enclosing the new cemetery by a suitable iron railing or other fence'.

The Commissioners authorised payment of a first instalment of £2,000 'as soon as it might be required' on 2 November 1826 (CCALSS Z TRB 57, fo 33), suggesting that work was in progress or was about to start. On 28 June 1827 the sub-committee noted that the parishioners were dissatisfied over the delays in building and agreed that the Church Building Commissioners should be notified of their concern.

At all events the laying of the foundation stone took place three and a half months later on 12 October 1827. The ceremony was performed by the Bishop of Chester, Dr C J Blomfield, spreading mortar with a silver trowel on a plinth stone and reading a dedicatory prayer for the church. There was a brass plate fixed to the stone, recording the event and noting the names of the architect and the builder. Possibly because of age — he was 83 and would die in March 1829 and be buried in the new cemetery — Harrison was not responsible for the design, which was the work of one of his pupils, William Cole the younger. The builder was John Wright.

According to the report in the *Chronicle* of 19 October, the ceremony was preceded by a procession from the Exchange, where those present were 'regaled with negus, cake etc'. Those taking part in the procession included the boys of the Blue Coat School, Poor Gownsmen, William Cole and Joseph (*sic*) Wright 'carrying the trowel', the churchwardens, the clergy in their canonicals two by two, the mayor and Corporation in their robes and a band. The Chronicle also had to report with regret that during the ceremony part of the crowd 'behaved with extreme indecorum, pushing each other and shouting to the annoyance of the venerable prelate and the respectable portion of the individuals present'.

As designed by William Cole, the church measured 87' x 51'. It had doric pilasters supporting a pediment at the west end, and a cupola supported on ionic columns above (Ill V.6). The building, according to Ormerod (1882, **1**, 341), was 'a plain oblong structure with a neat light and airy interior, but with no architectural grace to recommend it. There was a gallery at the west end, a painted roof and a coloured east window representing the Ascension'. Its classical design met with mixed opinions; to Hemingway (1831, **2**, 116) it was 'executed in a superior of elegance', but in Thomas Hughes' eyes (1856, 61) it had 'none of the characteristics of a Christian church and might easily be mistaken for some pagan temple'. Hemingway also pointed out that, 'although the parish of St Bridget's was wholly within the city, the church itself was neither in the parish nor the city, but altogether within the county palatine'. In fact there had been a clause in the act regarding the re-building specifying that after its consecration the church 'for all purposes, and to all intents whatsoever, shall be deemed part of and situate within the parish of St Bridget's and within the city of Chester'.

The church was consecrated on 5 August 1829 by the bishop, John B Sumner, who had succeeded Blomfield in 1828 on the latter's translation to London. The ceremony was pre-ceded, as with the laying of the foundation stone, by the mayor and other members of the Corporation processing from the Exchange, dressed in their official robes and accompanied with a band. The *Courant* in its report of 11 August, true to form in missing no opportunity to discredit the Corporation, said that 'it would be difficult to imagine a more motley or grotesque group … The inhabitants thought the occasion too opportune to pass without manifesting *their* estimation of the body corporate, which they did by the most marked contempt'.

The church was said to be two-thirds filled 'by a very respectable congregation, who contributed silver at the doors as they entered'. This had the effect, according to the *Chronicle* in its report of 7 August, of 'preventing an indiscriminate and inconvenient crowd and at the same time furnished the sum of upwards of £30'. In the afternoon a dinner was

Ill V.6 The Castle and St Bridget's Church. (Chester: Seacome. *In:* Views of Chester: volume of prints in Chester Archaeological Society Library. Reproduced with permission)

provided by Mr Ebrey at the Globe Inn, attended by some twenty-five persons, parishioners and those connected with 'raising the elegant edifice'. During the evening 'the most pleasant hilarity prevailed — several good songs were sung and the usual toasts were received and celebrated with enthusiasm'.

The new burial ground had been consecrated on the same day as the laying of the foundation stone. The size of the original piece of land granted for this had been the subject of some concern to the vestry, 'considering the removals which must take place'. Accordingly on 23 November 1826 they had resolved to ask the magistrates to sell a portion of county land adjoining the north side of the piece already granted. This sale was agreed on 22 March 1827, and the parish acquired a plot of ground measuring 753 square yards, together with another of 693 square yards, the latter for the purpose of making an exchange with the gas works garden. Mr Hinckes, the owner of the garden, and the Gas Light Company, the lessees, had agreed to the exchange provided the parish met all costs. These amounted to £204 6s 0d, made up of £144 6s 0d for the ground, £20 for enclosing the new gas works garden and £40 for the necessary conveyances (CCALSS Z TRB 82). As a result of these additions the area of the new site extended to 3,569 square yards, of which 2,989 square yards were used as the cemetery (Ill V.7). In response to pressure from the bishop to complete the deal so that the cemetery could be consecrated, the vestry on 7 July 1827 agreed to accept an offer from the bank of an advance of £200 against a promissory note signed by the churchwardens. The terms of repayment were £50 pa over four years, commencing in February 1828, but the account was in fact settled in full in 1830.

Some income had been obtained from the sale of goods from the old church, the churchwardens being empowered on 25 March 1827 to sell the two bells, the shandeliers (*sic*) and any other articles there. However, on 14 March 1829 the vestry, being faced with the need to settle various tradesmen's bills, decided to raise £800 by a mortgage on the church rates. On 18 October it was agreed that a further £200 would be required, which should also be secured by the assignment of the church rates. On 4 December, therefore, in return for £400, an assignment of the rates was made to Sarah Poole, and an offer by the rector, Richard Massie, of a loan of the balance of £600 from his two spinster daughters was accepted. The Massies were to have preference in repayment, and Sarah Poole was not repaid until 2 February 1861, when the agents for her representatives received the balance owing, plus interest, of £115 16s 0d (CCALSS P 15/8/2).

The new church remained in use until 1892, when it was demolished following the establishment of St Mary-on-the-Hill as the parish church for the united parish of St Bridget and St Martin, which had itself been formed in 1842. The cemetery survived until the construction of the inner ring road in 1972, when most of the site and that of the church disappeared under the roundabout at its junction with Grosvenor Street. In the cemetery were a number of brick-lined vaults. Above one was a stone slab in which was set a marble tablet inscribed 'Thomas Harrison's vault, died 29 March 1829 age 85'. The vault contained three coffins, two of lead and one of wood, but with no indication as to which was Harrison's. These coffins, together with the other remains from the cemetery, were re-interred at Blacon, although the memorial obelisk to Matthew Henry and several flat gravestones were retained and remain within the grassed-over centre of the roundabout.

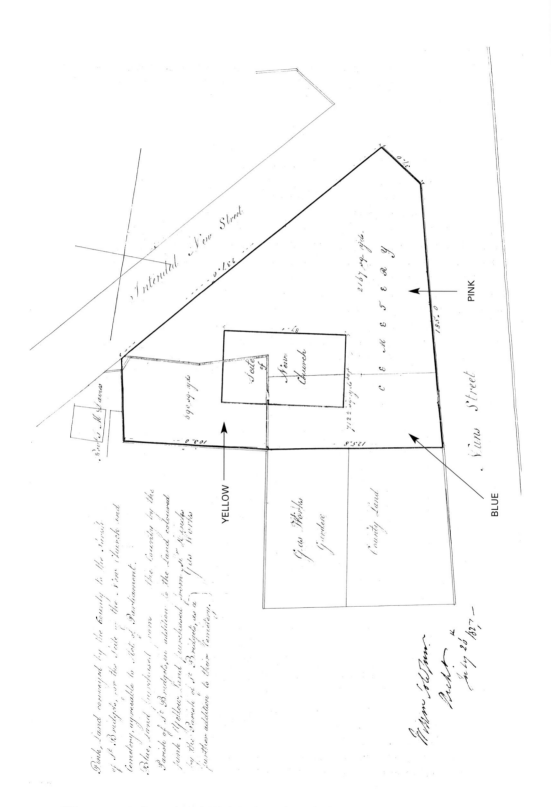

Appendix 1

Schedule of Houses and other Premises proposed to be purchased and used for the purposes of the Act 6 Geo IV *c* 175. (Reproduced by permission of Cheshire County Council)

The SCHEDULE referred to by the aforegoing ACT.

Of Houses and other Premises proposed to be purchased and used for the purposes of this Act.

Where situate.	Description of Premises.	Names of Owners or reputed Owners.	Occupiers' Name.
In the parish of Saint Bridget, in the city of Chester	Saint Bridget's church	Reverend Richard Massie / John McKinlay / Thomas Clayton	Minister.
Ditto	Shop, and rooms over		Churchwardens.
Ditto	Counting-house	Mr. John Brown	
Ditto	Dwelling-house, shop and offices	ditto	Edward Hughes.
Ditto	Parts of dwelling-house, outbuildings and yard	David Francis Jones, esq.	Self.
Ditto	Currier's workshop, closet and room over	Mr. Charles Worrall Leadbeater	John Ward.
Ditto	Two dwelling-houses, offices and yard	Mr. Edward Roberts	Simeon Williams.
Ditto	Dwelling-house, outbuildings, offices and yard	ditto	Elizabeth Parry.
Ditto	Privies, yard, &c.	ditto	Isabella Berry.
Ditto	Dwelling-house, &c.	ditto	William Jones.
Ditto	Dwelling-house, yard and offices	Mrs. Wrench	ditto – and others.
Ditto	Dwelling-house, yard and offices	ditto	(Untenanted.)
Ditto	Dwelling-house, yard and offices	ditto	Daniel Roberts.
Ditto	Dwelling-house, yard and offices	ditto	Matthew Davies.
Ditto	Dwelling-house, yard and offices	ditto	Anne Barnes.
Ditto	Dwelling-house, yard and offices	ditto	Samuel Dod.
Ditto	Dwelling-house, yard and offices	Earl Grosvenor	Jane Davies.
Ditto	Dwelling-house, yard and offices	ditto	Robert Jones.
Ditto	Coachmaker's shop	ditto	John Davies.
In the parish of Saint Mary-on-the-Hill, in the city of Chester	Parts of yard and shed	Miss Ratcliffe	Richard Snelson.
In the said parish of Saint Bridget, in the city of Chester	Dwelling-house, offices and garden	Mrs. Mary Blower	Self.
Ditto	Public-house, yard and offices	Earl Grosvenor	Edward Davies.
In the said parishes of Saint Bridget and Saint Mary-on-the-Hill, or one of them, in the city of Chester	Dwelling-house, yard, &c.	ditto	Morris Williams.
Ditto	Dwelling-house, yard, &c.	ditto	John Price.
In the said parish of Saint Bridget, in the city of Chester	Dwelling-house, yard, and offices	Mr. Samuel Oaks	John Williams.
Ditto	Dwelling-house, &c.	Mrs. Humphreys	Robert Williams.
Ditto	Dwelling-house, yard, &c.	ditto	Robert Hughes.

left: Ill V.7 St Bridget's church: site plan showing land granted and purchased for the new burial ground. (CCALSS EDP 72/4. Reproduced by permission of Cheshire County Council)

Where situate.	Description of Premises.	Names of Owners or reputed Owners.	Occupiers Names.
In the parish of Saint Michael, in the city of Chester	Dwelling-house, yard and offices	Mr. John Baron	Self.
Ditto	Garden house and part of garden	Sir John Williams, bart.	Dr. Cummins.
In the said parish of Saint Mary-on-the-Hill, in the city of Chester	Dwelling-house, yard and offices	Hugh Roberts	Self.
Ditto	Dwelling-house, yard and offices	Samuel Davies	David Pugh.
Ditto	Dwelling-house, yard and offices	Mary Morris	Robert Leake.
Ditto	Dwelling-house, yard and offices	Mr. John Moss	William Parry.
Ditto	Dwelling-house, yard and offices	Paul Price	John Grindley.
Ditto	Dwelling-house, yard and offices	Richard Denson	Self.
Ditto	Dwelling-house, buildings and yard	Samuel Oaks	Self.
In the said parish of Saint Mary on-the-Hill, in the County Palatine of Chester	Yard and buildings	The Custos Rotulorum of the County Palatine of Chester, in trust for the inhabitants of the said county	Samuel Oaks.
Ditto	Dwelling-house, &c.	ditto	Eleanor Salisbury.
Ditto	Land	ditto	Untenanted.
In the said parish of Saint Mary-on-the-Hill, in the city of Chester	Land	Reverend Thomas Davies	Untenanted
Ditto	Kelp mill, buildings and land	The Dean and Chapter of Chester	Messrs. Hodson & Witter.
Ditto	Land	Reverend Thomas Davies	Untenanted.
In the parish of Saint Martin, in the city of Chester	Part of garden	John Hinckes, esq.	Gas Light Company.
In the said parishes of Saint Martin and Saint Mary-on-the-Hill, in the County Palatine of Chester	Land	The Custos Rotulorum of the County Palatine of Chester, in trust for the inhabitants of the said county	Untenanted.
In the said parish of Saint Mary-on-the-Hill, in the County Palatine of Chester	Land	ditto	Mr. Dunstan.
In the said parish of Saint Mary-on-the-Hill, in the county of the city of Chester	The city wall	The Corporation of Chester	Untenanted.
Ditto	Land	The King	William Jones.
Ditto	Land	The Corporation of Chester	ditto.
Ditto	The River Dee.		

		The Corporation of Chester	
In the said parish of St. Mary-on-the-Hill, in the county of the city of Chester -	Land	The Corporation of Chester	Untenanted.
Ditto	Part of a garden	James Bingley	Self.
Ditto	Part of a garden	James Mainwaring, esq.	Thomas Weaver.
Ditto	Dwelling-house, offices and garden	John Edwards, esq.	Thomas Speed.
Ditto	Dwelling-house, offices, garden and land	ditto	William Davies.
Ditto	Dwelling-house, offices, &c.	ditto	Edward Jones.
Ditto	Dwelling-house, &c.	ditto	Late Thomas Foster, now untenanted.
Ditto	Dwelling-house, &c.	ditto	Untenanted.
Ditto	Dwelling-house, &c.	ditto	Thomas Price.
Ditto	Dwelling-house, out-buildings, offices and garden ground	ditto	John Phillips.
Ditto	Dwelling-house and buildings	Rebekah Shone	Self.
Ditto	Dwelling-house and building	Edward Phillips	Joseph Wainwright.
Ditto	Dwelling-house, offices and garden ground	John Edwards, esq.	Thomas Whittakers.
Ditto	Garden ground	ditto	Samuel Saunders.
Ditto	Garden ground	ditto	John Rogers.
Ditto	Dwelling-house, offices and garden	ditto	Richard Bellis.
Ditto	Dwelling-house, buildings, offices and garden	ditto	Randle Bellis.
Ditto	Land	The Corporation of Chester	Untenanted.
Ditto	Dwelling-house, garden, &c.	John Edwards, esq.	John Bellis.
Ditto	Garden ground	ditto	Thomas Davies.
Ditto	Dwelling-house, offices, garden, &c.	Earl Grosvenor	Joseph Vaughan.
Ditto	Dwelling-house, offices, garden, &c.	ditto	Edward Price.
Ditto	Dwelling-house, offices, garden, &c.	ditto	Griffith Jones.
Ditto	Dwelling-house, offices, garden, &c.	ditto	Samuel Fairbrother
Ditto	Dwelling-house, offices, &c.	Mr. Joseph Jones	Anna Actop
Ditto	Dwelling-house, buildings, &c.	ditto	John Cottgrave.
Ditto	Dwelling-house, buildings, &c.	ditto	William Davies.
Ditto	Dwelling-house, buildings, &c.	ditto	Michael Gerrard.
Ditto	Dwelling-house, buildings, &c.	ditto	Samuel Saunders.
Ditto	Dwelling-house, buildings, &c.	ditto	Thomas Price.
Ditto	Dwelling-house, buildings, garden, &c.	ditto	Thomas Davies.
Ditto	Dwelling-house, buildings, &c.	ditto	Edward Thomas.
Ditto	Dwelling-house, buildings, &c.	ditto	Thomas Ridgway.
Ditto	Dwelling-house, buildings, &c.	ditto	George Worrall.

Appendix 2

Valuation of property to be purchased for forming the new street between Bridge Street and Bunce Street in the city of Chester as per annext plan* excepting St. Bridget's Church.

David F. Jones Esq.	a House	£450	-	Materials off £90 -	£360
Messrs. Brown's	Shop	£430	-	Materials £80 -	£350
Chas. Leadbeater Stables and Room		£200	-	Land & Improvements £120 £80	
Edw. Roberts Part of a house, poor shippon and very small cottage		£270	-	Improvement £200 -	£70
Wrench Esq.	a cottage		-	Improvement considered — £50	
Mrs. Blower	a house	£360	-	Materials £60 -	£300
# William Cooper & others	a house	£350	-	Land & Materials £120 —	£230
Sir J. Williams	a bit of land				£35

Earl Grosvenor	two back houses	£12 per year	
	public house	14	
	smithy	7	
	2 houses 4 (?)	18	

£51 at 15 years value 760 (*sic*)

Improvements off 100 ——	£665 sic	
	2140	
Earl Grosvenor's donation 665)		
Sir J. Williams do 35)	-700	1440

Total of land purchased by the County from the Crown

	4163 yards @ 2/- — 416 — 6 — 0
Part of Farecloughs	1188 yards @ 7/- — 415 —16 — 0
To be purchased	Gas Co. Garden — 90 — 0 — 0
	922 — 2 — 0
Building land off	400 — 0 — 0
Differance (*sic*) to County	522 — 2 — 0

* The plan is missing

Not named in the Schedule or on the plan reference Z TRB 190

Source: CCALSS Z TRB 147

Notes

[1]   6 Geo IV *c* 125 (reprinted as a foreword to the Minutes of the Dee Bridge Commissioners: Cheshire and Chester Archives and Local Studies Service (hereafter CCALSS) Z TRB 57

[2]   George Harrison's Account Book 1811–37: CCALSS Z D/HS 516. Brunel was engineer to the tunnel, a project without precedent. Physical problems when the Thames broke in on more than one occasion and financial difficulties led to construction being abandoned for long periods, and the work was not completed until 1843.

[3]   The correspondence between Harrison and Brunel from 18 November 1825 to 3 January 1826 was entered in the Minute Book of the Dee Bridge Commissioners, following a directive made at their meeting of 5 January 1826: CCALSS Z TRB 57 fo 15v.

[4]   Brunel's presence at the Rotherhithe tunnel as it slowly progressed and problems arose was crucial and clearly took first priority with him. Symptomatic perhaps of his absorption there is that he misdated his letter to the Commissioners as 7 January.

[5]   The collapse began when a portion of the south side fell into the street. No-one was injured but it was reported that a Sal Adams, who was reputed to be 'a practitioner in things relating to the other world — a Meg Merrilees in whose hands fate had placed the destiny of the world' was sitting in an upper room in a chair within six inches of the wall which fell down. The report concluded 'this does not augur well for her foresight'.

[6]   As is evident both from Ormerod's description and Batenham's etching, St Bridget's did not have a steeple in the modern sense of a spire surmounting a tower. It must be presumed the vestry were following the not uncommon practice of the day in using 'steeple' as the equivalent to 'tower'.

Bibliography

Batenham, G 1816   A series of etchings of churches, gates and other parts of Chester

Clarke, J W 1958   The building of the Grosvenor Bridge. *J Chester Archaeol Soc* new ser **45**, 43–55

Clements, P 1970   Marc Isambard Brunel. Harlow: Longmans

Goulbourne, K &   Chester: a portrait in old picture postcards.
Jackson, G 1987   Market Drayton: S B Publications

Hemingway, J 1831   History of the city of Chester. 2 vols. Chester: Fletcher

Hughes, T 1956   The stranger's handbook to Chester: London: J R Smith

Ormerod, G 1882   History of the county palatine and city of Chester. Ed 2, rev Helsby, T. 3 vols. London: Routledge

Council and Officers for the Year 1999/2000

Council and Officers for the Year 2000/2001

Index